Michael Madden 01/02/2024

AGAINST ALL ODDS

AGAINST ALL ODDS

A True Story of
Ultimate Courage and Survival
in World War II

★

ALEX KERSHAW

CALIBER

DUTTON CALIBER

An imprint of Penguin Random House LLC
penguinrandomhouse.com

Maps by Chris Erichson

LIBRARY OF CONGRESS CATALOGING-IN-PUBLICATION DATA
has been applied for.

ISBN 9780593183748 (hardcover)
ISBN 9780593183762 (ebook)

Printed in the United States of America
1st Printing

In memory of Jim Hornfischer

CONTENTS

AGAINST
ALL
ODDS

PART ONE

The Mediterranean

CHAPTER 1

Baptism of Fire

THE SILENCE WAS unnerving after several days at sea, crossing from America with the constant grinding of the ship's engines, quiet now in the Atlantic waters off North Africa. But it didn't last long. In the early hours, bells clanged and then soldiers heard an anchor chain's rattle, barked orders, heavy and frantic footsteps, power winches whirring as they started to lower landing craft into the whitecapped water.

A radio played. Twenty-four-year-old Lieutenant Maurice "Footsie" Britt to his surprise heard the voice of President Franklin D. Roosevelt announce that the invasion of North Africa had already begun. "We figured he had jumped the gun a little," Britt later remembered. "After all, we were still eight miles from shore."[1] Then blond-haired Britt, all two hundred twenty pounds of him, took his place in his landing craft. Finally, the craft headed toward the shore.

The seas as far as the horizon were dotted with transports. Britt belonged to the 3rd Division's 30th Infantry Regiment, whose motto was "Our country, not ourselves."[2] He was one of thirty-five thousand green American troops in Western Task Force, commanded by General George S. Patton, one of three forces attacking French Morocco and Algeria in three areas of a thousand-mile-long coastline, stretching all the way from Safi on the Atlantic to Algiers. The arrival of the first Americans in Europe to fight the Axis powers came at a critical point in the war. After enjoying stunning success against the British 8th Army through 1941 and much of 1942, General Erwin Rommel and his famed Afrika Korps were now on the defensive, having been defeated at El Alamein in Egypt less than a week earlier.

In all, the Torch Landings, the first joint operation of the war by the Americans and the British, comprised more than a hundred thousand troops backed by three hundred fifty warships from seven Allied navies. The Americans had tried to negotiate an armistice with the French in recent days but to no avail, and so an order had come from on high to Britt's division: "Okay, boys, let's play ball."[3]

Dawn was now breaking off the coast of North Africa. In the far distance, men could make out the steeple of a Catholic church rising above the port of Fedala.[4] There was the sound of machine-gun fire. Bright red tracers spat across the lightening sky. Ahead loomed a flat, broad beach a couple of miles to the east of Fedala.

Britt heard the drone of French bombers and then saw "huge

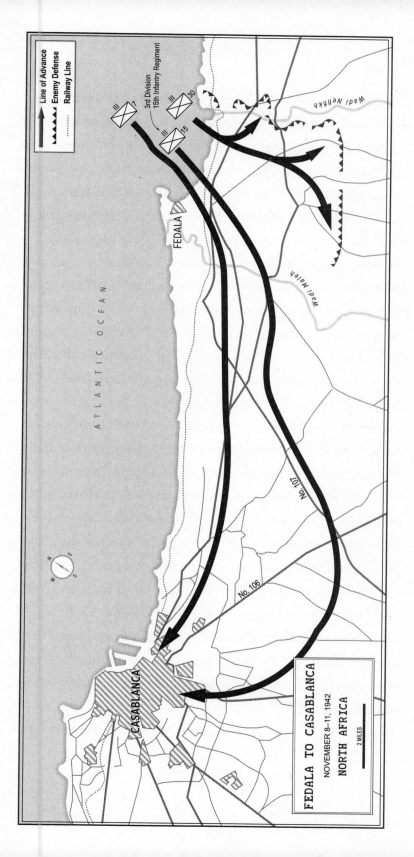

FEDALA TO CASABLANCA
NOVEMBER 8–11, 1942
NORTH AFRICA

2 MILES

Line of Advance
Enemy Defense
Railway Line

3rd Division
15th Infantry Regiment

ATLANTIC OCEAN

FEDALA

CASABLANCA

Wadi Nefikh

Wadi Maleh

No. 107

No. 106

fountains of spray" as bombs crashed into the sea. "It was a pretty sight," he remembered, "until suddenly we realized, with a sickening feeling, that the men in these bombers were trying to kill us. No lectures on the subject, no crawling under carefully aimed machine gunfire, will ever make a soldier. He becomes one the instant he realizes the gunfire he hears is intended to kill him."[5]

Britt's landing craft ground ashore. Men began to unload it but then there was a "deafening rattle of fire" and Britt looked up and saw a French plane diving toward him, strafing his regiment. There had been no preinvasion bombardment in the hopes that the French would not put up any resistance. Many of Britt's fellow invaders carried American flags, figuring the French would be less likely to fire on US troops. The flags made no difference.

Britt and his men stopped unloading the craft, headed for safety across the beach, and then moved inland. By midday they had reached a preassigned assembly area near a road bridge. Then Britt returned to the beach with a sergeant to salvage the jeeps and equipment he'd been forced to leave in the landing craft. "The first edge of my excitement was beginning to dull and when another strafing plane came over I hit the beach in utter terror, digging madly into the sand."

The plane soon passed over, in search of more targets. For five long minutes, Britt lay flat, terrified, trying to summon the courage to get back on his feet. He then found his landing craft. But before he and the sergeant could pull off several guns and two remaining jeeps, the landing craft sank in the rough seas. There was more bad news. Britt learned that a "submarine torpedo [had] hit our transport standing off shore and all our equipment went down with it. We lost all our barracks bags, food, kitchens, and other equipment. All we had left was the clothes on our backs and the rations we carried. We were tired, sick, and disgusted."[6]

Britt and the sergeant had no option but to walk back across the beach and rejoin their company at the assembly point by the road bridge. By early afternoon, Fedala was in American hands, and Britt and his company were marching toward Casablanca, sixteen miles to the southwest. Britt's regiment encountered minimal resistance while taking dozens of French soldiers as prisoners.

Allied Supreme Commander Dwight Eisenhower arranged a cease-fire with Vichy French forces forty-eight hours later, on November 10, and Casablanca was occupied with fewer than seventy men killed from Britt's division, although by the time the guns fell silent in all of Morocco, there had been some fifteen hundred Allied casualties. Britt and his fellow "Marne men," as the 3rd Division soldiers were known, had been initiated into the full chaos and confusion of combat in a couple of hectic, feverish days. They'd fought with barely any armored support yet had successfully spearheaded the first US invasion of the war. "My biggest thrill," Britt wrote his wife, "and one that I'm sure I'll never recapture, was when my boys performed so heroically that at least three will be decorated for outstanding bravery."[7]

Far bloodier battlefields and much greater danger were in

store for Maurice Britt but, unlike so many of his fellow junior officers, his background and training had prepared him to endure the ordeals ahead. Britt had in fact trained for combat since the harshest days of the Great Depression when he first donned an army uniform in 1937 as a freshman in the ROTC program at the University of Arkansas. He was quick-witted, tough, and humble, with no airs or graces, an optimist by necessity, having grown up dirt-poor in rural Arkansas. He was born in the small town of Carlisle, in the state's rice-growing region, and already knew what death meant. When he was nine, his father was badly hurt in an industrial accident and given less than five years to live. He lasted four.

Britt's mother was left with two boys, nine-year-old Basil and thirteen-year-old Maurice, to bring up on her own. Each cent counted and Britt worked every hour he could, stacking wood, picking fruit, chopping cotton.[8] In high school, he was an exceptional athlete, playing basketball and football and starring on the track team. His teammates nicknamed him Footsie because he had such big feet—"size 12, double E."

He studied as hard as he worked to feed his family, graduating in 1937 as his high school's valedictorian. He never forgot his mother's delight when he won a football scholarship to the University of Arkansas, where he majored in journalism, hoping one day to become a sportswriter if he didn't make the cut as a professional athlete.[9] As in high school, Britt was again both a star athlete and a superb scholar, gaining a 5.5 grade point average in his freshman year while winning plaudits for the college's Razorback football team as a nimble, quick-thinking defensive and offensive end. Before his senior year, he'd attended a reserve officers' training camp at Fort Leavenworth in Kansas—what he regarded, on the cusp of his first combat, as "a priceless experience."[10]

Aged twenty-two, Britt fell in love with a high-spirited, beautiful freshman called Nancy Mitchell. After he received his commission as a second lieutenant upon graduating, he and eighteen-year-old Nancy were married on June 8, 1941. "Life was simple and serene in those days, six months before Pearl Harbor," he reminisced. "We went on a honeymoon tour of the Ozarks and in the fall we went to Detroit, where I had an offer to try out with the Detroit Lions professional football team."

Britt was selected for one of six roster spots and soon became a regular starter, a professional football player in the NFL. The Lions were a woeful team, losing most of their games, but Britt was highly respected by both fans and teammates for his dedication and endurance. "He could take any amount of punishment and he was a sixty-minute man," recalled fellow Lion O'Neale Adams. "I always thought he would make a leader."[11] Another of Britt's teammates was Byron White, a future Supreme Court justice, rumored to be the best-paid player in the NFL. "There were stories that [White] was making $1000 a game, which was fantastic money," remembered Britt. "None of us knew if it was true and no one asked. We were just glad to have him on our side. . . . It wasn't hard to see that this man was going places."[12]

The same could have been said for Britt. But then, a few weeks before the end of the 1941 season, he received a letter from the War Department calling him to active duty.[13] Britt turned up at

Camp Robinson in Arkansas on December 5, 1941, and was told to make his way to Fort Lewis in Washington State. He was listening to the radio, driving across the Arizona desert with his wife, when he heard that Pearl Harbor had been attacked and that the United States had entered the war.

Certain he'd be shipped to the Pacific in a matter of days, Britt's first impulse was to pull his coupe over at the next town and send his bride home, but she insisted on crossing the Rockies with him. It was a fraught journey as her husband kept putting his foot to the gas, eager to get to the West Coast. The police stopped Britt several times for speeding and he earnestly explained he was in a rush to get the war won. He didn't pick up a single ticket. In Fort Lewis, an officer in a tank unit quickly sized him up—he stood 6 feet 3.5 inches: "You're too big," the officer told him. "You look like you might be some good in the infantry."[14]

So it was that Britt ended up in the 3rd Division, the legendary "Rock of the Marne" outfit that had saved Paris in July 1918 by blocking the last great German offensive of World War I. Dubbed "the Blue and White Devils" because of the blue and white stripes on their insignia, the Marne men had boasted among their ranks between the wars none less than Dwight Eisenhower—the future Allied supreme commander—and George Marshall, US Army chief of staff.[15]

LATER THAT NOVEMBER 1942, as Hitler sent more men to North Africa to bolster Rommel's Afrika Korps, Britt was detailed with his battalion to set up security for one of the most important conferences of World War II in Casablanca, the first port on the

Atlantic that could receive troops and supplies directly from the United States. It was dull work but Britt and his company found time to barter with the local Arabs, he recalled, "for eggs and other food to supplement our rations. One lucky fellow in our company had come ashore with a box of red, white and blue poker chips. The Arabs thought these were worth more than silver money, and our man almost had a corner on the Moroccan egg market."[16]

From January 8 to 23, 1943, Britt and his fellow Marne men kept a tight cordon around the elegant Anfa Hotel as Prime Minister Winston Churchill and President Roosevelt and their military staffs planned strategy for defeating the Axis in North Africa and then in mainland Europe. "Britt personally met his Commander in Chief," it was later reported, as well as "Churchill, De Gaulle, Marshall, and others."[17]

The Torch Landings had been opposed by the US chiefs of staff, who feared being dragged into what they saw as a vaguely planned Mediterranean sideshow, designed to further Churchill's imperialist aims. But Roosevelt was under intense pressure to commit more men and matériel to the fight against the Axis. It had been impossible to invade northwest Europe in 1942 and thereby open a second front as Stalin demanded. To maintain momentum in the war, Roosevelt now agreed to Churchill's calls for a strike to the "soft underbelly" of the Third Reich in the Mediterranean.[18] At Roosevelt's insistence, it was also decided at Casablanca that there would be no negotiating with Hitler and the Axis powers; only unconditional surrender would be acceptable.

Once the dignitaries had left Casablanca, Britt and his

battalion bade adieu to the port with its ancient medinas, gut-rotting chicory coffee, armies of beggars, and surly French colonials. They were sent to the windswept Spanish-Moroccan border, where they again performed guard duty. Spring arrived and men no longer shivered so much as they stood at sentry posts at night. On March 7, 1943, they received a new division commander, forty-eight-year-old Major General Lucian Truscott, a chain-smoking aesthete who'd left American shores with a copy of *War and Peace* and a bottle of booze stowed in his kit bag. A former schoolteacher from Texas, the son of a country doctor, aged twenty-three he'd enlisted in the cavalry and become a superb polo player. Famously short-tempered and bull-headed, he would soon dole out fifty-year sentences to men who shot themselves in the foot to avoid combat.

Truscott took charge at a turning point in the North Africa campaign. The Allies had hoped for a quick victory following Operation Torch but Rommel's forces proved infuriatingly hard to defeat. Rains lashed the mosquito-plagued invaders and deep mud along coastal highways slowed Allied tanks. Then came a stunning victory against the green Americans at Kasserine Pass. Six US battalions were destroyed in two days.

It was a woeful performance, leading to sniping from the British. But Kasserine was a necessary blooding that led to a shake-up in the US Army, sackings and reassignment of men and commands. And now, that spring of 1943, the Allies were back on the offensive, better organized and with new generals such as Truscott in charge. Record numbers of enemy ships were being sunk, strangling supply lines across the Mediterranean.

That April 22, the Allies launched a decisive offensive. Tunis fell as two once mighty German Panzer armies fell apart, and by May 13, what was left of Rommel's Afrika Korps was defeated and 238,000 Germans and Italians were taken prisoner.

Lucian Truscott gathered his officers for a pep talk. The Germans were no supermen. When the American soldier was daring, organized, and highly aggressive, he could beat his German foe, always called the Boche by Truscott. Barely a week later, Truscott ordered his regimental commanders to move to Arzew, a training center in Algeria.[19] "While Allied forces were driving Marshal Rommel back from the gates of Egypt and the Germans were being cornered in Tunisia," recalled Britt, "our division was rehearsing for [an] invasion. Over and over we practiced beach landings. It was dangerous work but the men who formed combat teams were generally volunteers. They got no extra pay."[20]

Truscott was ruthlessly determined to knock the Marne men into tiptop shape, telling regimental commanders to send them on long forced marches at maximum speed so they could learn what would be called the Truscott trot. "Have you heard what that new hard-ass general wants us to do?" asked some officers. The US Army field manual stated that troops march at 2.5 miles per hour. Truscott demanded four. A colonel dared to show Truscott the manual. "Colonel," growled Truscott, "you can throw that in the wastebasket."[21]

Truscott wanted men to cover as much ground as fast possible, to pivot and dash with the speed of cavalry. He knew the Allies' next amphibious operation would happen that summer in baking heat in rough terrain unsuited to tank warfare. The objective had been decided at the Casablanca conference. The Marne men would be heading to Sicily.

Late that June, Lieutenant Britt and his company were finally able to rest. They were in superb shape, better conditioned for killing than they would be at any stage in the war. On July 3, Britt stood in a parched olive grove in Tunisia. It was late afternoon when Britt, his face deeply tanned, gathered with officers from the 3rd Division in a large semicircle. Many men, uniforms stained with sweat, then sat down on their helmets beneath a scorching sun.

The Marne men's division chief of staff, Colonel Don Carleton, heavyset with a sunburned face and bristling mustache, stepped up to the microphone.

There was a sudden gust of hot wind.

"Gentlemen," said Carleton, "the first Sirocco. A hot wind that sweeps north across the sands of the Sahara, with the heat of a furnace, to die over the Mediterranean. A good omen."

Some men laughed halfheartedly.

Then Carleton saw that General Truscott was approaching.

"Attention!"

Men scrambled to their feet.

"Gentlemen, the Commanding General."

Lucian Truscott stood before a microphone. The sun shone in his broad face, making him squint. "Gentlemen," said Truscott, "we are on the eve of a great adventure. We are about to set forth upon the greatest amphibious expedition the world has ever known. . . . We find ourselves anticipating success or . . . failure?

No, instead we anticipate success, or success beyond our utmost expectations. We do not know the word 'failure.'"

The next day, Independence Day, Truscott made a shorter, more emphatic speech, directing his comments at every man with blue and white stripes on his shoulder: "You are going to meet the 'Boche'! Carve your name on his face!"[22]

CHAPTER 2

Sicily

NEPTUNE WAS ANGRY. A fierce storm the previous night had buffeted the invasion fleet, threatening to defeat the Allies before they even stepped ashore. The force seven gale had abated, but high waves still slapped against landing craft as they plowed toward the shore. It was early on July 10, 1943, off the southern coast of Sicily. In one craft stood a nineteen-year-old private called Audie Murphy, army serial number 18093707. Men beside him from B Company of the 15th Infantry Regiment were bent over, puking. The five-foot-seven-inch Texan, weighing in at all of 138 pounds, a steel helmet strapped to his back, stood looking ahead at the soft golden sands of Yellow Beach, to the east of the port of Licata.

The craft bounced up and down, buffeted by the stiff wind—what the Sicilians, so often invaded over the centuries, called a *tramontana*. Men kept puking. They were at the start of the Allied liberation of Europe, the first wave in the largest amphibious invasion in history to date, involving sixty-six thousand of their fellow Americans and almost twice as many British troops and twenty-six hundred navy ships. According to their division commander, Lucian Truscott, the Marne men were "anxious to get the job done—and get home."[1]

Aboard the USS *Biscayne*, a few thousand yards offshore from Yellow Beach, Truscott was dressed for battle, wearing his trademark leather jacket and silk cravat. In the long hours before dawn, he had been "concerned with his own thoughts," haunted by memories of the failed Dieppe raid of August 1942, which he'd witnessed. He remembered the excruciating tension before launching Operation Torch, the invasion of North Africa, the previous November.

"What was to be the result?"[2] Truscott wondered.

The Germans would not be taken by surprise. Albert Kesselring, in command of German forces in Sicily and Italy, had expected an Allied landing and had prepared accordingly. The fifty-seven-year-old ex–artillery man had reinforced the Axis garrison. The coastal defenses in Sicily were still pathetic, however, "a pretty sugar pastry," and he had no faith whatsoever in the Italian defenders—congenital cowards, espresso-loving womanizers. But neither the thin crust of defenses nor the Italians mattered. Kesselring's Panzer divisions would wait for General George Patton's Americans and for the British and Canadians, led by General Bernard Montgomery, to move inland and then counterattack, throwing them back into the Mediterranean. Before the war was over, Kesselring would kill more of Truscott's men than any other German warlord.

It didn't feel as if he was approaching a "sugar pastry" to

Private Audie Murphy, desperate to get ashore. Whatever Kesselring had in mind for him and his fellow invaders, it couldn't have been worse than being cramped in a troopship and then a bucking landing craft. Finally, he was almost at Yellow Beach, yards away from surf crashing onto golden sands.

The ramp was down. Murphy made it onto the beach. There was scant opposition other than a few desultory artillery shells fired by terrified Italians. Then he saw his first dead American, blown apart by shrapnel.[3] It was still early morning. Murphy looked around and saw bodies dotted along the beach. It seemed as if the men who had landed before him had been slaughtered. But then he realized the soldiers were lying down, taking a quick breather before pushing inland.[4]

Murphy sprinted across the beach and then through a gap cut in barbed wire. An enemy machine gun cackled and was soon silenced. Murphy felt disappointed. He'd expected far more excitement. The feeling passed quickly. Gunfire erupted once more. He sensed, for the first time, that another human being was trying to kill him. This was deadly work. He'd need to take it seriously to survive. And never before had he wanted so badly to stay alive.

A shell exploded. Murphy felt the earth tremble. He looked up and spotted a three-hundred-foot-high ridge inland, Saffarello Hill. A second explosion was much closer. Men were nearby, taking cover, coughing from the clouds of powder from the shell explosion. Murphy spotted a redheaded soldier who'd fallen from a rock. Blood seeped from his ears and nose. A soldier who'd fought in North Africa scrambled forward. He got to the redhead and then turned to another man close by, a greenhorn, and told him to grab the redhead's ammunition. The redhead wouldn't be needing it. Someone else sure as hell soon would.

The greenhorn started to strip ammunition from the dead man's cartridge belt. Someone said the dead man had two kids and a wife back home.

A soldier covered his body with a cape to stop it from being eaten by flies.

"Flies go to work on 'em right away," said the soldier. "Fellow from the last war told me they well up like balloons."[5]

Murphy moved on into the hills, drenched in sweat.

"Where is the glamour in blistered feet and a growling stomach?" wondered Murphy. "And where is the expected adventure?"[6]

Lieutenant Maurice Britt also arrived at Licata that morning, coming ashore with I Company of the 30th Infantry. He and his unit had practiced landings so often, and there was so little opposition, that it all felt like an anticlimax. The preinvasion bombing was perfectly timed, and thanks to a plethora of photographs and intelligence reports, Britt almost felt as if he'd visited Licata before.

With Britt's company was a large, irascible German shepherd called Chips. Back in the US, the dog had mauled a sailor almost to death. Now, incredibly, Chips did the same to the enemy. After moving off Blue Beach, to the east of Licata, Britt and I Company were held up by machine-gun fire erupting from a pillbox.[7] The canine spotted the gun and, trained to attack any man wielding a weapon, escaped his handler and sprinted forward. He tore its hot muzzle from the slit in a pillbox and then, smelling Germans, bounded to its rear and inside. Before long a petrified German staggered outside, hysterical, his arm almost chewed off. When the handler caught up, he found Chips at another German's throat, with two men cowering nearby. Chips would later have the Silver Star pinned to his collar by Truscott.[8]

Audie Murphy meanwhile moved on, a couple of miles to the west of Britt, beneath the harsh midday sun. He walked past scrubby Saffarello Hill and across the Ginisi Plain, a few miles of dusty flat ground. Scouting parties from the 15th Infantry Regiment forged ahead, looking for water. Men dropped their packs and heavy equipment, to be brought to them later, so they could march as fast and light as possible, carrying only six clips of ammunition each and a single day's rations. Italian soldiers surrendered in droves to their American invaders, yelling, *"Me bambine!"*[9] They all had many children back home, cursed Mussolini, hated the Germans even more, and sang and smiled as they trotted toward a POW compound.

A few weeks earlier, Murphy had written his family in Texas, telling them he'd never felt better. The army had been the making of him. He'd not asked after his father in the letter. Short, heavyset, barely literate, a violent abuser, especially of his wife, Josie Bell, Emmitt Pat Murphy had not been in his son's life for a long time. Murphy never forgave him for what he'd done to Audie's mother, to his siblings, to himself. "Every time my old man couldn't beat the kids he had," he recalled, "he got himself another one."[10]

At the height of the Depression, in 1933, Audie's father had moved his wife and eleven children to Celeste, Texas. They lived in a cotton picker's shack without plumbing, lit by bare lightbulbs hung from wires dangling from the ceilings. Harder and harder years had followed. In 1940, as Hitler's forces stormed across Europe, Murphy's father abandoned him and his siblings. "When my dad left," recalled daughter Nadene Murphy, "it was a cold icy night, and I saw him . . . he got up and put on all the clothes he could, walked out the door . . . that was the last time I saw him."[11]

Murphy did what he could but there were too many mouths to feed, no matter how many rabbits and squirrels he killed with his .22 rifle. "My mother, attempting to keep her brood together, worked harder than ever," he remembered. "But illness overtook her. Gradually she grew weaker and sadder. And when I was sixteen she died."[12] It broke something deep inside him—watching her collapse, aged forty-nine, under the strain, then seeing his three youngest siblings sent to an orphanage, four others fending for themselves, the family scattered like so much cottonseed. According to his sister Nadene, their mother's sudden death "tore him up because he wanted her to live so he could do something for her."[13]

Murphy worked any odd job he could find but often went hungry. His violent mood swings led him to pick fights on the slightest pretense. War couldn't have come quick enough for Audie Murphy. When the Japanese attacked Pearl Harbor, he was "half-wild with frustration" because he was too young to join up.[14] He wanted so badly to put on a uniform and fight, as much to serve his country as to vent his burning rage. Pretending to be eighteen, although a year younger in fact, he went to a Marine Corps recruiting station. A sergeant gave Murphy one look and rejected him as too small and thin. If only he'd done what some other kids his age and weight had done and drunk a pint of milk and gorged on bananas before stepping on the scales.

America was at war. The army would surely not be so picky. Ten days after being rejected by the marines, Murphy stood by a road, trying to hitch a ride from Farmersville to go join up in Dallas. Someone stopped and gave him a ride. He tipped the scales at 112 pounds but was accepted into the 3rd Division as the lowest form of grunt, a replacement. He'd never been more than a hundred miles from home. On his first practice drill, he passed out. Some soldier. They started calling him "baby" in basic training but that was before he crossed the Atlantic, before he landed in Casablanca that February, before he began to serve under Captain Keith Ware in B Company.[15] No one called him baby anymore.

Murphy put one rubber-soled boot in front of the other, ready to hunt Germans, to start paying back for all that the world had taken from him. Licata was behind him, the first town in Europe to be liberated by his regiment. He moved on, heading inland. The humidity and the Sicilian landscape were reminiscent of the region of northeastern Texas where he'd grown up.

One fall at age twelve, Murphy had worked in a field full of fluffy cotton; he'd been born a sharecropper's kid, after all. He toiled beside an old man, a veteran of World War I. The veteran warned him about war. It was a ghastly business, nothing to glorify. The old man had been gassed by the Germans. He'd been a machine gunner. He'd killed many times.

"Someday, I aim to be a soldier," Murphy told him.

The old man looked at him with disdain.

What the hell for?

————

KESSELRING WAS RIGHT about the Italians. There was no serious opposition from them as the 15th Infantry Regiment moved ashore.[16] "The Italians were caught by surprise," remembered one man. "Some sleeping in pill boxes never opened their eyes to see light of day again. They were killed before they ever awakened."[17]

Both the German and Italian defenses were minimal, much to the delight of Truscott—his ten thousand troops suffered fewer than a hundred casualties that morning. In planning, as much as twenty percent in losses had been expected. Within an hour of the first wave arriving, all his objectives for D Day had been seized—the local airport, the port and town of Licata itself. One relieved officer told Truscott: "Fighting the battle was a damn sight easier than training for it."[18]

Audie Murphy ended his first day in combat with a stomach-ache, having gorged on too many tomatoes and green melons in the fields north of Licata. The next morning, Murphy examined his surroundings just as he'd surveyed new ground when hunting to feed his family as a boy. This was not the verdant Sicily he'd seen in picture postcards. This southern slice of the island was mostly a drab patchwork of wheat fields and scraggly olive orchards. Murphy had been selected to work as a runner for the commander of B Company, twenty-seven-year-old Captain Keith Ware. That meant jogging and sprinting between platoons with orders, reporting back on progress, and that morning B Company set a brisk pace as it advanced farther inland, passing the odd patch of green—vineyards and even some cotton fields.

In Captain Ware's eyes, Murphy looked far too young to be in combat. He was eighteen, remembered Ware, but appeared "three or four years younger."[19] Like Murphy, Ware was a neophyte in the ways of war, undergoing his greatest test leading two hundred men into action. Nothing in his background suggested he might fail. But every officer going into battle for the first time could not help but wonder if he had the right stuff.

Like Murphy, Ware didn't look cut out for killing. According to one account, he was "dour" and "shy," an unassuming bachelor who squinted "at the world through sedate, rimless glasses. His voice [was] soft, his language reserved."[20] But like his young runner, he had an inner strength forged by loss and hardship that belied his appearance.

When Ware was twelve years old, his father—a chain-smoking traveling salesman—had died of throat cancer. Medical bills left Ware and his mother and sister penniless, so poor at one stage that Ware and his sister subsisted on raw oatmeal. Ware worked any job he could find after his father's death. He delivered newspapers before school and each night would clean up in a grocery store, sweeping up blood-soaked sawdust in the meat department.

Ware's sister, who was four years older than him, found a job with the telephone company, AT&T, and the family moved to California with her. After graduating from high school, Ware worked in a department store in Glendale, eventually becoming a manager. Then war broke out and Ware was drafted. Because of his high intelligence and managerial experience, he was selected to attend Officer Training School, where he excelled. Aware, no doubt, of his lowly status as a "ninety day wonder" among his fellow officers, he was about to show he was as capable as any West Pointer.

Later, on the second day of combat, as they marched north, some of Ware's men were pinned down by machine-gun fire, bullets whipping all around. The Germans were fighting back, not the Italians. It was the first time B Company had encountered Kesselring's troops. They wouldn't be quite so eager to throw their hands up in the air.

A Sherman tank rolled up, tracks clanking, and fired at the German position with a jolting bark. Ware ordered Company B to move fast across open ground and then to get to the other side of some rail tracks and find cover. They were to stop for no reason. Murphy and the others did as Ware ordered and sprinted forward.

Two men fell, hit by gunfire. A grenade exploded close by, but Murphy kept running, firing his carbine from the hip, shouting for others to follow him. Then he jumped across the rail tracks and found cover in a shallow ditch, out of the line of fire. Something heavy dropped on top of him—it was a private called Joe Sieja. The chain-smoking Pole must have relished this first encounter with the Krauts. He harbored a raging hatred for the Germans, who had invaded his beloved homeland in 1939, just a year after he'd emigrated to America. Every goddamn one was a sonofabitch as far as Sieja was concerned. The only good Kraut was a dead one.

Ware pushed B Company on toward the next village, Campobello, leading the First Battalion's advance. As Ware's men neared a German strongpoint, bullets slashed through the air. Six of Ware's men were wounded. Ware organized his men, sending a private with a Browning Automatic Rifle ahead to lay down fire on the enemy position while others pulled the wounded to safety.[21] Then Ware led his men across open ground and the strongpoint was knocked out. The First Battalion could advance once more. He had passed his first true test, earning the Silver Star on only his second day in combat.[22]

As Audie Murphy moved ahead that afternoon on a scouting patrol, he spotted two enemy officers trying to escape on white horses. He raised his carbine and toppled both in swift succession with uncanny deadly accuracy. He felt no guilt at taking his first lives, "no qualms, no pride, no remorse," merely a "weary indifference."

"Now why did you do that?" a soldier asked Murphy. "You shouldn't have fired."

"That's our job, isn't it? They would have killed us if they'd had the chance. That's their job. Or have I been wrongly informed?"[23]

The sun began to set.[24] Trucks had churned up the dry mud, and now clouds of gray dust shrouded everything, giving the Marne men a deathly complexion until they could wash away the grime. But there was no time to get clean. General Truscott wanted to keep his regiments on the move, constantly harrying the retreating Germans.[25]

THEY WERE TWO titans of the US Army, hard-charging, short-tempered cavalrymen with great swagger and style. On July 14, Truscott and General George Patton, the 7th Army commander, met for the first time in Licata to discuss strategy. After stopping a German counterattack at Gela, where he had come ashore, Patton was eager to make his mark and destroy German and Italian resistance in all of Western Sicily.

Truscott knew that Patton had his eye on Palermo, Sicily's largest city, with its famous waterfront and Norman-Byzantine Cathedral of Monreale, one of the finest in Europe. It drew him "like a lodestar," remembered Truscott, who offered to send a reconnaissance force to probe enemy resistance to its south.[26]

The gesture was appreciated. A few days later, Patton ordered Truscott to get his entire division to Sicily's capital as fast as possible. Truscott called together his regimental commanders and opened a bottle of whisky, offering them a drink.

"I want you to be in Palermo in five days!"[27]

The city was a hundred miles away. The roads were poor and there was scant chance of finding clean water in the hinterland. Lieutenant Maurice Britt vividly recalled the "foot race" that ensued. "We left our anti-tank guns behind but carried bazookas and anti-tank rifles and the usual mortars and machine guns. There were no roads, not even paths, on this march, and the country was rugged—worse than the Ozark mountains of my home state. After each hour we rested about ten minutes, about as long as it takes to smoke one cigarette slowly."

Men staggered to their feet, adjusted their packs, and resumed the Truscott trot, passing singed fields of cactus, dry riverbeds, and thickets of cork oak. There was no singing, not a word wasted as the horizon shimmered and the weakest began to wilt.

Britt saved his breath as he struggled under the weight of his pack. He started to feel dizzy with fatigue even though he was in better condition than most. Before long, men dropped to the ground and were left behind, lips parched and faces burned deep red. "Going up hills was the worst," remembered Britt. "When my own lungs felt like bursting, I kept my eyes on some little city fellow, trudging along, suffering, I knew, with every step."[28]

Britt's company reached their first objective—a key road used by the enemy—in less than two days, subsisting on the rations they carried. "Then we settled down for our fight, taking positions to cover the road. The Italians, who never knew what to do when their plans are upset, were so surprised to see us so far inland that 1,000 of them surrendered."[29]

Meanwhile, Captain Ware's B Company and the 15th Infantry Regiment stomped forward on half rations, scavenging for grapes and other fruit when they could, for fifty-four miles in thirty-three hours—a record in World War II for US foot soldiers—and coughing from the clouds of dust that contained crushed chalk and cow dung, which compounded their thirst.[30] Jeeps trundled alongside columns and a few lucky GIs, tongues swollen, handed over their canteens to be filled without breaking step.

A private under Ware's command in B Company noted in his diary on the evening of July 19: "What a day. We covered thirty miles through the dust and heat of the Sicilian summer. Our feet are covered in blisters. The roads are rocky and that makes it hard walking. The enemy is retreating so fast, we can't contact him. We are walking at a rate of 4.5 miles an hour. Boy are my dogs barking now."[31]

B Company reached the village of Santo Stefano Quisquina, a two-day march from Palermo, on July 20, and Ware finally allowed his men to rest for a few hours. General Truscott had followed their advance with growing pride. All the hard training in North Africa was paying off. "In blistering heat and stifling dust," Truscott recalled, "these soldiers plowed their way forward like waves beating on an ocean beach and at a rate which Roman legions never excelled."[32]

The Marne men were, however, denied the honor of being the first to enter Palermo, the first major city in Europe to be liberated from German occupation. Patton ordered Truscott to stop short so that he himself could be photographed on July 22 welcoming Sherman tanks from the 2nd Armored Division as they clanked into the ruined city.

Banners flew.

"DOWN WITH MUSSOLINI!"

"LONG LIVE AMERICA!"[33]

Boys with stick-thin legs, malnourished, threw fresh lemons and bunches of grapes at the Americans.

"Caramelli! Caramelli! Caramelli!"[34]

Candies! Candies! Candies!

Camera shutters clicked.

The famed war photographer Robert Capa, working for *Life* magazine, watched the ensuing victory procession: "The road leading into the city was lined with tens of thousands of frantic Sicilians waving white sheets and homemade American flags with not enough stars and too many stripes. Everyone had a cousin in Brook-a-leen."[35]

Truscott and Patton met the day after Palermo was liberated.

Patton looked delighted.

"Well, the Truscott trot sure got us here in a damn hurry," said Patton.[36]

There followed a week's rest for Ware, Murphy, and Britt. B Company was stationed at first in an abandoned aircraft factory. Seaplanes needing only guns to be mounted stood silent guard.[37] Then Ware moved his men to a municipal building in the heart of Palermo. In streets nearby, soldiers lined up patiently outside whorehouses. Only a quarter of the population remained, more than a hundred fifty thousand civilians having fled bombing. Ware's men wandered down the narrow passages between collapsed homes, past the propaganda signs declaring *Duce! Duce! Duce!* and along the Via Libertà in search of decent chow and coffee.

If they were lucky, officers might get a table at the Grand Hotel Excelsior. The minestrone soup was too watery, the steak sliced too thin, but at least the fruit was fresh. Dogfaces had to make do with *caffè surrogato*, an almost palatable mix of chicory and beans. There was no espresso, no cappuccino. Italians hadn't tasted real coffee for three years. And the people of Palermo hadn't seen a loaf of bread for over a week. They were desperately hungry. Everywhere Americans ventured, they met locals who repeated one word.

"Pane, pane, pane!"

Bread . . .

"When will you Americans bring us food?"[38]

No one knew for sure. Then, on July 26, radio broadcasts from Rome announced that Il Duce—Mussolini—had been placed under arrest. King Victor Emmanuel had told him: "We cannot go on much longer. Sicily has gone." And so ended twenty-one years of fascism in Italy. A new government, under Marshal Pietro Badoglio, formed and pledged to fight on with Germany, redoubling its efforts. No one was convinced, least of all Hitler. Badoglio was bluffing, having already told Emmanuel that the war was *perduto, perdutissimo*—totally lost.[39]

Hitler considered replacing Badoglio but was persuaded to wait. He didn't waste any time in contacting Kesselring, however, and telling him to consider pulling all German troops out of Sicily. Kesselring had already made contingency plans and ordered operations officers from the Wehrmacht divisions still in combat to fly to his headquarters so they could arrange Operation Lehrgang, a mass evacuation. It would prove a smashing success.

Back in Palermo, Patton basked in his newfound fame as the conqueror of Western Sicily, ensconced in the Royal Palace with its Palatine Chapel, where he prayed devoutly when not impatiently pacing red-carpeted hallways. His face was on the covers of *Newsweek* and *Time* magazines that month but he yearned for ever greater glory on the battlefield—it was preordained. He knew it. So did God. The battle maps Patton pored over showed that his 7th Army had occupied more than half of Sicily. The crayon markings also revealed that Montgomery's 8th Army was making slow progress, in the lee of Mount Etna, along the southeastern coast of Sicily.

General Harold Alexander, commander of Allied forces in Sicily, looked at different maps, but they told the same story: Montgomery's forces needed help. And so he ordered Patton, in command of some two hundred thousand men, to attack eastward toward Messina along Sicily's northern shore. Whichever general reached Messina first would be able to declare victory in the Sicilian campaign.

Patton wasn't about to end this contest in second place, certainly not behind Montgomery. "This is a horse race," he told Troy Middleton, commander of the 45th Division, "in which the prestige of the US Army is at stake. We must take Messina before the British."[40] But it wasn't Middleton to whom Patton turned to win the race. That privilege was reserved for Lucian Truscott and his Marne men. They would spearhead the 7th Army's strike toward Messina, Patton's ultimate prize, a hundred forty miles away along the Via Valeria, an ancient coastal road.

CAPTAIN KEITH WARE had a problem—a soldier in B Company called Audie Murphy. Ware didn't want him in the front lines, however deadly a shot he had proved. He couldn't see beyond Private Murphy's "cursed baby face," in Murphy's words, and so Ware had transferred Murphy to his headquarters staff. Murphy should have been grateful but instead he slipped away several times to join dangerous patrols.

An exasperated Ware confronted Murphy.

"I hear you can't stay away from the front?"

"Yes, sir."

"What's wrong with you? You want to get killed?"

"No, sir."

"I'm going to do myself a favor. I'm putting you back in the lines, and you'll stay there until you're so sick of action you'll want to vomit."

"Yes, sir."

"And, incidentally," Ware added, "you've been made a corporal."[41]

Corporal Murphy found himself bent over, vomiting, not from revulsion at killing but rather from the dehydration he suffered. The temperature topped 110 Fahrenheit, with a hundred percent humidity. "It was a common sight to approach large groups of men clustered around a small pipe cemented into the side of a rocky cliffside," recalled Eugene Salet, one of Ware's fellow officers, "from which a small trickle of cold water flowed. These men would edge their way in an attempt to fill their canteens, then they would double-time for several hundred yards to arrive, soaked with perspiration and covered with a film of dust, back in place in their rapidly marching columns."[42]

Finding clean water, remembered Salet, often became "a life and death matter." The Germans had poisoned many water supplies and booby-trapped wells. Men were constantly thirsty, their throats "clogged with dust," losing a pound in weight each day because of the "muggy, sticky, smothering weather."[43] Mosquitoes descended whenever men made camp, and to quench their thirst, some gladly accepted jugs of unsanitary water from locals. Before long, some units were losing more men to diarrhea and malaria than to German bullets and mines.[44]

The road to Messina wound along a rocky and beautiful coastline, cutting through lemon groves. It was skirted by bushes of white oleander and pink bougainvillea. "If you could only travel this road in peacetime it would be a nice vacation, wouldn't it?" quipped one GI.[45] The Tyrrhenian Sea beat against narrow beaches. In many places, there were sheer drop-offs to the indigo blue waves below. Mountains bordered the shell-cratered road, providing superb observation for German mortar and artillery crews.

When B Company's Captain Ware and other commanders opted to outflank roadblocks by moving inland, through the mountains, it was as if they had been transported back to the Wild West. Now the most useful dogfaces were the country boys who knew how to handle mules and strap on saddles. Each mule could carry three to four forty-pound boxes of rations, enough to feed a company for a day. Some trails were so steep that the mules staggered and fell to their deaths, their braying and screaming echoing across valleys. When mules collapsed with exhaustion, soldiers finished them off with merciful pistol shots and then pushed them aside or tipped them over ledges.[46]

On August 2, B Company approached the town of San Fratello, perched in the Nebrodi Mountains, midway between Palermo and Messina. The town provided a perfect base for German artillery fire and for observation of the coastal road leading to Messina. Overlooked by a large outcrop of twenty-two-hundred-foot white rock called Monte San Fratello, the town could be reached only by a single winding road. The Germans blew up approaching bridges, mined the road, and set booby traps. They were not going to run again. This time, they would hold almost to the last man. The 15th Infantry Regiment's toughest and costliest battle in Sicily was about to begin.

Following a 2.5-hour barrage, B Company attacked on August 3 but was halted. What was the problem? There had been several casualties. Captain Ware decided to find out. It was vital to examine the craggy heights for snipers and to look down for mines—the Germans had seeded the entire area with them. He found some of his men positioned on a mountainside. On the other side of a valley, a mile or so across a river, were combat-hardened Germans from the Assietta Division well dug in on barren slopes. For every ten men, they had two machine guns, some with telescopic sights.

Ware selected several men for a patrol. He wanted an even closer look at the enemy. The Germans had set up excellent positions with machine guns and mortars covering the river. He ordered the patrol to be vigilant in case the Germans launched a counterattack after dark. Then he returned to his command post. Men began to dig in. As if on cue, a shell exploded, killing one of Ware's best sergeants and stunning others in the patrol. Pfc. Vert Enis scrambled back to inform Ware, covered in dirt from the explosion.[47] "I was so dirty," Enis noted in his diary, "that Ware didn't recognize me when I came into the command post. I was so nervous they sent me to the battalion aid station where I stayed the night."[48]

The fighting intensified the next day. The regiment's third battalion seized high ground overlooking San Fratello but came under savage counterattack. Ammunition ran low. Soldiers stripped their carbine clips and shared the bullets with any man who could fire an M-1 rifle—wiremen, runners, and radiomen. Finally, there were no more slugs to pass around. With bare hands, rocks, and bayonets, they held their ground.

The wounded could not be pulled out, so intense was the artillery and mortar fire. Shallow holes were hacked hastily in the rocky slopes and those who stood a chance of living were laid down, out of the line of fire, and given direct blood transfusions.

There was no plasma. That too had run out. Ravenous men, stranded for days without rations, trapped goats and sheep, slit their throats, and curbed hunger pains.[49]

Audie Murphy witnessed much of the fighting from a machine-gun nest he'd been ordered to protect. He watched as a smoke screen was laid down, shrouding the river below. As B Company attacked, Murphy lay in a vineyard, eating grapes. He could see his company, which had crossed the river, under fire in the distance. The Marne men were taking casualties but still advancing, pushing the Assietta Division from their positions, eventually seizing the town of San Fratello.

The 15th Infantry Regiment had passed its greatest test yet. It had stood strong against an entire German division, under constant fire. Hunger and heat and terror had pushed many to the edge and beyond. One man had dug up a can of hash he'd nonchalantly thrown away days before, scraped away the flies and ants, and wolfed it down. Men were "hysterical with joy and relief," it was reported, when a mule train finally arrived, carrying medical supplies, fresh water, and ammunition.[50] "I contributed little to the battle," remembered Audie Murphy. "I acquired a healthy respect for the Germans as fighters; an insight into the fury of mass combat; and a bad case of diarrhea. I had eaten too many grapes."[51]

THERE WOULD BE no letup. Those were the orders coming from the top. With the British finally making steady progress along the southern coast, Truscott was under intense pressure from Patton to get to Messina. Kesselring had ensured that the Via Valeria was superbly defended in key places, so Patton devised a clever but potentially costly plan to leapfrog particularly strong German positions. He demanded that Truscott provide a battalion to support an end-run landing at Brolo, around forty miles west of Messina. Truscott pleaded with Patton for a twenty-four-hour delay so he could arrange for artillery support. The division had suffered high casualties in the last two weeks and Truscott wanted to save lives.

Patton could not have cared less. On Tuesday evening, August 10, he arrived at Truscott's headquarters at an olive oil factory near a small village called Terranova. According to Patton, Truscott was "walking up and down and looking futile."[52]

"What's the matter with you, Lucian?" Patton shrilled. "Are you afraid to fight?"

"General, you know that's ridiculous and insulting."

"General Truscott, if your conscience will not let you conduct this operation, I will relieve you and put someone in command who will."

"General, it is your privilege to reduce me whenever you want to."

"I don't want to. You are too old an athlete to believe it is possible to postpone a match."

"You are an old enough athlete to know that sometimes they are postponed."

"This one won't be. Remember Frederick the Great: *L'audace, toujours l'audace!* I know you will win."[53]

Patton put his arm around Truscott's shoulder.

"Let's have a drink—of your liquor."[54]

Later that day, Patton picked up his diary at his headquarters at the Royal Palace in Palermo. "I may have been bull-headed," he jotted, referring to his encounter with Truscott.[55] He had been indeed. Truscott's battalion was quickly in serious trouble, almost surrounded. At the eleventh hour, troops sent by Truscott came to its relief but four fine officers and thirty-seven men lost their lives.

Captain Ware meanwhile led his weary men through the mountains toward Messina, the loud crackling of cicadas interrupted by the echo of explosions thundering and rumbling across narrow valleys. "If enemy gunners spotted you going up the mountainside," recalled one man, "you were either a dead duck or a badly frightened one." The 88mm, the finest German weapon of the war, was particularly lethal. Men never knew when a "stomp" of shells might land, "atomizing" and "vaporizing" soldiers in the blink of an eye.[56]

At 5 P.M. on August 13, as the afternoon heat began to wane, Ware's company began an all-night march, resting for two hours to draw rations, before finally digging in at six the next morning. "The outfit as a whole is about dead," noted Pfc. Vert Enis in his diary. "Our feet are worn out. The rumors are going around that the Battle of Sicily will be over in two or three days. OK by me."[57] To the south, far off in the distance, stood the volcano, Mount Etna, almost eleven thousand feet, the tallest peak in Italy south of the Alps.

Thankfully, German opposition lessened as B Company trekked farther east, uniforms sagging, coated in dust.[58] Ware passed abandoned half-tracks and supply dumps. By August 16, his men were rolling in trucks along the Via Valeria toward Messina. Ware was ordered to set up positions to the south. That night, other units from the 3rd Division entered the city.

After daylight the following morning, the last German troops escaped from Sicily across the Messina Strait to mainland Italy, two miles distant. Operation Lehrgang was a spectacular success. Forty thousand German troops and some ten thousand vehicles, as well as thousands of tons of ammunition and fuel, had been evacuated in six days and seven nights. It had been, according to one German general, Fridolin von Senger, a "glorious retreat."[59] Von Senger and others reporting to Kesselring had delayed the Allied advance with consummate timing and skill, allowing their forces to fight another day in Italy.

General Truscott had pushed the 3rd Division hard. He had carried out Patton's every command. By rights, he should have led his men into Messina and received the city's official surrender. Yet again, glory was denied him.

Patton asked Truscott to wait on a road leading into the outskirts of Messina. Patton duly turned up in a jeep with a pack of correspondents in tow.

"What in the hell are you all standing around for?" barked Patton.

Truscott kept his counsel and then Patton was off, rolling into Messina to have his photograph taken and to make headlines around the globe. He had beaten the British to the city by a couple of hours.[60]

Starving Italians emerged from the ruins of their homes and lined the streets.

"*Viva, viva!*" they cried.

Old women, clad in black, threw paper flowers and roses.

"*Tanto tempo vi abbiamo aspettato!*"[61]

We've waited so long for you to arrive.

The Battle for Sicily had lasted thirty-eight days and cost twenty-five thousand Allied casualties. Almost a hundred fifty thousand Italians had surrendered. Crucially, Axis forces were no longer able to control the Mediterranean. Yet some of those who had fought their way along the bloody but beautiful Via Valeria would later consider the entire Sicilian campaign to be a bitter victory, given that so many of the enemy had escaped unscathed. "We should have murdered them," one American officer lamented after reaching the ruins of Messina. "It would have saved us a hell of lot of trouble later on."[62]

While Patton enjoyed his glory hour, Truscott and his staff drove back along the Via Valeria to their headquarters in Palermo. It had taken Truscott's division almost three weeks of savage fighting to get from Palermo to Messina. The journey along the winding coastal road, which boasted several new bridges, took three hours. From Palermo, Truscott headed farther west along the coast to the port of Trapani, at the far western tip of Sicily's northern coastline, where his division would finally gather to rest.

Patton would always be grateful to Truscott for getting him to Messina first, rating him fifth out of the 153 general officers who served under him in World War II. On August 25, he sent Truscott a congratulatory barrel of cognac. "On the barrel is the division insignia about a foot square," Truscott wrote his wife. It had a banner—"First in Messina."[63]

For B Company commander Keith Ware and Corporal Audie Murphy, Trapani was a welcome relief from the slog through mountains in oppressive heat. The evenings were cool and men wrapped themselves in blankets and slept under the stars rather than in tents. The hazelnut and almond season was at its peak and many dogfaces could be seen carrying bags of nuts, breaking them against rocks, chomping away as if Christmas had arrived early.

Rumors abounded. The 3rd Division would be heading to England or perhaps even to China. Others said they were going to stay on and garrison Sicily under Patton's command. Everyone wanted to believe the ships massing in the nearby harbor were to take them home to the States. On September 9, it was announced that Italian armed forces had surrendered to the Allies. In Sicily, they'd barely put up a fight. The Germans had done most of the killing. Hitler and Kesselring reacted swiftly, occupying most of Italy, defeating Italian resistance, freeing Mussolini, and setting up a puppet government in Rome. The Italians were no longer a threat but the Germans, in far greater numbers, would now have to be defeated on the mainland.

IT WAS TOO good to last—lounging in the sun, eating fresh fruit, reading comics, and dreaming of home. At B Company headquarters, Captain Keith Ware gathered his men on September 14, 1943. He had big news. The Marne men had already been transferred from Patton's 7th Army to General Mark Clark's 5th

Army. Audie Murphy and his comrades listened as Ware now said they were going to move to a staging area the next day. B Company's dogfaces, the "vinegar taken from their spirit," as Murphy put it, would play their part in yet another amphibious operation, this time to breach Fortress Europe itself by invading mainland Italy.[64]

"We are going there to fight, boys," said Ware, "and I ask you to do as good a job there as you have here."[65]

B Company was told to pack and then dismissed.

By 6 P.M. that day, Ware's men were on trucks, rolling toward Palermo.[66]

Meanwhile, Lieutenant Maurice Britt in I Company had a surprise visitor.

A colonel stood before Britt and told him he wanted Britt to take over command of his battalion's L Company.

"Sir, I don't think I'm up to the job," Britt replied.

The colonel knew he was asking a lot and appeared sympathetic but irritated.

Britt had not given the expected answer.

"If I didn't think you were able to do it, I wouldn't put you in command," said the colonel briskly.

Britt's first duty was to brief L Company on the change in command. He told the most senior sergeant to gather the men. He was as nervous as he'd ever been, his throat tight as he saw all two hundred fall into line. They looked in superb fighting form. "We were all in good shape," recalled Britt, "because we had been resting in an olive grove for several weeks after the end of the campaign in Sicily. We had oranges and lemons to eat, a rare treat for soldiers and the last oranges we saw for a long time."

In Britt's mind, it seemed that they looked at him, lined up in two perfect rows, with suspicion if not resentment.

Who the hell did he think he was?

L Company was regarded as one of the finest units in the 3rd Division if not the entire United States Army.

"Sir, the company is formed," said the sergeant.

"At ease," said Britt.

Britt took a breath and composed himself. This was going to be one hell of a team talk. He did not recall exactly what he said, only that he gave it his all, speaking from the heart. He then introduced a fellow lieutenant, called Jack Miller, from Vincennes, Indiana, who'd been assigned to L Company as its executive officer.[67] During the trek across Sicily, Miller had served as a grave registration officer, what Britt regarded as "the hardest job in the army," which had often meant removing watches and rings from those dead friends who could be identified, who had not been blown to chunks, and then searching through blood-stained pockets for "snapshots of wives and babies" that would then be sent to the bereaved.

The men listened politely to Britt but did not look overly impressed.

"We sure got a cold reception," Britt later told Miller.

Miller tried his best to cheer Britt up but the Arkansan looked glum. He knew he was replacing a highly respected officer, Captain George Butler, who'd been forced to miss the upcoming invasion having fallen sick. Butler had earned the Silver Star as he had pushed L Company along the northern coast to Messina. He had rarely had to bark an order, leading through suggestion and example. "The men would go to hell and back for him," remembered Britt.[68]

Would they do the same for Britt? In less than twenty-four hours, on a distant shore, he would find out.

CHAPTER 3

Mud, Mules, and Mountains

EVIDENCE OF FIERCE fighting lay all around as Lieutenant Maurice Britt came ashore, leading L Company, south of the port of Salerno on September 19, 1943. The beachhead that Britt passed through, strewn with abandoned equipment and burned wreckage, had been saved in bitter fighting only a few days before. On September 15, "Black Wednesday," it had looked for several hours as if the Salerno venture would be the first major defeat for US forces in Europe in World War II.

So grave had the situation become that the 3rd Division, placed initially in reserve, had been sent in to support the 45th and 36th Divisions, both of which had taken a beating but had nonetheless held against counterattacks from Kesselring's forces. Had Kesselring been allowed to call on his own reserves, he would easily have destroyed the precarious bridgehead. Instead, two days earlier, on September 17, the Americans and British had linked up and the crisis had passed but at the cost of more than twelve thousand Allied casualties.

Britt advanced toward the railroad town of Battipaglia. Ahead loomed a ridge of mountains, the Apennines. Mercifully, there was no enemy resistance as Britt led his men toward the rugged horizon. But those peaks ahead, where the Germans were waiting, looked to be higher than in Sicily, more forbidding. Battipaglia was little more than scorched earth, pounded to rubble by the 12th Air Force. "The destruction there was fantastic," recalled one soldier. "Rails were torn up and stood in great loops in the air as though some giant had twisted them into weird shapes."[1]

Britt moved on toward a town called Acerno, the spearhead of the 3rd Division's advance. There were vague plans, he had learned, about pushing the Germans back to Naples and then eventually to Rome.

"Where will it end?" some men wondered.

"When will it end?" others asked.

Will I be there when it does end?[2]

Britt was leading an infantry company for the first time but he knew what it took to motivate young men to believe they could win, to find the will to fight back against an opponent. He'd tested himself over and over in a violent sport. "He had the ability," his college coach would later recall, "to make snap decisions in a crisis and the ability to think out problems in advance."[3]

There were those heady days of being worshipped by so many co-eds screaming his name as he ran with the pigskin for the University of Arkansas. There was that cold November afternoon in 1941 when he'd played for the Detroit Lions. They were trailing the Philadelphia Eagles by three points in the fourth quarter. Then the ball arced through the air and Britt plucked it from the sky and charged forward, the roar of the crowd louder each yard as he dodged and sprinted to the end zone for a forty-five-yard touchdown. The Lions finished the game victors, 21–17, but Britt never made a reception again—three weeks later, the Japanese bombed Pearl Harbor and the majority of NFL players, including Britt, hung up their cleats and headed to war.

Those glory days belonged to another life as Britt led L Company along a dusty road toward Acerno, twelve miles inland from the Salerno beaches. As Britt approached the town, the Germans showed their hand, blowing bridges ahead of him, and so his first day as L Company's new commander was spent going almost nowhere. Two days later, he and his men were finally able to see the town, some twenty-four hundred feet above sea level, lying in the lee of slopes thick with maple, oak, and chestnut trees. In peacetime wild cats roamed there as golden eagles soared above.

Britt's orders were to seize Acerno as fast as he could. Then the entire Salerno bridgehead would be secure and the Allies could push north, take Naples, and head along the Liri Valley to Rome. He'd been told the Germans had committed as many as a dozen tanks and several hundred men to the town's defense. His plan was to seize a hill above it and then enter Acerno itself after crossing several fields and orchards. That evening, Britt learned that L Company and he were to jump off the next morning, September 22, at 7 A.M. Before he attacked, there would be

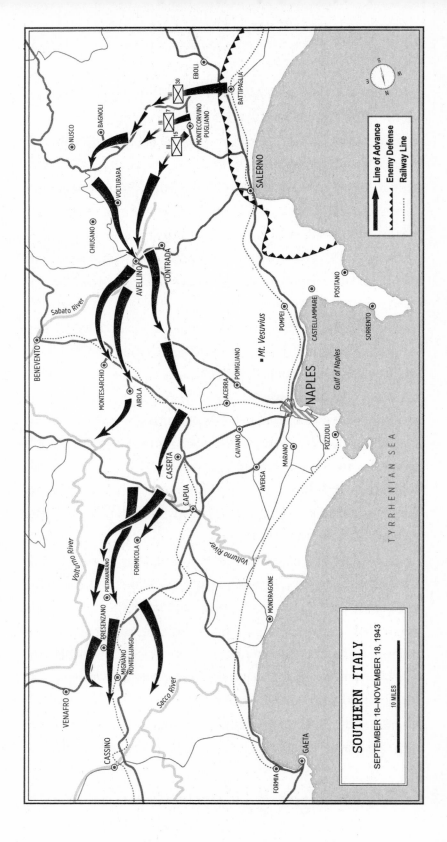

SOUTHERN ITALY

SEPTEMBER 18–NOVEMBER 18, 1943

10 MILES

Line of Advance
Enemy Defense
Railway Line

TYRRHENIAN SEA

Gulf of Naples

EBOLI
BATTIPAGLIA
MONTECORVINO PUGLIANO
SALERNO
NUSCO
BAGNOLI
VOLTURARA
CHIUSANO
CONTRADA
AVELLINO
POSITANO
SORRENTO
CASTELLAMMARE
POMPEI
Mt. Vesuvius
Sabato River
BENEVENTO
MONTESARCHIO
AIROLA
POMIGLIANO
ACERRA
NAPLES
CAIVANO
AVERSA
MARANO
POZZUOLI
CASERTA
CAPUA
Volturno River
FORMICOLA
PIETRAVAIRANO
PRESENZANO
MIGNANO
MONTELLUNGO
Sacco River
VENAFRO
CASSINO
MONDRAGONE
FORMIA
GAETA

a ten-minute artillery barrage to soften up German defenses and then a smoke screen would be laid down.

That night, Britt and his men advanced in single file and headed toward a gorge. They waded across a fast-flowing stream, its cold water chilling them. The men carrying the heavy base plates of mortars had a particularly grueling time getting across and then up the other side of the steep gorge. By 3 A.M., Britt and his men had reached their assigned jump-off positions. Sure enough, as promised, the battalion's artillery started up at 7 A.M., and after the smoke shells had been fired, Britt ordered his company into action.

"It was my first attack as a commanding officer," he recalled, "and I wanted so much to win the men's confidence that I think I forgot to be very scared."

The enemy pulled back as the Marne men crossed a cornfield beside a road leading into Acerno. Britt came under fire and felt a sharp pain above his knee. A piece of mortar shrapnel had struck him. But he was too excited to let it bother him as he saw Germans advancing and then setting up machine guns. Before long, one of the guns was sending volleys of bullets toward Britt. He and his men dropped to the ground and were quickly pinned down in the cornfield. In the words of one of Britt's fellow officers, the first "serious blood-letting" for the 3rd Division in Italy had begun.[4]

Britt told a man with a rifle grenade to go to the left to take out the German machine gun, but before long he returned, saying he couldn't locate the German position. Then Britt sent another man to the right but again he had no luck. The Germans were well camouflaged.

Britt turned to a GI with a grenade launcher.

"That's a nice instrument you got there."

"Oh yeah."

"That thing will toss a grenade forty yards?"

"Yeah, if you know how to handle it."

"Gimme."

Britt grabbed the grenade launcher and crawled forward. "I tried to follow the ripples of the mounds of earth, but the dried cornstalks didn't provide much cover, and soon the machine gun opened up," he remembered. "I heard the bullets whistling over my head and the crackle as they occasionally hit a cornstalk. A German mortar squad must have spotted me, because shells started falling nearby."

Britt had never been more aware of his height. He was almost six foot four inches in his stocking feet—a large target. He pressed his face to the soil and then began to crawl on his belly again. It seemed like an eternity but in fact it was less than five minutes before he got close enough to hit the German machine gun. "I pulled up on one knee, aimed quickly, and fired the rifle grenade. It flew about 60 yards, a beautiful and lucky shot that landed directly on the target. The machine gun stopped; two Germans firing it were both killed."[5]

L Company could move forward once more. Acerno fell after bitter fighting, and dozens of casualties, to the 30th Infantry Regiment later that afternoon—the "first major action," it was reported, of Mark Clark's 5th Army as it advanced toward Naples.[6] The next day, Britt had his wound treated. He'd earned his first Purple Heart and would receive the Silver Star for his performance with the rifle grenade: "I was glad to get the medal, of course, but what pleased me most was the feeling that I had made 'the first team' as far as Company L was concerned."[7]

THE PUSH NORTH, up the jagged spine of Italy, continued. On September 26, the autumn rains began. They would continue, ceaselessly it seemed, until the following spring. Before 1943 was over, a depressing twenty inches would fall. "The country was shockingly beautiful," recalled the journalist Ernie Pyle, "and as shockingly hard to capture from the enemy."[8] As the pace of advance slowed and the maple and oak leaves began to turn color on the heights of the Apennines, the fighting got tougher and tougher.

Casualties mounted and the grave registration squads began to stuff mangled corpses into mattress covers before sending them for burial.[9] Audie Murphy remembered "undue optimism" after the Battle of Salerno and being "prepared for a quick dash to Rome." But by October the advance had slowed to a "walk," then to a "push," and finally to a crawl.[10] The suffocating heat and swarms of black flies of the summer were long gone. The air was crisp, heralding winter.

Lieutenant Maurice Britt wrote to his wife, Nancy, back in Arkansas, describing a visit to the front lines by no less than Allied Supreme Commander Dwight Eisenhower. Wanting to "sustain morale amidst the inescapably miserable conditions," as he put it, Eisenhower had inspected Britt's L Company and others.[11] Britt was proud to report home that Eisenhower had congratulated him and his men on the "wonderful job" they had done with "four campaigns under their belt."[12]

The next challenge would be to cross the Volturno River, some hundred miles south of Rome. The river had steep banks, was in full flood, and at points was more than fifty yards wide as it snaked toward the Tyrrhenian Sea.

Under cover of darkness, Murphy and his platoon from B Company occupied a dank, recently abandoned German dugout by the river. Willow and poplar trees had been shredded by shellfire, thousands of rounds per day fired by the Allies. In B Company's area, just one tree had survived. It was pitch-black inside the dugout and it reeked of rotten food, Teutonic sweat, and old clothing. The Germans were infamous for their lack of hygiene but admired for their dugouts and other shelters, which were remarkably resilient—they had to be, given that in Italy the Allies fired ten shells for each one that Kesselring could throw back.

Among Murphy's closest comrades that fall were private Joe Sieja and a corporal called Lattie Tipton. Three months in combat, from Sicily to the Italian mainland, dodging artillery shells and watching his fellow soldiers die, had done nothing to dampen Sieja's hatred of the Germans. When Murphy looked at him, he sometimes saw "a strange, broken light" in the young man's eyes that made him look particularly sad. Both Sieja and Tipton had long since confided in Murphy, expressing their deepest feelings. Whenever they talked about women, Murphy complained that he'd never had time to fall in love and besides he'd been "too damned proud to let a girl see the patches on [his] pants."[13]

Tipton had often read out letters from his nine-year-old daughter, Claudean.

Dear daddy i am in school but the teacher is not looking . . . when are you coming home i miss you . . .[14]

Murphy and Tipton, in particular, were "like brothers," as Murphy put it. Every time Murphy went into combat at Tipton's side, he pictured Claudean, "the eyes, eager with life; her pert freckled nose; her pigtails with bows at the ends."[15] Murphy was determined to do all he could to protect Tipton so he'd see his daughter again.

Tipton had also received mail from his ex-wife. "We got married too young," Tipton confided, "and the big things I planned didn't pan out."

On the morning of October 12, at a press briefing, a senior officer laid out the challenge facing the Allies.

"You all know what's planned for tonight," he began. "We're going across the Volturno."

This was no ordinary river.

"It's got the damnedest banks you ever saw, at some places as steep as forty-five degrees. Those banks are mined."

Kesselring knew where they could cross and had planned accordingly.

"What we're up against is to get the infantry across and far enough in, so the bridges can be put across."

Three German divisions were waiting on the other side of the river.

"We can't be too optimistic. . . . It's going to be a tough scrap. One of the handicaps is that we can't use air support because of the weather."[16]

That afternoon and evening, men prepared for their assault.

"Sleep, swine," called out Germans on the northern banks. "We kill you all before breakfast."[17]

No doubt to Audie Murphy's relief, B Company was going to be held in reserve. He could stay in his dugout for a while longer, sheltered from the rain and German shell bursts. This time, other companies from the 15th Infantry would go first.

The two bridges in the 3rd Division's sector had been blown, so assault boats would be needed, but there were not enough on hand. And so the Marne men improvised, using whatever they could scrounge: rubber pontoons from the navy and even hastily assembled rafts with water cans and gasoline tins used as floats. Of the four US infantry divisions in VI Corps, the Marne men would bear the brunt of the operation. To give them a starting chance, Truscott ordered that a massive smoke screen be laid down on enemy positions and the river itself before H Hour— 2 A.M. on October 13—when his troops would start to cross.

Beneath the milky white clouds of the smoke screen, in the first minutes of October 13, the first wave of troops gathered from the 15th Infantry Regiment. Captain Arlo Olson, commander of F Company, led his men in hushed silence toward the southern banks of the Volturno, on a stretch of the river running east to west, about a mile from a small village called Triflisco.

A graduate of the University of South Dakota, twenty-five-year-old Olson had slogged for thirteen days straight for thirty miles across nameless mountains and torrential streams. It was raining hard when Olson arrived at the southern bank of the Volturno at 2 A.M. The river was in full flow, spilling over rocks with ominous force. Flares soared above the German positions, bright green and red. Olson began to cross, the roiling waters reaching his chest. The last few weeks had taken their toll and his face was no longer boyish. Gone was his usual smile, the bright eyes.

There was the steady hacking of machine-gun fire. White and blue tracers stitched from German bunkers. Thankfully, the smoke screen shrouded the river from German forward artillery observers on high ground a few hundred yards to the north. Olson waded through the cold floodwaters, carbine above his head. But then Germans spotted him and bullets were zipping into the torrents around him. He kept going, making agonizingly slow progress, more bullets whistling past him as he headed toward a machine-gun nest. Finally, he was across but then had to climb several feet to get to the top of the northern bank. The German fire was relentless.

Olson pulled a pin from a grenade and then from another and tossed both at the nearest German machine-gun nest. He heard loud explosions as the grenades killed the men who'd tried to cut him down as he crossed the river. But there were other machine-gun nests dotted along the northern banks, and the Germans opened up as Olson's men struggled to ford the river. Olson kept moving along the bank toward the next enemy position. He did not run. He did not dive for cover when the bullets stuttered his way. He walked slowly, deliberately, back straight, as if immortal, taking his time, drawing the hypnotic blue and white tracers, a sacrificial decoy, hell-bent on saving his boys.[18]

Five Germans, it was later reported, tossed potato-masher grenades at him. He carried on, closing on the enemy until he was just twenty yards away, before opening up with his carbine and slaughtering them. Then he ran out of ammunition. On the soft, muddy ground he saw a German machine pistol, a highly effective weapon at close range. He picked it up and walked on. The machine pistol held thirty-two rounds when fully loaded. Hopefully, there were plenty of bullets left. Olson was merciless, drilling nine more Germans, the machine pistol making a velvet purr. His men were soon across the river with minimal casualties, thanks to his courage and aggression, for which he would receive the Medal of Honor.

As dawn broke, General Lucian Truscott stood at the river's edge, anguished, his face creased with worry. White smoke hung over the churning waters, a fragile veil. Crimson tracers from American machine guns, which had a lower rate of fire than Germans MG-42s, skimmed across the river above men wading, wearing life vests, grabbing onto ropes. Truscott was anxious, above all, for armored support to get across and support five battalions that were, by first light, already on the northern side of the river. If the Germans counterattacked with Panzers, his division would be ripped to shreds.

"Hurry!" barked Truscott. "Hurry! . . . Get those damn tank destroyers and tanks across. . . . Goddamit, get up ahead and fire at some targets of opportunity. Fire at anything shooting our men. . . . What do you mean it can't be done? Have you tried it?"[19]

Armored units crossed that morning and more infantry followed all day, including Captain Ware's B Company, and within twenty-four hours, Truscott's troops were in control of the entire Volturno Valley. According to the commander of the German Tenth Army, Heinrich von Vietinghoff, the 3rd Division had done well to lose only around three hundred men.[20]

The Germans pulled back along a crucial road, Highway 6, to what Kesselring called the Reinhard position: heavily defended mountains on either side of the Mignano Pass.[21] Some twenty miles farther north of the Reinhard position lay the even more formidable Gustav Line, which the Germans believed was impassable in bad weather.

Truscott wasn't about to lose momentum and drove his men onward, hoping to break the Reinhard position and then the Gustav Line before the winter set in. Maurice Britt, leading L Company, tried to bolster his men's spirits as they traipsed through ruined villages with pieces of red roof tiles scattered everywhere, along goat trails, through groves of cypresses and stone pines seeded with antipersonnel mines, and past rotting corpses of German youths from the 3rd Panzergrenadier Division.

Four out of ten American casualties in Italy were caused by mines: large ones that could blow up a truck, wooden ones that were difficult to detect, and castrators, which did exactly as their name advertised. The Allied advance could be traced by a gory wake of body pieces and bloodied shreds of uniforms and twisted equipment.

Why should Britt's men care about Italy? At times, it all seemed so utterly futile. Almost every day, Britt had to tell his platoon leaders their next goal would yet another goddamn hill in what was labeled on their maps as "mountainous hinterland."

"One more hill," Britt would say.

"Yes, Captain, one more hill."

There was no anger or bitterness when platoon sergeants said this. Men were too cold and exhausted, often drenched to the skin by the constant rain, so they simply mumbled their replies forlornly until "one more hill" was a sad running joke, a motto for L Company.

Britt would send an advance patrol of ten men—the point of his company—to scout out the next hill. They moved around four hundred yards ahead of L Company's forward platoon and were led by a sergeant who could be trusted not to panic. It was lethal work and Britt rotated the advance squad as often as he could, wanting to give men a decent chance of surviving at least a week on the line. It seemed bitterly unfair that Britt's L Company was more often than not chosen to be the spearhead for his battalion because his point men were so good.

Each man's death deeply affected Britt. It was particularly hard to see the heartbreak and anguish of men who lost a foxhole friend. "To lose a buddy was the worst that could happen," he remembered. "We had a pair of twins, who of course were even more than buddies. One was killed. When I saw the stricken look in his brother's eyes, I sent him back to rest camp immediately."[22]

One day that October, Britt and his company seized high ground above a village and then Britt was told to push on another mile or so to another town. A road lay between the village and the next town, but it was thought to be mined. And so Britt set off across a terraced vineyard. The rain began again, a chilling "drizzle" that seemed to soak into the marrow of their bones. Their boots squelched in the ankle-deep mud. Every few minutes, a man would trip over wires holding up vines and fall flat on his face.

After a few hours, Britt realized that he was lost. For a moment, he began to panic. Then he pulled out his map and held it under a blanket to keep it from getting wet and to shade the glare from his flashlight. He contacted battalion headquarters and reported his position as shown on his creased map. A colonel was called to the radio. "Britt!" he shouted. "Do you realize what you've done? You've passed up the battalion objective. You've passed up the regimental objective, and you've taken part of the divisional objective. Hold on there as long as you can and we'll try to relieve you."

It was a long wait until daylight. Eventually, the rest of Britt's battalion reached his position and the Germans pulled back, even leaving behind mortars and machine guns, shocked that the Americans had penetrated so far so fast.

According to Britt, General Truscott was delighted when he learned of the advance. From division HQ, Truscott sent a message of congratulation: "Britt, that was a marvelous piece of work that your company did. I want you to pass it along to your men that you have speeded up our schedule by two days."

Britt wisely chose not to reply: "If I had told the general I was lost I might have been court-martialed. My achievement was entirely accidental. It might as easily have been disastrous for all my men."[23]

———

BRITT'S UNINTENDED PROGRESS was unusual. By late fall, the Allied advance averaged a glacial two miles a week. To kill one of Kesselring's men cost an estimated $25,000 in shells. Had not Napoléon warned that the only way to invade the country was from the north? Hannibal had, after all, crossed the Alps in winter with elephants rather than approach Rome along the Apennines. "Rain, rain, rain," a dejected Allied commander jotted in his diary. "The roads are so deep in mud that moving troops and supplies forward is a terrific job. Enemy resistance is not nearly as great as that of Mother Nature, who certainly seems to be fighting on the side of the German."[24]

Despite the worsening conditions, the poor bloody infantry marched on. The 15th Infantry Regiment's Captain Arlo Olson, having earned the Medal of Honor at the Volturno, once again stepped up and showed the way, heading northwest, toward a ridge of mountains whose most ominous peak was called Mount Nicola. For two weeks, Olson crept through thick brush, avoiding S mines and booby traps, moving like a ghost ahead of his men in the cold darkness, probing, harassing German patrols.

The leaves were falling from trees on the upper heights, which meant Olson had to be vigilant, making sure his men did not expose themselves unnecessarily. They should avoid skylines, daub their helmets with mud so they did not shine when the sun dared to peek from behind the clouds. On October 27, he came under fire and crawled forward until he was around twenty yards from the enemy. Then he stood up and charged. A machine gun cackled and bullets flew close but Olson got to the nest and killed the crew with his pistol.

His men caught up with him. Olson pushed on but the Hermann Göring Division fought back hard, laying down a blanket of fire. Then Olson's luck ran out and he was hit badly. Although in excruciating pain, he refused medical aid and made sure his men could defend themselves from further counterattacks. Only then was he placed on a stretcher and carried down the mountain. He didn't live to see the bottom.[25]

In the early hours of October 28, the day after Olson's death, Lieutenant Maurice Britt arrived at the base of Mount Nicola. Dawn came and with it a massive half hour bombardment from German dugouts on a ridge above. When it ended, he took his cue and led his men upward. Still wearing summer fatigues— winter wear had yet to arrive—they formed a skirmish line, he recalled, "much like the men in the Civil war." His company seized the ridge with a few casualties. Then he ordered his men to dig slit trenches long enough so they could lie down, deep enough so that flying white-hot shards of shrapnel would not slice and dice them.

The slit trenches were arranged so that each man would have a field of fire. Britt knew only too well what was coming. The Germans would strike when it was darkest and his men most tired. It was the deadly pattern of war in these infernal mountains. "All that night we waited, permitting no one to sleep, but the Germans failed to show up. It started to drizzle, a clammy Italian drizzle that always made us wonder who started the expression 'sunny Italy.'"

Exhausted, Britt and his men climbed out of their slit trenches at daylight. There was a wide valley below and beyond it another ridge. The entire area was shrouded in a thick mist. A gust broke up the mist for a few seconds. Britt spotted several dozen Germans busy laying mines and unrolling barbed wire. When the mist settled again, Britt headed down into the valley but the Germans had vanished. They'd not yet finished burying several mines and Britt's men removed their detonators, crossed the valley, and began to climb through ferns, shoulders hunched, and through stubby trees and thorny brush once more.

Time to set a trap of his own. Britt had picked up a German machine pistol. As his forward platoon neared Germans on the next ridge, he pressed the trigger, hoping he'd fool the enemy into thinking he was a German officer giving the signal for them to open fire. It worked. Bullets flew. Britt's men were well concealed in bushes and the Germans had revealed their positions.

Britt and his men attacked through the bushes and twisted trees.

A German cried out: "Hahnds oop."

Britt instinctively turned and was about to shoot when he saw his radio operator pull out his pistol and aim it at three tall Germans armed with rifles.

"Hands up yourself," snapped the radio operator.

The Germans dropped their weapons.

When Britt reached the top of the ridge, he discovered that the enemy had pulled back. His men again dug in where they could, amid large boulders and slippery rocks. They were at the limit of their endurance after three days without rest, getting by on cold K rations and the rare swig from almost empty canteens.

"Our mouths were so dry that cigarettes tasted like dust," remembered Britt. "We tried to wet our tongues, but there was no saliva. Our lips were crusted and cracked. Our stomachs had an empty, drawn feeling."[26]

The rains returned. Some men tried to collect water in a blanket and then squeezed out drops into a helmet. Others in L Company thankfully carried tins containing Crisco, a cooking grease. They'd saved the grease in better days, after feasting on a slaughtered pig, and scooped out pork-flavored globs and swallowed them for energy.

The following morning, one of Britt's men fell down a steep slope. It was best to wait until after dark to go fetch him—in daylight snipers would pick off men if they exposed themselves. But Britt wasn't going to let one of his men die alone on a lousy mountain thousands of miles from home. He clambered down the slope, reached the stricken soldier, and then carried him out of the line of fire so he didn't bleed to death, in the process earning the Bronze Star with V for Valor.

The next day, Britt and his men climbed down through the brush, reaching a monastery on the outskirts of a town called Pietravairano, perched on a mountainside.[27] To his relief, Britt learned that the Germans had abandoned the town and the Santa Maria Della Vigna monastery, its mossy walls dating to 1372.[28] "But they left some deadly souvenirs," he recalled. "As we entered, two Italian civilians told us 'Mines, mines,' with much gesticulating toward the town. We took the hint and spent the night in some ancient or medieval ruins on the hill."

Tragedy ensued. "Next morning," remembered Britt, "some of the civilians of the town, who had huddled in [the monastery] through the fighting on the ridge, returned to their homes." But they hadn't counted on the malevolence—the pure evil—of the retreating Boche, who had left booby traps in many streets. Many were blown to shreds, including mothers and their small children. "We were as accustomed to death as men can ever get, but this made us sick. When our medics came up, they took care of the injured people, and we gave the civilians what food we could spare."[29]

MOUNT NICOLA HAD fallen but to the north lay yet another mountain range, wreathed in ghostlike clouds and soaking mists. The slog continued, the ordeal seemingly without end, surely designed to break the spirit. Britt's division commander, Lucian Truscott, agonized and wondered how much more his men could take. Companies like Britt's could endure only so much.

On November 5, after dark, Truscott's immediate superior, VI Corps commander Major General John Lucas, called Truscott on the telephone. The fifty-three-year-old West Pointer, a grandfatherly, pipe-smoking pessimist who had once commanded the 3rd Division, was the bearer of bad news. Fifth Army chief Mark Clark wanted the 3rd Division to launch yet another attack to help the British by dislodging Germans holding two natural fortresses: Mount Lungo and Mount Rotondo. These mountains flanked Highway 6, twenty miles south of the town of Cassino. The valley between the peaks was the Mignano Gap—in Audie Murphy's words: "a nightmare for offensive troops."[30]

Truscott was no pushover. He'd already lost half of his

division's most junior officers—second lieutenants—since arriving at Salerno almost two months before. And his regiments were fragile. There'd been almost nine thousand casualties. Three out of four men had been killed, wounded, captured, or pulled off the line with trench foot, battle fatigue, frostbite, and exposure.

Truscott didn't want to throw away what good men he had left.

What support would they have, Truscott demanded, if they climbed yet again out of foxholes and ran into a hail of machine-gun fire?

Had Lucas thought this through?

What reconnaissance had been done?

Truscott told Lucas he wanted to speak with Mark Clark himself.

Lucas was infuriated. He was already in Clark's bad books. He'd failed to move his corps fast enough and far enough, as Clark saw it, and he didn't want to lose his command.

"Damn it," snapped Lucas. "You know the position I'm in with him. That would only make it worse, and put me in a helluva hole. You have got to do it."[31]

"I still think it's wrong," replied Truscott, but he wasn't in a position to disobey an order from his corps commander.

Reconnaissance patrols brought back unsettling news about Kesselring's Reinhard position that Lucas wanted Truscott's battered regiments to seize as fast as possible. Mount Lungo and Mount Rotondo, rising like camel humps on each side of Highway 6, were studded with gun positions, and the southern approach to the Mignano Gap was blocked by tank traps and seeded with countless mines.

The only way to seize the mountains, decided Truscott, was to attack them from their flanks. Doing so, according to the 3rd Division's official history, would prove "to be the most heart-breaking, nerve-wracking venture" of the war so far.[32]

To soften up German defenses on Mount Rotondo, which would be attacked first, Truscott's supporting artillery launched an extraordinary barrage. In less than twenty-four hours, more than nine hundred 155mm Long Toms fired a hundred sixty thousand rounds, filling the sullen skies with an unending screeching and thunder, a hail of steel. An impressed German wrote home, boasting that he and his comrades were "retreating victoriously" under constant fire. The Americans were "no sissies . . . The amount of material [they] are using seems incredible . . . we get tears in our eyes."[33]

Lieutenant Maurice Britt was in no doubt that taking Mount Rotondo would be the greatest challenge yet for his company. The Germans had spent all that fall turning the barren peak into a death trap. And it seemed that Kesselring's finest were prepared for a long and bitter battle. "Their pillboxes were well stocked with ammunition and canned food and they had comfortable bunks," Britt recalled. "On the floors of the forts they had rugs which they had stolen from the Italians."[34]

CHAPTER 4

Bloody Ridge

MIST AND FOG shrouded the approach to the Mignano Gap as Lieutenant Maurice Britt awaited the order to attack. Some men could not see a comrade twenty feet from them. As Britt readied his men, a few miles away Corporal Audie Murphy led a platoon on a scouting mission to probe defenses at the base of Mount Rotondo. His days of hunting as a boy had been superb training. He instinctively understood the landscape and how to use it to his advantage, for cover and protection. Blessed with superb eyesight, Murphy could scan a mountainside and immediately assess where the Germans might be hidden.

As Murphy scrambled across rocks and through brush, he looked barely human to his buddies, more like a feral predator. "Audie had a peculiar walk," noted B Company's Private Albert L. Pyle. "It reminded me of someone slipping up on an object, slipping up on game, whatever that game might be. It was sort of a crouch of his own. That might have saved his life a lot of times."[1]

Murphy's reconnaissance confirmed what Lieutenant Britt already assumed. Mount Rotondo was a formidable fortress. Parts of the climb were so steep and difficult that Murphy and his friends had to carry equipment on their backs, crawling along like beetles on all fours.

On November 8, Britt set out with his company. His orders were to move without being spotted along a valley and then take up positions on the eastern side of Mount Rotondo before launching an attack with two other companies.[2] The rain lashed down and Britt's boots sank into the mud, slowing him. They pushed through bushes so thick that any exposed skin was covered in bruises and scratches. It took all day to trudge two miles.

Britt and his men finally approached enemy defenses— barbed wire rolls and a tank trap. The Germans opened fire with rifles and machine pistols. Two of Britt's men were killed and three wounded as Britt and others hit the ground and then hid in the thick undergrowth. They expected more Germans to attack any second. What to do with the wounded men? They couldn't be moved while it was still light. The minutes passed slowly. The Germans did not return. The wounded lay in agony until darkness and then several men took off their muddied overcoats, scoured the undergrowth for dead branches, and then slipped the boughs through sleeves to make litters. The wounded were then carried down to an aid station.

Britt and his men picked themselves up and started to climb again. The rain beat down from the dark skies. The Germans lay in wait. But the downpour was so heavy, the patter of drops on leaves so constant, that Britt and his men could not be heard. It was midnight when they reached their assigned position high on the eastern slope of Mount Rotondo. Before daylight, they would jump off and attack, securing the mountain. A long night lay ahead.

In the early hours, Britt discovered he had no contact with battalion headquarters. Men had unraveled telephone wire all the previous day but when someone attempted to contact the battalion commander, Lt. Colonel Edgar Doleman, there was no reply. The line was dead. When a soldier tried a radio, it didn't work. The rain, guessed Britt, had wrecked the batteries. He was cut off with no means of communication. Two rifle companies were supposed to be following them up the mountain. Were they doing so? Had they run into trouble?

Dawn brought relief. The two companies arrived. But then L Company's commanding officer, Captain Butler, was hit in the arm by a sniper and carried back down the mountain for medical aid.[3] That meant Lieutenant Britt had to take charge of what was left of L Company. There was no time to give a pep talk. They were to make their planned attack, however miserable they were, however depleted their ranks.

The Germans had noted the arrival of the two supporting companies, and as Britt's men moved forward, they fired mortars. They sounded at first, remembered one soldier, "like a distant lark but then, with a pulsing flutter, the mortar bombs landed with ferocious blasts."[4] Pieces of shrapnel ricocheted off rocks and gouged deep into tree trunks, leaving white scars. The air was thick with shreds of foliage. Then there was the "chug,

chug, chug" of machine-gun fire, the dashed lines of tracers.[5] To make matters worse, American artillery began to tear up the upper slopes of Mount Rotondo. The cacophony was pierced by the sound of German Nebelwerfer rockets that began as a soft whoosh and then became shrieks that turned to a deadly quacking as the rockets exploded.

Britt's company charged forward, laying down heavy fire, and seized several strongpoints from their rear. Truscott's strategy of outflanking the German positions had worked. Once the heights had been seized, Britt found himself with fewer than sixty men in his company, a quarter of its full strength. They would have to beat back inevitable German counterattacks and hold until relieved.[6] Battalion commander Lt. Colonel Doleman, positioned lower down on the mountain, knew how few men Britt had left. They could easily be overwhelmed—they were spread far too thin, across six hundred yards of a thickly wooded mountainside.[7] "When I inspected our line I could see the men were worried," recalled Britt. "I was worried, too."

There had been many occasions in the last year when Britt had asked God to spare him, when he had prayed he would survive.[8] Now he beseeched the Almighty on behalf of his men.

"Lord, lead me. Don't let me do anything that will cause any of these boys to be killed unnecessarily."[9]

Prayers would not be enough. Later that night, more than a hundred Germans slipped through a gap between Britt's positions and those of K Company. "We had no outposts to warn us," remembered Britt. "We couldn't spare anybody to man them."[10] At dawn, the Germans attacked. Corporal Audie Murphy and his B Company were on Mount Rotondo but not close enough to provide help. Britt knew that as the entire division's most advanced unit, he and his men had to hold up the Germans for as long as possible so that other companies on the mountain stood a fighting chance.[11]

Several of Britt's men, manning lookouts, were taken prisoner. Then the Germans stormed forward once more, firing from the hip. They quickly seized positions to Britt's left. He decided to split the men beside him into two groups. "You take six men and I'll take six," he told his executive officer, Lieutenant Miller. "You go up the left side and I'll take the right."

Britt and Miller each carried five clips for their carbines. They'd need every bullet. Britt picked up another seven men as he ran to his right. The bushes were so thick, he couldn't see any actual Germans.

"Don't shoot," shouted an American fifty yards or so distant.

"We're prisoners," yelled another. "They're using us as shields. There're lots of them and they're all around you."

"Run away," Britt shouted back. "Try to escape!"

The enemy kept coming, charging toward Britt. He lifted his carbine and pressed the trigger. Bullets flew back and forth. Two of the American prisoners were wounded by Britt's men in the confusion but the others managed to run away. Britt heard the familiar snarl of an MG-42 machine gun. The Germans had brought up the heavy stuff. They meant business.

A bullet grazed Britt's shoulder. A second hit him in the side of his abdomen.[12] He grabbed his side and told a machine gunner nearby to fire faster. Then he fell to the ground, pressing his helmet and face into the rocky soil. His shoulder burned and he felt a fierce sting in his side. A bubbling sound. There was some-thing warm trickling down his leg.

I'm bleeding to death. This is a hell of a way to die.

The blood kept flowing. The wound was serious, possibly fatal.

How long before he bled out? How many seconds, or minutes, until he blacked out and life ended . . . ?

The blood flow was slowing.

The bubbling sound stopped.

He was conscious. He could move his hand. He examined his side. He still had one. That was something. It hadn't been blown away. It was a bullet hole, not a shell wound. Then his fingers came across his canteen. He examined it—another bullet had left a gaping hole in it. Water still trickled from it, like the bright red stuff seeping from his side.

Adrenaline coursed through him. Some of his men were nearby and saw Britt get to his feet as if given a new lease on life, a massive injection of stimulant.

He was holding up his bullet-holed canteen.

Liquid trickled from it.

"It's water!" cried Britt. "It's water!"

He checked his carbine. No bullets left. There was a wounded man on the ground nearby. He grabbed his M-1 rifle and took aim. He aimed and fired until again he had run out of ammuni-tion. Germans were running, firing, killing, charging, hurling potato-masher grenades. One exploded as it hit Britt in the shoulder. It should have finished him off but only a couple of steel fragments pierced his back, although he was rendered deaf

in his left ear for the next few minutes. Nearby, unexploded grenades lay on the ground, their detonation times set for several
seconds, long enough for Britt and other men to hurl them
back.[13]

At some point, Britt spotted one of his men, Corporal Eric G.
Gibson of Chicago. He was hurrying toward him, carrying two
burlap bags crammed with grenades. Britt turned to a private,
Gunter L. Schleimer of New York City, and ordered him and
Corporal Gibson to take out the machine gun that had earlier
wounded Britt in the abdomen. The words were barely out of
Britt's mouth when the German gunner sent more volleys of
bullets flying their way.

Britt began to pull grenades from the burlap bags. The grenades were timed to explode after five seconds—enough time for
the Germans to pick them up and throw them back. Britt and
his two men—Corporal Gibson and Private Schleimer—pulled
the pin on each grenade and held it for three seconds before
hurling it.

To Britt's rear lay open ground. His men would be easily
picked off if they ran across it. He turned to his front again and
saw yet more Germans closing in fast and in large numbers. The
fanatics in dark camouflage, members of a parachute battalion
wearing round helmets and wielding machine pistols, seemed to
be everywhere.[14]

Britt looked at Gibson and Schleimer.

Ready to go?

"Lead the way, Lieutenant."

Gibson and Schleimer were forgotten as Britt went on a

rampage, intent on winning this deadly game, it seemed, all on his own, fighting through a wooded area, buying his men time as he broke up the German attack. Britt tossed one grenade after another. Over and over, the explosions ripped around him. When he ran out of ammunition, he picked up any weapon he could find, German or American, so long as it held bullets.

Britt killed several Germans in a machine-gun nest and moved on to another. A sergeant saw that Britt's canteen and the case for his field glasses had been punctured by bullets. A private watched as Britt ran back and forth, firing every time he glimpsed a German or thought he heard one. How on earth was Britt not killed? Concussion grenades were exploding all around him. Blood was seeping from a half-inch-wide wound on his left side, above his hip, and his jacket was drenched in his blood but still he kept fighting.

Britt spotted one of his corporals. He was in charge of a machine-gun crew. German grenades were exploding around the crew, showering them with rocks and dirt. The concussion from some blasts knocked their gun over but they had it back up and running in a few seconds. The Germans got to within ten yards but the corporal sprayed wherever he saw movement, sending bullets streaming in one direction after another, grabbing the weapon by its burning-hot barrel to move it. He was Britt's last hope. Then the gun jammed. The corporal and other men stood up, exposing themselves, to fix it. Then they got back to work, firing with such accuracy and in so many directions that the Germans must have thought Britt's men had several machine guns, not one.

Britt meanwhile kept lobbing grenades. One hit a tree and fell back and landed feet from him. He jumped away and then dived to the ground, somehow escaping the blast. Then he threw yet more grenades, making sure he missed nearby tree trunks. He finally ran out and then one of his men saw him pick up rocks and hurl them instead.

At some point, Britt realized the Germans were no longer trying to kill him. Then he saw several of them in the distance. They were fleeing.

Close by, covered in dirt, was a sergeant, a New Yorker from Brooklyn.

"Hell," said the sergeant, "we let them get away."[15]

LIEUTENANT MAURICE BRITT roamed in a daze around the shredded brush and woods, counting thirty-five German corpses. Four Germans lay wounded, left behind by their comrades. He talked with one of them and learned that there had been a hundred others in the attack, far outnumbering Britt and the Americans who had fought alongside him that afternoon. "When I heard that," Britt remembered, "I got really frightened."[16]

Later that afternoon, 3rd Battalion commander Lt. Colonel Doleman found Britt on the upper slopes of Mount Rotondo. Britt was barely recognizable, his face covered in scratches and bruises.

"Lieutenant," said Doleman, a proud New Jersey native.

"Yes, sir, Colonel Doleman."

"What are you doing up front here? You're wounded."

"It's nothing, sir."

"Cut it out. Don't pull that stuff on me. I can see blood in four places. Go down to the battalion aid station. That's an order."

Britt found himself standing inside the entrance to a medical tent, reporting to the commanding medical officer, Captain Roy Hanford of Sandpoint, Idaho. Hanford would never forget first laying eyes on Britt: "A tall, well-built first lieutenant with burly hands, young tugboats for feet, and the glazed eyes of a combat soldier."[17]

Britt sat down and said nothing.

Was there anything, asked Hanford, he could do for Britt?

"Go ahead and finish with your other patients," replied Britt. "I've got a little scratch here that I'd like you to look at when you've got the time."

Britt was seated on an empty K ration box. Men stared at him in awe. He still held his canteen, which looked like a sieve, holed by German slugs.

His chest was soaked in blood.

Captain Hanford finally got to examine Britt.

"Well, that one there is more than a scratch, Lieutenant."

Hanford turned to a medic nearby.

"Got his emergency tag?"

"Yes, sir."

The doctor read it: "Elliptical avulsion down to the muscles. One inch long, half inch wide on left side. Danger of infection."

"Elliptical avulsion?" asked Britt.

"Your side's all torn apart."

Hanford told Britt he would need to be evacuated to the rear, to a base hospital.

Britt didn't like the sound of that.

"Hey, wait a minute, Captain. I don't need that."

"What do you mean?"

"I'm going to no hospital. I've got a date, back up on that hill, with my guys."[18]

Britt was more seriously wounded than he had revealed to the doctor. Hanford remembered: "Lieutenant Britt didn't show me that piece of hand grenade embedded in one of his chest muscles until after we were relieved, several days later."[19]

Britt made his way back up the shell-ravaged mountainside to rejoin the remnants of his company. He looked at the young Americans who'd survived that day's fighting, battered and bruised, sodden uniforms clinging to their arms and legs. Several were so traumatized they would have to be pulled off the line with combat fatigue. Never would they or Britt forget the immense violence of the battle for Mount Rotondo. They had gone well beyond the call of duty. They'd been on the line for seven weeks before fighting for the last nine days straight. They prepared their foxholes and slit trenches, grieving, famished, nerves worn raw. A platoon belatedly arrived to reinforce them. "There were no reserve units available in the regiment," remembered Britt, "so the platoon was made up of clerks, messengers, cooks, and anti-tank gunners from headquarters company."

The next day was as bleak, as wet, and as cold as those before it. But there was, finally, some good news. Mail from home had arrived at 3rd Battalion headquarters down in the valley below. Because of Britt's position high on the mountain, a party could reach what was left of his company with either mail or rations, not both. Britt consulted his sergeants. Which was it to be? There was no question. Mail came first. Most of Britt's survivors received something but a few did not. Girlfriends and wives had probably become impatient and sent Dear John letters months back. A forlorn teenager burst into tears. Britt opened a package from his wife. There were twenty-four bars of chocolate inside. Every man received an equal share.

Britt and his fellow Marne men had carried out their orders. Five of them from L Company would receive the Silver Star. They'd taken Mount Rotondo. They'd delivered for Truscott, Lucas, and Clark. "It was like a nightmare that is quickly forgotten unless you write it down as soon as you awake," remembered Britt. "But some things that happened I can never forget."[20]

Their German foe, drawn from a battalion of paratroopers, among the best soldiers in the Wehrmacht, had been decimated. It was a decisive defeat, noted at the highest levels of the Wehrmacht. "A local failure of the Panzer Grenadiers," recalled Kesselring, "gave the enemy possession of the massif and a counter-attack by the only parachute battalion at my disposal failed to recapture it."[21] The Americans were remarkably resilient, worryingly so.

After learning that his men had seized Mount Rotondo, a deeply moved General Lucian Truscott wrote his wife. Time had ceased to have meaning. The booze supply at his command post had been restocked with thirty-five bottles of cognac. He needed all the Dutch courage he could get. "I only pray," he confided to his wife, "that I can live and measure up to what my lads seem to expect of me."[22]

For his extraordinary courage on November 10, one of Truscott's finest surviving lads—Lieutenant Maurice Britt—would receive the Military Cross from the appreciative British, an Oak-Leaf Cluster to his Purple Heart, and the Congressional Medal of Honor.[23]

CHAPTER 5

Naples

HE WAS TALL and thin and had a haughty manner—vain, egotistical, hated by many of the press, cursed by more and more of his soldiers, but nevertheless doing his best to salvage a botched job. Forty-seven-year-old 5th Army commander Mark Clark, destined to become the youngest four-star general in World War II, had been given far too few men and resources. He had been saddled with a half-baked plan, carried out on a shoestring, with no clearly defined goal. And now, the day after Lieutenant Maurice Britt's heroics on Mount Rotondo, he stood in a cemetery amid hundreds of white crosses south of Naples. How many more American corpses would be planted in this accursed foreign soil?

It was November 11, 1943, exactly twenty-five years since the end of the last bloodbath that had engulfed Europe.

"Here we are, a quarter century later, with the same Allies as before, fighting the same mad dogs that were loose in 1918," said

Clark, who had been seriously wounded by shrapnel, hit in the upper back and shoulder, in that last war.

Clark looked at the fallen, the forever young, lined up obediently in neat rows before him.

"They gave their lives," he said, "so that the people at home can pursue the life which we have always wanted—a happy life—and so that their children could go to the schools and churches they want, and follow the line of work they want. And we are fighting, first, to save our own land from devastation like this in Italy."

Clark finally addressed the dignitaries and press gathered nearby: "We must not think about going home. None of us is going home until it's over. We've caught the torch that these men have flung us, and we'll carry it to Berlin and to the great victory—a complete victory—which the united nations deserve."[1]

Clark sounded and looked ebullient, but he knew only too well that his forces and Kesselring's were exhausted, punch-drunk, slumped on the ropes. Kesselring had hoped that Clark's divisions would "break their teeth" on his mountain defenses, and that had been the case.[2] At the town of Cassino and other places along the Gustav Line, the war had ground to an ever-more-tragic standstill. There were as many stretcher-bearers and porters, stooped men acting as pack mules, as there were soldiers in combat, and most of Clark's latest replacements had no training in mountain warfare. Trench foot was epidemic. Supplies brought from Naples's ruined docks, where the Mafia flourished once more, were woeful, as Lieutenant Britt knew only too well, having survived on a third of standard rations for week after week. Not one American grunt on the front lines had received a winter uniform.

Lucian Truscott talked to the press about the Gustav Line at his headquarters on November 15. Several reporters had begun to call him Iron Man. The attrition in the mountains, said Truscott, was beginning to look a lot like the static warfare of the Great War when he'd served in the cavalry.

"It's by far the strongest area of defense we've run into so far in Italy," explained Truscott. "But it is in no way comparable to the Western Front in the last war, because now I could send a small patrol to pierce the defenses at any point; I could take Cassino tomorrow if I wanted to make the expenditure of men."

And once Cassino was finally taken?

It would be a straight shot to Rome?

"No, this kind of country is too easy to defend," Truscott said, "and the Boche is still a good soldier. We mustn't kid ourselves about the fact that there's still a lot of fight left in the old son of a bitch."[3]

That day, Clark ordered a moratorium. There would be a two-week rest before returning to the offensive. VI Corps commander, Major General John P. Lucas, would later insist that had he been given one new division, the Allies could have prevailed in Italy that fall of 1943 and pushed to Rome. But there was no fresh blood, no backup, only endless mountains and mud.

"Wars," Lucas noted in his diary, "should be fought in better country than this."[4]

The following day, November 16, a badly mauled 3rd Division was finally pulled off the line. The dogface soldiers had set a record for continuous combat in Europe for Americans—sixty days of straight fighting—longer in hell than any other US division. More than twenty-five hundred of their fellow Marne men had been wounded and almost seven hundred had been killed.

It was a sunny morning when Audie Murphy and Lattie Tipton in B Company learned that the nightmare was finally over. They climbed down from their position. Burial units were busy at work, scurrying like termites across the slopes that would so quickly be forgotten.[5] Murphy and his fellow dogfaces traipsed down a road, potholed by shellfire, littered with grim wreckage, skirted by the scorched skeletons of trees. Some were heady with happiness and others dumbstruck, overwhelmed by the realization that they were alive and would stay so until asked to go back.

Keith Ware, who had commanded Murphy's B Company in Sicily, came down from the mountains too. He had been promoted to major and was a battalion executive officer in the 15th Infantry Regiment, responsible for managing a combat unit of more than eight hundred men. He would have been able to see the full extent of their fatigue as they headed to rest areas. Amid the thousands of other Marne men in Truscott's division there were so many red-eyed, bearded soldiers who had clenched their jaws in fear and grief for several weeks and had thousand-yard stares. Now their jaws were slack, mouths gaping open, as their facial muscles finally began to relax.

Even though it was winter in the Italian mountains, the bright sunlight made men feel as if it were spring. The Marne men marched toward showers, real beds, hot chow, their boots on firm ground, no stones sliding beneath them. There was a soft wind, blowing the memories and trauma away for a while, cleansing. Replacements—fresh meat—stomped along the road going the other way, up into the mountains, toward death. Nice clean uniforms, polished buttons. Nervous boys gripping weapons they had never used to actually kill, plodding toward the dull thuds over the horizon, wondering who among them would end up wrapped in a mattress cover, dirt and rocks piled above.

Lieutenant Maurice Britt saw the sun warm his men, the fifty or so left from L Company, as they made their way away from the Mignano Gap and toward Naples. Brown leaves lifted in the breeze and the last clouds disappeared. The sky was an immense, startling blue. "We were ragged," he remembered, "dirty, greasy, bearded, and only half conscious. Our walking wounded trudged along with us. We were the infantry, coming out of the line. For us, it meant an end to 59 nights in foxholes, slit trenches and on the ground; an end to canned rations, an end to bailing out foxholes with helmets, an end to living like rats."[6]

It was a long march to safety, ten miles distant, with each step taking more effort than the last. Finally, Britt and his men arrived in the small town of Pietravairano, which they had set free earlier that month. In sucking mud, dogfaces set up eight-man tents and dumped gravel to make walkways. With their last energy, they knocked together bunks from empty ammunition crates and laid a blanket of hay on top. New mattress covers were issued.

Before collapsing onto their ammunition crates covered in deloused hay, some of Britt's men lined up one last time and took a shower with hot water courtesy of a fire stoked beneath a large barrel. The tents were flimsy protection from cold gusts but the Marne men were masters of improvisation and created chimneys and stoves from food tins and scrounged charcoal from locals. Then most men slept better than they had in years, without worrying about shellfire. They shaved off their ragged beards using hot water the next morning, looking into grimy mirrors, trying to recognize their former selves in the faces of the old men staring back.

EARLY THAT DECEMBER, Britt and his fellow officers received five-day passes that allowed them to get some "rest and recreation" in Naples, some forty miles to the southwest.[7] When they ventured into the city, it was obvious there was but one master in this capital of the Baroque, once home to Caravaggio, where time bombs planted by Kesselring's men still exploded now and again. Hunger ruled the third-largest city in Italy with no mercy. Children with faces the color of paste were pushed in front of their liberators, their black eyes pleading as they then clutched at the sleeves of the latest arrivals in green uniforms.

Pimps stood at corners.

"You want a nice girl?"

"Biftek, spaghetti. Verra cheap."

"Good brandy? Only five hundred lire."

"Beautiful signorina."[8]

Piles of masonry, sometimes twenty feet high, served as dusty monuments to Allied bombing, testaments to the silver fortresses that left lazy white contrails far above. The stench of death, of feces, of deprivation, hung in the air. Hunchbacks were bizarrely common, some legless, believed by the locals to bring luck. Neapolitans touched them on their humps and prayed as they stroked their deformities.

All the exotic fish in the Naples aquarium were gone, cooked and scarfed before the Allies came. To celebrate Mark Clark's arrival in the city, officials had bizarrely provided a baked baby manatee—the aquarium's star attraction—because they'd heard he liked seafood. Many families were living in a single window-less room in terrible poverty. And yet there was wonderful music played in the streets and at the grand opera house, and superb food and wine for those who could afford black-market prices.

The city was at once utterly squalid and splendid. "A huge pulsing crowd moved up and down the Via Roma," remembered the Australian journalist Alan Moorehead, "among the bright silks and the flowers and the pimps. The whole motif was that of a gaudy tropical flower that springs out of decay and smells rotten in its heart."[9]

Audie Murphy and Lattie Tipton visited Naples several times, Murphy later recalling that he became infatuated with a teenage girl called Maria. But the city's delights were to be all too brief a distraction. While Truscott's men knocked back vino rosso and caught the clap, Winston Churchill pored over maps of Italy and decided it was time to break the stalemate in the mountains south of Rome once and for all. An amphibious landing at An-zio, thirty-five miles from the Eternal City, would throw Kes-selring off-balance, dividing his forces, allowing Clark's stalled 5th Army to push north.

There was one problem. Mark Clark had already decided against it. He'd explored the possibility of landing a force at An-zio and concluded such an end run would succeed only once the 5th Army had broken through Kesselring's Gustav Line at Cassino. But his army had not even reached the Gustav Line, let alone breached it. There were, as always, too few troops available, too few landing craft, and too few supplies. Churchill was not to be denied, however, and so a reluctant Clark began organizing the Anzio adventure, code-named Shingle, an operation he'd dismissed weeks before. Clark had no choice if he wanted to retain his command. Churchill, he jotted in his diary, had placed a "pistol" to his head.[10]

Meanwhile, Clark's most experienced troops, the Marne men, prepared to celebrate Christmas. "We made elaborate preparations," remembered Maurice Britt. "There were no company funds, but we took up a collection, and sent a detail to Naples to buy oranges, apples, and nuts. They returned with a jeep load. Another detail went scouting for wine, but found only five gallons at a place where they thought they could buy 1,000 gallons."

Britt's executive officer, Lieutenant Miller, was particularly resourceful, persuading local families to bake cakes and cherry pies in their ovens. Someone even managed to rustle up a cow so Britt and his men could eat steak for Christmas dinner. One morning, at roll call, Britt asked anyone who had worked in a butcher's shop to step forward. Four men did so and before long the cow was in finely cut pieces.

Bags of Christmas mail and packages arrived. Men read letters from their wives, children, and parents; stuck Christmas cards up by their cots; and gleefully ripped open gift packages stuffed with goodies like real chocolate and chewing gum, dividing the contents with their buddies. Their former lives felt farther away and more precious than ever. "We longed for the usual things about life at home," noted Britt, "like going to a movie down at the corner, or eating hamburgers at the kitchen table. Christmas Eve was especially lonesome. We sang carols and other old songs, and felt a little sorry for ourselves. We wondered if we ever would get home."

On Christmas Day, Britt was summoned to a nearby airfield. His steak would have to wait. He watched a Piper Cub airplane descend and then land. Britt could barely believe it when six-foot-four-inch General Mark Clark climbed out. Britt was told to stand in a line with several other officers. Clark, with his Roman nose and angular features, loped over to the line and shook hands with each officer.

Clark looked Britt in the eye and handed him the silver bards of a captain.

"Here's a little present for you," said Clark.

Back at his company headquarters, newly promoted Captain Britt skipped the army's meager turkey ration and gorged on roast beef from the butchered cow.

The Christmas cheer didn't last long. Legions or replacements arrived to fill the gaps in Britt's company and so many others. They were raw and unnervingly young and naive. Britt and his fellow officers immediately began rigorous training programs. "This was hard on the men who had come out of combat," recalled Britt, "but there was surprisingly little griping."[11]

The old-timers knew their lives depended on knocking the greenhorns into shape as fast as they could. Most days, Britt made his men practice river crossings—those were his orders from on high. Of all places, they found themselves back at the Volturno River, its waters as bone-chilling and swift as the previous October when so many had lost their lives trying to get across. Britt guessed they would be sent north to cross the Rapido River, south of Cassino. On New Year's Day 1944, he knew that wouldn't be the case. He and his fellow officers in the 3rd Division received orders to break camp and move to an assembly area near Naples.

It was one of the coldest days on record as men boarded trucks in the frozen mud of Pietravairano.[12] It began to sleet and snow. A fierce wind blew down many tents, an unsettling harbinger. "We turned the tents back to the quartermaster with some sadness," recalled Britt. "We knew we were going back to war." At the new training area, Mad di Quarto, in swampy terrain near Naples, Britt and his men began to train for an amphibious landing—what would be his fourth. "Sometimes we worked 18 hours a day, hitting the beach again and again. In odd moments we speculated on what country's beaches we were going to invade. Most of us thought it would be France. At least we hoped so."[13]

A couple of weeks after arriving at Mad di Quarto, Truscott learned from Clark that his division alone would invade Anzio. Truscott was appalled. "We are perfectly willing to undertake the operation," Truscott told Clark, "if we are ordered to do so and we will maintain ourselves to the last round of ammunition. But if we do undertake it, you are going to destroy the best damned division in the United States Army for there will be no survivors."[14]

Clark added another division, the British 1st, and nine battalions of Rangers, commandos, and paratroopers. Truscott was far from reassured and ordered his entire division to make a practice invasion run. He was as ever a stickler for fitness and a superb planner. What he saw left him even more concerned. There was considerable chaos and confusion. Thousands of men had never seen action, had never learned the Truscott trot. Truscott begged Mark Clark for another rehearsal. His men needed another go. Clark turned him down, saying there was no time.

On a cold morning in late January, Truscott stood in his leather bomber jacket, his vocal cords strained, on the deck of the USS *Biscayne*, and watched his men assemble on the docks in Naples. He had done his best to get them ready, to break in the legions of green replacements. Once again, his "lads" looked magnificent, their regimental flags snapping in the wind as the 3rd Division band gave them a rousing send-off, playing "Dogface Soldier," the division's anthem.

The Marne men broke into song:

> *I'm just a dogface soldier with a rifle on my shoulder*
> *And I eat a Kraut for breakfast every day.*

ABOARD THE USS *Biscayne* was Clark's chosen commander of the upcoming operation, Major General Lucas, bespectacled, struggling to stay calm, convinced that failure loomed ahead.

"Don't stick your neck out, Johnny," Clark had warned Lucas. "I did at Salerno and got into trouble."[15]

Lucas wasn't about to disobey.

CHAPTER 6

The Agony of Anzio

CAPTAIN MAURICE BRITT stood in his landing craft, in the first wave of invading Marne men, as he neared a beach fronting the seaside town of Nettuno. The weather was mild and the seas were calm. He'd hoped the craft would ferry him and his men to France, but when secret orders were revealed the day before, he'd discovered he was bound once more for combat in Italy. A flotilla carrying rockets approached the shore. The sky lit up as the rockets launched and then landed with such devastating power that the concussion could be felt by US sailors in transports three miles out to sea.[1]

A waning moon was visible in the night sky. Then the ramp was down. There was no stutter of German machine guns, no screaming of enemy artillery as Britt crossed the firm, coarse sand, leading L Company. His orders were to move inland four miles, dig in, and then wait for the Germans to strike back. At 7:31 A.M., the sun appeared over the horizon, and in the light of dawn, Marne men could see, a couple of miles distant, the fishing port of Anzio, birthplace of Caligula and Nero.

It was a cakewalk, disconcertingly so. There had to be a catch. Britt organized his platoons and advanced with his company the four miles, past drab buildings with peeling stucco daubed with fascist graffiti, through pine woods, and into open farmland. No heart-jolting snap of sniper fire—the least Britt could have expected in enemy territory. No coughing mortars. By sundown, as Britt and his men took shelter, thirteen Allied soldiers had been killed among the thirty-six thousand who had landed that day. "After the almost disastrous performance during the rehearsal," General Truscott noted, the actual landings were "unbelievably smooth and accurate."[2] Yet already the Germans were reacting with, it was later reported, "lightning speed," rushing twenty thousand troops to Anzio within twenty-four hours of the Allies' arrival.[3]

Meanwhile, Corporal Audie Murphy lay in a hospital in Naples, suffering from malaria he'd contracted in Sicily, a thermometer showing a fever of 105 degrees. He'd refused medical help, not wanting his buddy Lattie Tipton and the others to go fight without him, but he had become so sick, he could barely stand and had been ordered to the hospital.

It seemed as night descended on January 22 that Captain Britt and his fellow 3rd Division invaders would be able to stroll in a day or two to Rome, normally less than a couple of hours away by truck. The following morning, Britt moved confidently across the Mussolini Canal, over a hundred feet wide, constructed in the thirties, providing drainage to the Pontine

Marshes until the Germans had arrived and promptly flooded the area, returning much of it to a malarial swamp.

The nearest town, Cisterna, lay several miles to Britt's north. The farmland stretching toward it was barren and gray, criss-crossed with deep drainage ditches called wadis and dotted here and there with modern brick buildings, many painted a jolly bright blue. In the distance, to the northeast, loomed the Alban Hills, rising several hundred feet. If the Germans were any-where, Britt knew, they'd be in those hazy heights, looking down through binoculars, able to see any movement he and his men made aboveground.

Britt was told to seize a critical junction to the north of the Mussolini Canal. Patrols reported that the Germans were mov-ing supplies through the junction. They were in fact reinforcing their positions, intending to hold the line at the Mussolini Ca-nal, buying time for elements of four Wehrmacht divisions to arrive from elsewhere in Italy and then help wipe out the Marne men.[4] A couple of tanks had been spotted. When Britt got closer, he discovered that the junction was protected by three platoons of SS, Hitler's elite fighting force, backed by mobile 88mm guns and five tanks. Britt's L Company was no match.

Before Britt could call for backup, he heard the roar and scream of artillery shells. German observers were in those roll-ing green hills and were directing fire from the SS's tanks. Caught in the open, Britt barked orders and ran for the nearest cover, a brick farmhouse. Explosions ripped across the nearby wadis and fields as the German tankers found their range, zero-ing in on L Company.

"This probably is the hottest spot on the beachhead," said a sergeant.[5]

No one disagreed.

Where exactly were the German tanks? Britt needed to know before calling battalion headquarters to ask for support from tank destroyers. He started to climb a stairway. He'd have a good view from the floor above. There was a deafening explosion—a shell from a German tank made a direct hit on the house, shaking it to the foundation. Britt was dazed but unhurt. Then the building began to collapse, rafters and walls falling. He stayed put on the stairs, which somehow still stood, as the wall nearest him crumbled away, leaving him with a clear view of the battlefield. He was quickly on the radio, contacting his regiment's tank destroyers, which landed shell after shell until the German tanks pulled back.[6]

Britt left the shattered building and ordered his men to continue to the critical road junction on the northern side of the Mussolini Canal.[7] They hadn't gone far when dozens of Germans from the Hermann Göring Division charged, under orders to push Britt and his men back into the sea. They'd tangled with the Marne men before, in the mountains to the south and in Sicily. Time to finish them off.

Machine-gun bullets cracked overhead. When Britt dared lift his head from the ground, he saw that many of his men were pinned down. Volleys of bullets filled the air. Several of Britt's men were hit. He couldn't see the German gun, so he got up and walked into the open and then leapt up and down, doing two jumping jacks, shouting and clapping his hands as if he was warming up for a big game with the Detroit Lions.[8]

It didn't take long for the bullets to come snapping his way. Britt knew where the machine gun was and sprinted toward it, carrying a radio on his back, covering seventy-five yards as fast as he'd ever crossed a gridiron. Then he found cover, dropped to his knees, and called in supporting fire. To his relief, he heard the hiss of American mortars and the German machine-gun position was destroyed.

Later that day, Britt's regimental commander, Lt. Colonel McGarr, found him in a culvert beside a road. McGarr gave a few words of advice but it was clear Britt and his executive officer, Lieutenant Miller, didn't need any encouragement. No "pushing" was required. They were calm and decisive, McGarr noted, even as "sniper bullets cut the ground along the banks and chipped concrete inches from their heads."[9]

The push toward the junction continued. A hundred yards away stood another farmhouse. From a distance, it appeared empty. Were the Germans lying inside, wondered Britt, waiting for L Company to get close so they could slaughter them? A couple of L Company soldiers dropped to the ground and crawled closer. Grenades were tossed inside. There was a strange sound, surely not human, then an agonized bellowing. The source was not a maimed SS soldier, rather a wounded Italian cow, quickly put out of her misery with a merciful rifle shot.

That night was pitch-black. Britt felt uneasy, knowing the SS often fought most effectively after dark, their favorite time to strike. He ordered a platoon forward but as soon as his men exposed themselves the Germans opened fire. Britt saw a stream of tracer bullets smack into a haystack nearby. Flames leapt into the air, silhouetting Britt and his men, making them easy targets.

There was a terrifying sound high above, as if the skies were moaning. Britt looked up. A German bomber, riddled by Allied antiaircraft fire, was spiraling down toward him. It crashed and burst into flames that lit the entire area as if someone had snapped on an arc light.

There was no option but to stay put until the gaseous flames died down. Britt got on the radio. He needed armored support badly. A few hours later, to his relief, he heard the sound of four tank destroyers, their engines growling as they crawled closer. Now he'd get to see what he could do with their firepower for the first time in combat. He'd never fought alongside armor before.

At first light, Britt got to work, directing his tank destroyers' fire at German strongpoints. Then a German shell hit one of the tank destroyers. Britt heard ammunition pop off and then the tank exploded, killing two men. He crawled forward until he was less than a hundred yards from the road junction. The enemy fire intensified. A young corporal saw to his horror that his foot had been blown off. Blood gushed, yet despite the wound, he somehow managed to hobble to where Britt and his executive officer, Lieutenant Jack Miller, had taken cover.

"I'm killed, sir," said the corporal. "I don't want to die."

Miller pulled off his belt and wrapped it tight around the kid's leg, stanching the blood.

"I don't want to die."

To his dismay, Britt learned that the tank destroyers supporting his company had been called away to help elsewhere. He watched them trundle off, trailing exhaust fumes, and then stared forlornly at the burned hulk of the tank destroyer that had exploded earlier. He and his men were on their own.

Was there a way to get to the junction without being seen? He'd noticed a swamp nearby and so he ordered a platoon to cross it, hoping the SS would not notice. As the platoon waded forward, Britt ordered his men to open fire to distract the SS. It worked. His platoon, undetected, emerged from the swamp, legs blackened with slime, and closed on the junction. "Then the Germans woke up," remembered Britt. "Frantically they brought up a flak wagon, which poured 20 millimeter antiaircraft shells into our men. It was one of the few times that infantrymen have had to take such punishment. The murderous fire killed five of our men and wounded six others. But they stood fast."[10]

Britt spotted a badly wounded soldier. He'd fallen around seventy yards away and would bleed out if he didn't get help fast. Jack Miller watched in wonder as Britt ran to the downed soldier and picked him up, "carrying him in his arms like a baby," braving relentless fire, saving the soldier's life.[11] It was one of many occasions when Britt, Miller later said, laid his life on the line and didn't receive a medal.

The clatter and crackle of small-arms fire finally died down. The SS had abandoned the junction. Britt and his men finally took over the junction. Dead SS soldiers, corpses stiffening, faces yellowing as blood drained away, lay scattered around. To Britt's pride he noted his men had killed twice as many of Hitler's boys as he had lost, even though the SS had had a larger force.

It had been a horrific ordeal. Ammunition was low. Men were utterly drained, having slept no more than a few minutes, if at all, since arriving at Anzio. With their last strength, they dug positions around the junction and waited to be relieved. The bloody crossroads would be known throughout the upcoming four-month Battle of Anzio as Britt's Junction.

At last, Britt and his men were trucked to a beach near Anzio to rearm and rest, perhaps for a few days if they were lucky. A few thoughtful men had not forgotten to bring along the cow they'd killed, and they butchered it. Numbed men gorged on fresh Italian steak, united by something holy, by pride and trauma, by too much spilled blood. "It was another infantry job when Company L fought to secure that road junction," noted Britt. "But it meant a lot to us. We had lost some good friends, some good soldiers. We knew what lay behind the war department telegrams that soon would be going home."

In grief, stomachs filled with beef, Britt and his men dropped down into nearby dugouts and were finally able to sleep. The darkness returned and the war with it. A shell landed close by and killed two more of Britt's men. At daylight, Britt received fresh orders. His company was to support an attack by the division's 7th Regiment, whose turn it was to enter the maw. Britt and his men pulled themselves together and set out, heading for a spot on Britt's map two long miles beyond the crossroads they'd finally secured the day before.

Later that day, Britt passed the junction. Artillery fire landed and explosions ripped all around. Having survived the last few days of carnage, another six of Britt's men fell, killed or wounded. A German machine gun stuttered to life. Britt and his men slithered on their bellies along a ditch. A squad of Germans fled from a farmhouse that Britt then took over. From an upstairs window, Britt had a superb view of Cisterna and several roads. Shell craters pockmarked the entire area like the surface of the moon.

It got dark. "The tension of our nerves had been so great that I think we all got a little hysterical," recalled Britt. He considered pulling his company off the line, out of combat, but then extra ammunition arrived with much-appreciated rations and twenty-five new men. "We didn't have their names on the roster," he remembered, "but we were so tired that I told Lieutenant Miller to put them on the line and we'd get their names in the morning. The new men were recruits who had never fired a gun at the enemy. Their uniforms were clean; they were polite and eager, but very scared."

German fire continued sporadically through the night, and by the next morning, six of the greenhorns had been killed before Britt even knew their names. "Then we entered them on our roster," he recalled. "They, too, were members of Company L."

Britt wanted to move. His instinct told him to find a safer command post. But he didn't want to do so in the open in daylight, risking the loss of yet more of his men. Better to stay put and wait, counting the hours yet again until twilight.

It was a mistake.

From a window, Britt spotted six German tanks.

"They're coming this way," a man shouted. "Fall back, fall back."

Another soldier stared at the enemy tanks.

"Six Nazi tanks looking at us," he said. "Six Nazi tanks, five hundred yards, coming up."

"You out of your mind?" said Britt. "That's no five hundred yards."

"Well . . . how much do you make it?"

"I can only figure distance by figuring how many football fields it is. From us to those tanks it's no more than three football fields."

"Whatever the distance, they've got a range."

"Gimme that phone."

Britt grabbed the handpiece and tried to direct fire. A German tank trundled forward. It was some three hundred yards from Britt. Standing out of a window on the second floor, he looked through his field glasses. He lifted his arm to point out a target when a massive blast rocked the building. Then another shell exploded, making a direct hit, shrapnel destroying the casement of the window through which Britt was looking, peppering those in the room inside.

Britt was thrown to the floor. He was dimly aware of plaster dust and debris settling after the explosion.

A voice.

"It was a tank."[12]

His right arm was missing. It had been blown off at the elbow. Every bone in one of his feet was broken. A lieutenant lay dead a few feet away. Others were severely wounded, sprawled nearby, moaning, their blood spattered all around.

Britt could move his left hand. There was something in the rubble close by. He reached out and picked up his right hand with his left.

This is it. . . .[13]

Someone was moving. A private was kneeling, applying a tourniquet to Britt's arm using the nearest thing to be found, a heavy rope. Britt was in severe shock but the pain had not begun to kick in. The private found water and got Britt to drink it and to swallow six sulfa tablets to prevent infection.

Britt turned to another private and asked him to remove his shoe because his foot felt numb.

"It's as good as off now, sir," said the private.

Britt looked down and saw that the sole of his foot had been stripped off.

He had a desperate craving for a cigarette.

Someone gave him one and lit it for him.

A sergeant dropped down beside Britt.

"Captain, I'm sorry," he said. "What are your orders?"[14]

Hold the position. Hand over command of L Company to a lieutenant called Ivorson. That was if he hadn't bought it too.

Lieutenant Miller lay nearby, badly wounded but conscious.

Who else was hit? asked Britt.

Miller mentioned some names.

Britt was too far gone to register them.

Fifteen men had been in the room with Britt when it was hit. Only three were unhurt. Five lay dead. Seven, including Britt and Miller, were seriously injured.

Britt spoke to Miller again.

He could trust him with a last wish. He'd fought at his side for so long.

"Tell my wife I love her," mumbled Britt before falling unconscious. His last thought before the darkness was that he was dying.

When Britt awoke, he was in a tent hospital near Anzio. He had received five lifesaving blood transfusions. He was, according to a wounded soldier in a cot beside him, "out of it . . . utterly demoralized, his spirit broken."

At some point Britt started to feel a little better. He saw a pretty Red Cross nurse approaching him and gave her a broad grin. She had tended to him earlier.

"Feel better, Captain?"

"I feel OK. I would like to take you up on that offer."

"Which one was that?"

"Didn't you say that you'd take a letter for me if I dictated it?"

"At your service."

"It's my wife. Her name is Nancy Britt. Her address is 2100 North B Street."

Britt lay in the hospital bed. His side had been cut badly. A bullet had gone through his gut. He had grenade wounds to his face and hands. He had three broken toes and a missing right arm.

The Red Cross nurse wrote as Britt dictated.

"The Nazis finally got lucky and laid me up. However, the only permanent injury will be the loss of my old pitching arm, but I still have my left arm to give you plenty of big hugs and I will soon Nancy. I will soon."[15]

Nowhere was safe from German artillery at Anzio. A shell hit the tented hospital and Britt was thrown to the ground, screaming in pain. Then he blacked out. The next thing he knew, he was in the bottom of a landing craft, headed for yet another hospital, this time in Naples. A few months later, Britt lay in a cot on a packed hospital ship headed to the US. At some point he received a letter from Major General Lucian Truscott: "The news of your wounds and subsequent loss of your arm I felt most keenly for I had come to know you as a brave man, a fine officer, and a friend."[16]

When Britt arrived back in the United States, two generals greeted him at the bottom of a gantry as he disembarked from his ship. They had been sent by no less than General George Marshall, US Army chief of staff. A band played, welcoming him home.[17] From the East Coast, a train took Britt to Lawson General Hospital in Georgia. He was lying on an X-ray table, surrounded by reporters, when he was officially informed that he would receive the Medal of Honor for his actions in helping to save his regiment the previous November on Mount Rotondo. Major General Lucian Truscott had recommended Britt for the award with, as Truscott had told him, "intense pride and personal satisfaction."[18]

The press had been invited to record Britt's reaction to the news—already he was a vital propaganda figure, committed to a nationwide bond tour, a guest on coast-to-coast radio shows. The only other man from Arkansas to have received the ultimate award for valor in World War II was General Douglas MacArthur, commander of the Southwest Pacific, who had been recommended for it twice, during the Veracruz action of 1914 and in World War I when he had notched up an incredible seven Silver Stars. MacArthur's Medal of Honor, awarded in 1942, had not been for a specific action but for his leadership in the Philippines.

"How does it feel to rate a salute from the president?" asked a reporter.

Britt grinned, put his hand on his heart, and then chuckled. "Normal."[19]

A reporter read out the citation for Britt's medal. It concluded with the number of fragmentation grenades he had thrown that gut-wrenching morning on Mount Rotondo—exactly thirty-two.

"How the heck do they know how many grenades I threw?" guffawed Britt. "You can bet your bottom dollar I didn't have time to count them."[20]

The Medal of Honor meant that the "big, raw-boned captain from Arkansas rice country" was one of the most decorated soldiers of the war to date, lacking only the Distinguished Service Cross.[21] No soldier in US history had ever received every medal for valor in a single war. Britt was one award from immortality.

Presidents and MacArthur himself and all servicemen and -women would be obliged to salute the wisecracking, always smiling "Footsie" Britt. He would have a special pension, the right to be buried at Arlington National Cemetery, automatic invitation to presidential balls and inaugurations, an extra uniform allowance, and if he had children with his wife, Nancy, and they met qualification standards, they would be automatically admitted to any of the United States' service academies. Above all, the medal—first presented in 1863 to six US Army volunteers—conferred a priceless prestige. Whoever received it forever belonged in a hallowed pantheon of heroes.

The news that he was to receive the Medal of Honor made Britt famous overnight, a household name back in Arkansas, where he was already revered by many for his feats as a Razorback end on the gridiron. One day, Britt was photographed propped up in bed in the hospital. Nancy had come to visit him. Press again gathered around. His broad face was again lit up with a beaming smile.

Asked how he had lost his arm at Anzio, Britt put it down to extreme bad luck.

"They couldn't hit me again," he said, "if they fired at that window every day for two months."[22]

Britt looked as confident as ever, dressed in pajamas, as he gazed into five-foot-tall Nancy's blue eyes and then wittily recounted his actions in Italy for the adoring reporters, concealing any anguish at having been permanently maimed, his dreams of being a gridiron star brutally dashed.

"Britt's story sounds like something a Hollywood script writer might have dreamed up," gushed one reporter. "It makes better reading than all his football exploits put together. Better, for instance, than when he caught a touchdown pass in the last three minutes of play to beat the Philadelphia Eagles, 21–17. Or the afternoon he had snagged ten passes to set up all of Arkansas' touchdowns in a 27–12 victory over a great Tulsa team."[23]

Britt would never make another touchdown, but his stunning record on the battlefield, his extraordinary haul of medals, would surely be impossible to beat.

TWO DAYS AFTER Britt was maimed, a newly promoted Sergeant Audie Murphy arrived at Anzio on January 27. He knew things were going badly when he headed inland to rejoin B Company and saw "trailer-loads of corpses . . . the bodies, stacked like wood . . . covered with shelter-halves . . . arms and legs bobble[d] grotesquely over the sides of the vehicles."[24]

Fighting grew fiercer by the day as Kesselring reinforced his troops with armored divisions and batteries of artillery, creating a ring of iron around the Allies, trapping them on the Anzio plain. Major General John Lucas, commanding the invasion force, had followed Mark Clark's advice and avoided sticking his neck out, opting to consolidate his positions rather than push to Rome. He was justified in his caution, according to contemporaries, including General Truscott. The Marne men might have been able to reach the Eternal City, Truscott acknowledged, but would have been giddy conquerors for a day before being annihilated.

Grim news awaited Murphy at B Company. Joe Sieja had been killed in action. Thankfully, Murphy's other close friend, Corporal Lattie Tipton, was unscathed, one of the few recognizable faces among Company B, whose ranks had been filled with callow replacements.

Murphy had returned to the front, he recalled, "just before hell broke loose."[25] B Company was to be part of a concerted attack on Cisterna, from which a rail line and a road, Highway 7, led to Rome. Advance elements of the 3rd Division jumped off on January 19 but were stopped dead in two days as they crossed bare, open terrain. Enemy fire was so intense, it was reported, that "nothing could live without taking cover."[26] Kesselring's forces were "contesting every inch of ground bitterly."[27] For the first time, Murphy saw German 20mm antiaircraft fire ripping holes the size of footballs in dogfaces. A soldier was killed a few feet from Murphy, who was thrown to the ground. He blacked out for a short time before coming to with a bad nosebleed.

The failure to take Cisterna was a serious setback. The Allies clung to a bridgehead fourteen miles wide and ten miles deep, hemmed in on three sides, under constant observation. They confronted an enemy of equal strength in numbers of men and, crucially, armored support. Behind the Allies was the sea. There could be no retreat. As one soldier quipped, it was "a long swim back to Naples."[28] The Anzio venture, aimed at breaking the stalemate in Italy, had only compounded it. "We hoped to land a wild cat that would tear out the bowels of the Boche," complained Winston Churchill, prime architect of the entire Italian campaign. "Instead we have stranded a vast whale with its tail flopping about in the water."[29]

Audie Murphy and his buddies in B Company huddled together in foxholes, soaked and cold. The temperature fell below freezing some nights and it was an unusually wet winter; many dugouts had two or three feet of water in them. Trench foot decimated line companies as the battlefield became a vast quagmire.[30] Men knew they could be blown to shreds at any time. "Never before," it was reported, "had our men been under such intense, prolonged and deadly accurate artillery fire."[31]

Nowhere and nobody was safe from the German guns leveled at Anzio. Nurses were killed as they tended the dying. The constant threat of shelling wore away at everyone's nerves, from generals to messcooks. Men learned to walk or run bent as low as possible in what became known as the Anzio crouch. "Penned in as they were on the low-lying, notoriously unhealthy coast," remembered a smug Kesselring, "it must have been damned unpleasant; our heavy artillery and the Luftwaffe with its numerous flak batteries and bombers alone saw to it that even when 'resting' their soldiers had no rest."[32]

The German propaganda station, Axis Sally, reported with mock sympathy on the Marne men's plight, dedicating songs to them such as "Don't Get Around Much Anymore" before adding with Teutonic subtlety: "As long as there is blue and white paint, there'll always be a 3rd Division."[33] German counterattacks all along the Allied perimeter were stopped but at mounting cost. "The better part of thirteen German divisions sat in a watchful ring about that little patch of ground," recalled one man, "and did their best to make it the sort of inferno a native son of Italy had once described as awaiting the souls of those who sinned on earth. Dante's descriptions, however, were imaginary. Anzio's, unfortunately, was not."[34]

The most concerted German strike, Operation Fischfang, began on February 16. Not since the Blitzkrieg in 1940 had so many German forces been thrown at the Allies—more than a hundred thousand troops. Hitler had ordered Kesselring to "lance the abscess below Rome" and Kesselring was dead set on delivering for the Führer.[35] The main route of attack lay down a road called the Via Anziate.

As the German attack developed, involving six divisions smashing through lines, it seemed that the Allies were doomed. With immense sacrifice, in particular by the 45th Infantry Division, the Germans were stopped seven miles from the coast after a week of nonstop killing on an industrial scale. German veterans swore the fighting was fiercer even than at Stalingrad. When asked if his men had retreated during the onslaught, Assistant Division commander John O'Daniel shot back: "Not a Goddamn inch!"[36] One US battalion suffered seventy-five percent casualties. A British battalion from the Queen's Royal Regiment was utterly destroyed.

Once the crisis had passed, 5th Army commander Mark Clark

decided to ditch Lucas, the woeful leader of the beleaguered Allied forces at Anzio. Lucas had long expected to be replaced and it therefore came as little surprise when, as he put it, his head finally "fell in a basket."[37] The man Clark replaced him with was none other than the 3rd Division commander, Lucian Truscott, whose position was filled by fifty-year-old John O'Daniel, nicknamed Iron Mike, who was to prove as capable as Truscott.

Operation Fischfang had failed but only just. Kesselring's forces regrouped and attacked once more on February 29. This time Kesselring shifted the focus of his main attack, hurling three divisions at the 3rd Division south of Cisterna—wave after wave of troops backed by more than a hundred tanks. Near a village called Isola Bella, Sergeant Audie Murphy's battalion felt the full force of the German assault. Major Keith Ware and his colleagues at battalion headquarters organized a frantic defense, throwing tank destroyers into the battle and calling in artillery bombardments. Before long there were so many German dead near Isola Bella that the enemy stacked them up and then used bulldozers to bury the bodies in mass graves.[38]

Murphy found himself at the sharp end once more on March 2, leading Corporal Lattie Tipton and others in his platoon on the front line, a pistol tucked under his belt, an M-1 rifle slung over his shoulder, pockets full of grenades, carrying extra ammunition and a carbine, his favorite weapon. It had a wooden pistol grip and was shorter and lighter than the M-1. A clip held fifteen bullets, and if he chose to do so, he could tape it to another so he could, in theory, hit thirty-one targets in swift succession if he had a slug in the chamber.[39] Even though so heavily weighed down, he still moved remarkably fast.[40]

That night, Murphy took a patrol of six volunteers to probe
the German lines. In the darkness, he saw a German tank two
hundred yards away. It had been hit by Allied fire. Fearing that
Germans might be trying to repair the tank, he told his men to
stay put in a ditch and then he crawled through mud toward it.
"I was wishing my shirt didn't have any buttons so I could get
closer to the ground," he remembered. "When I was within 15 or
20 yards of the tank, I set up a grenade launcher, fired and scored
six hits."[41]

The Germans reacted viciously, firing from several directions, closing on the tank. Tracer fire zipped through the darkness, so many streams of glowing bullets that they crossed one
another inches above the ground, yards from Murphy, who
picked his moment and ran for his life, making "probably the
fastest 200-yard dash in history." He then led his men back to
Allied lines and later laughed with them about the close call.
"But for the half hour I was crawling toward that tank and firing
at it," he recalled, "there wasn't anything funny about it. That
was how I got the Bronze Star. 'Valorous conduct in action,' the
citation calls it. I think I was lucky."[42]

Still the Marne men held, battered and brutalized. Yet more
green replacements filled the ranks. They annoyed the old-
timers, even those who'd only been at the front a few weeks.
Their inexperience was demoralizing. They couldn't be trusted.
And there was no time to train them. Audie Murphy, as with so
many other platoon leaders, became increasingly short-tempered
when the latest batch of high school graduates didn't do exactly
what they were told. Other arrivals were in no fit state to fight,
still recovering from wounds. One day, Murphy raged at a

medical officer who'd sent him men who couldn't even walk because they still suffered from trench foot. On another occasion, he snapped when asked to make his platoon perform close drill, a pointless exercise that infuriated his fatigued men.

"We left regulations in the rear," spat Murphy. "They were too goddamned heavy to carry."[43]

Finally, Murphy passed the breaking point. He had been in combat for more than two hundred days. Anzio had become too much even for him. One day late that March, he discovered that dead cows, killed by artillery fire, lay near his men's positions, stomachs bloated, rotting in the unrelenting drizzle. Murphy told several men to dig holes and cover the corpses or the stench of death would be insufferable.

A replacement dared to disagree.

Others watched as Murphy punched the soldier in the stomach and the face and then smashed his head against a door. None questioned Murphy's blaze of violence. It was the same aggression that they needed to save them in tight corners on patrols, that they depended on in firefights, that they'd need to break out from Anzio.

CHAPTER 7

Breakout

WINTER FADED AND spring finally arrived. Streams were in full flood. On the few trees left at Anzio with branches, the first brave buds appeared. Life was returning to where Nero had once soothed his aching limbs. The ocean of mud had begun to dry and men could walk without jumping from plank to plank, even if they did have the Anzio stoop when they ventured aboveground, hunched down with shaking hands, their nerves ragged after weeks of shelling. "The roses are blooming in great profusion," General Truscott wrote his wife. "You know how I love them."[1]

As lime trees blossomed, the Allies began that April to amass huge quantities of matériel and to refill the ranks with yet more pallid replacements. Each night as temperatures got warmer, more and more artillery opened up on the Germans, always a harbinger of a major operation, this time to break out from

Anzio. The Allies could not countenance spending yet another season going nowhere. In England, millions of troops were massing for an imminent Normandy invasion. Italy could not remain a stalemate.

It was clear to the Marne men that the nightly poundings were to soften up the German defenses as well as to lure Kesselring's 19th Army into replying with tit-for-tat shelling, thereby running down their own supplies. There was no one area where the shelling was most intense—that would alert the Germans and lead them to further fortify already formidable positions.

Officers pored over updated maps and intelligence reports. By early May, they were intimately familiar with the vast acreage of minefields, the hundreds of machine-gun nests, and in particular the maze of heavily reinforced defenses around the town of Cisterna. Ware and his men had tried to take the town back in January with high losses. Other units from the 3rd Division had tried five times to reach the most heavily defended place on the Anzio plain. Each time, it was reported, the Marne men had "stumbled and stopped."[2] To break out, it was obvious, they would finally have to seize Cisterna, the most shelled place on the most shelled battlefield on earth.[3]

Ware in all likelihood knew that the Germans facing him were bound to fight harder than ever. And Kesselring would not fail to bring in his own reinforcements and supplies to stall any attempt to take Cisterna. Who would fight harder, Kesselring's hardened defenders or the war-weary Allies? Acutely aware of how much blood had already been spilled, Truscott obsessively studied the enemy's positions, paying particular attention to

Cisterna, where two battalions of Rangers had been tragically wiped out in late January. Less than a dozen men from the battalions, attached to Truscott's division at the time, had made it back to Allied lines. Hundreds of captured Rangers had been paraded before news cameras through the streets of Rome, humiliated pawns in the Nazi propaganda machine bound for POW camps.

Truscott had taken the loss hard, having fought with the lost Rangers in North Africa, Tunisia, Sicily, and southern Italy. He was now out for revenge. Every strongpoint and approach was examined. "Stone buildings and narrow streets were formidable obstacles to any attacking force," he recalled. "Extensive caverns underneath the town protected the defenders from our heaviest artillery and air bombardments."[4]

On May 20, the 15th Infantry Regiment's reserves were ordered to break camp and move forward. That night, Ware would have seen flashes in the clear sky from far to the south, near Cassino, where the Allies had been stalled since Christmas in a battle of attrition as bloody and heartbreaking as Anzio. A big push from the south, aimed at linking up with the Anzio forces, was also in the making.

The next day, May 21, 1944, a simple order came: "The regiment will move up tonight."[5] Ware's men in the 15th Infantry Regiment would not have to make a direct assault on Cisterna— that was the mission of the 7th Infantry Regiment. The 15th would slot in to the right of the 7th and skirt Cisterna to the southeast, taking positions along the critical Highway 7, which led to Rome, and cutting an equally important railway line.

Ware's men headed through a pine forest toward the front lines. Finally, after months of cold and rain, it was a balmy, sunny evening. Summer had arrived. Sheep grazed in fields nearby. The 3rd Division Band belted out "Dogface Soldier." Morale appeared to be high as men whistled and sang along. Then machines that created artificial smoke began pumping out sickly-sweet spumes of fog that screened the marching troops from German spotter planes and observers in the Alban Hills to the north. In the gathering darkness, Marne men kept moving along a road that led toward the jump-off point.

The sky filled with flashes from artillery fire. When men looked up, it was as if they were witnessing a biblical thunderstorm, lightning cracking every few seconds. They knew savage fighting lay ahead, probably even worse than in Sicily or in the mountains south of Rome. More than a thousand men from Ware's division had been killed in action since he had arrived at Anzio that January. There were bound to be plenty more.

IT WAS AN hour before sunrise. Truscott stood in an artillery post, clad in his usual leather jacket, silk scarf at his throat, close to the jump-off point for the 3rd Division. "Light rain had fallen during the night, but occasional stars gave promise of a clear day," he recalled. "There was no sight or sound to indicate that more than 150,000 men were tensely alert and waiting. For better or worse, the die was cast as the minute hands of watches moved slowly toward the zero hour."[6]

At 5:45 that May 23, the skies were torn asunder by the greatest Allied artillery barrage of the war to date, so powerful that it seemed to Audie Murphy and his men in B Company that "nothing could be left of the German lines." Few could hear others above the din and crash of thousands of artillery rounds. It was as if the heavens were screaming as a vast iron shutter was slammed down.

"Hitler, count your children!" shouted one man close to Murphy in B Company.[7]

Murphy and men from the 3rd Division crawled from their dugouts. Machine-gun bullets—aimed at the Germans, thankfully—snapped overhead. Truscott watched in awe as "a wall of fire appeared as our first salvos crashed into the enemy front lines, then tracers wove eerie patterns in streaks of light as hundreds of machine guns of every caliber poured a hail of steel into the enemy positions."

The ground beneath men's feet trembled as if in an earthquake. Then dawn arrived but the frontline troops could barely distinguish the enemy positions, so thick were the smoke and dust from explosions. It was almost 6:30 A.M. when Truscott saw aircraft dive on positions in and around Cisterna, "their silvery wings glinting in the morning light."[8]

Murphy and B Company were on the move as fast as their legs could carry them, across the fields dotted with violets and buttercups, hoping to break through while the Germans were dazed and panicked. But then Murphy heard the distinctive cackle of enemy machine guns and realized that Germans in his sector had survived the Allied shelling.

Success did not depend on the darting planes with silver underbellies, the vast tonnage of shells, nor the cleverly laid plans of Truscott. It was up to the infantrymen or rather key warriors who could lead others into the rain of enemy bullets, who could show the way, who were prepared to die to get this job done. Selfless men would make all the difference.

The 15th Infantry Regiment hit serious resistance from the start. L Company was reduced in a couple of hours from a hundred fifty men to around forty who were able to fight. Other companies suffered high casualties, hit by intense fire from heavily camouflaged dugouts so well prepared that only a direct hit could have stopped the seemingly constant streams of machine-gun bullets that raked the regiment's spearhead.

After ninety minutes, the Marne men had moved only about five hundred yards.

"It is going too slow," thundered their commander, "Iron Mike" O'Daniel.[9]

They had to get off the goddamn plain and into the hills, even if they were dying at the rate of one every four minutes.[10] By nightfall, they had moved almost a mile but had lost 995 fellow Americans, the highest casualties suffered by any US Army division on one day in World War II.[11] There were more wounded than there were medics to treat them and many bled to death amid the trampled cornstalks.

Cisterna was proving a tough nut to crack, as had been expected. The next morning, the 15th Infantry Regiment's A Company reached a railroad embankment on the outskirts but was then repulsed. It was the Germans' last line of defense, to be held at all costs. A Company had lost an officer and eight other men, and fifty-four were wounded trying to get to the embankment, let alone across the line itself.

Audie Murphy's B Company was next to try. As he approached the embankment, Murphy saw two German strongpoints a couple of hundred yards away. Ahead of Murphy were two other platoons from B Company. Then the men in field gray laid down vicious fire once again, trying to split the platoons up and create panic.

Murphy could see a sergeant in one of the platoons. He recognized him. Lutsky. A good-looking guy. A Pole from Ohio—twenty-seven-year-old Sylvester Antolak.

Murphy knew what Antolak must have been thinking.

If the platoons got split from each other, they'd all be done for. The Germans would mop them up, like wiping gravy from a mess tin with bread.

Murphy was closing on a strongpoint when he saw Antolak rush forward, a man truly possessed, demonic, sprinting two hundred yards. Antolak pumped bullets into a machine-gun nest. The Germans tried to drop him with intense small-arms fire and he was hit two times and knocked to the coverless ground, but then got up, as if immortal, and charged them again.

A German machine gun rattled from the right.

Brapp! Brapp!

Antolak was hit for the third time and went down. A corporal reached Antolak. "We urged Sergeant Antolak to take cover," recalled the corporal, "while we arranged to get him medical aid. He looked too weak from his wounds and loss of blood to keep on going."[12] Somehow, Antolak got to his feet. His right arm was a mangled mess. He had a deep wound in his shoulder. Blood soaked his upper body yet he staggered on, his carbine under his one good arm. Fifteen yards from the enemy, he pulled the trigger and killed two more Germans. Ten others decided to give up.[13]

"*Kamerad!*" they yelled.

It was wrong to execute men with their arms in the air, even if you did it with your last breath.

Antolak spared them.

Cisterna still had to be taken, even if it was a field of rubble. Germans still lurked under the ruins, in basements, in dugouts. Antolak started out for another strongpoint, about a hundred yards away. Incredibly, he almost reached it when he dropped to the ground, shot dead.[14] "This was how Lutsky," recalled Murphy, "helped buy the freedom that we cherish and abuse."[15] He would become the third man from the 15th Infantry Regiment to earn the Medal of Honor in the battle for Cisterna. In forty-eight hours, the regiment had notched up more Medals of Honor than the entire 101st Airborne Division, the legendary Screaming Eagles, would gain in World War II.[16]

The Germans were weakening at last. Some units had lost half their men. Dozens of Shermans from the 1st Armored Division were clanking forward, gears grinding, closing the noose on Cisterna. Kesselring, informed of the situation, conceded that "things do not look good."[17] Murphy and B Company kept fighting, moving closer and closer to the rail line. By noon on May 25, with the backing of tanks and intense artillery fire, B Company finally cut the line. Other units seized Cisterna itself, incurring heavy losses.

At Cisterna and elsewhere, the ring of iron around Anzio had been broken at long last. The 15th Infantry Regiment paused for a while in a wooded area to regroup. Abandoned German equipment lay under laurel trees. Men felt terribly thirsty and hungry. They had no food with them and scoured the ground and hunted through the trees for discarded German rations.

The Germans had spotted them and shells began to explode all around, shrapnel and countless shards of wood and pieces of rock flying. Murphy took cover in a German foxhole and rammed his head between his knees. A man jumped into the hole. Murphy knew him. He was nicknamed Horse Face. He looked terrified as he asked Murphy for a swig of water.

Murphy handed over his canteen but then Horse Face dropped it. What was wrong? Horse Face said he thought he'd hurt his back and then fell forward. Murphy pulled open the man's shirt and saw a wound in his shoulder. It was a scratch, said Horse Face. Murphy knew different. He climbed out of the foxhole and ran through the exploding shells to get a medic. But when he got back to the hole, his friend Horse Face, otherwise known as Private Abraham Homer Johnson, breathed no more.[18]

The shelling ended and the regiment headed north, pursuing the Germans, moving in columns up Highway 6, the main highway from Rome to Naples. But then there was the loud whine of engines far above—fighter planes. Their wings were spitting fire. They swooped down, streams of tracers ahead of them, strafing, killing dozens of men, inflicting more than a hundred casualties.[19] Then they climbed, white stars clearly visible on their wings. Damned American flyboys. Dead and dying Marne men lay in the road, groaning, screaming, bodies ripped apart by machine-gun bullets, so many slaughtered like cattle by their own side after so long, after finally breaking out from Anzio.

Survivors stood with mouths gaping, incredulous. Then came the rage, the barked curses, the shaking heads, the pity. Murphy and his infuriated buddies traipsed on and learned that the Germans were in fast retreat. They had to press the advantage. Besides, Rome beckoned, the Eternal City with its ancient wonders, its dago red wine and twenty-five-lire whores.[20]

All along the Anzio front, German forces were in full flight, trying to escape the Allies so they could regroup north of Rome and fight another day. In what would become one of the most controversial episodes of the war, 5th Army commander Mark Clark disobeyed a direct order from his superior, Harold Alexander. Rather than chase after Kesselring's legions, he diverted key forces toward Rome, to the outrage of Lucian Truscott and other commanders who saw the chance to deal a decisive defeat to the Germans in Italy. "The enemy behaved very much as I had expected," recalled Kesselring. "If he had immediately pushed forward on a wide front, sending his tank divisions on ahead along the roads, our Army Group west of the Tiber would have been placed in almost irreparable jeopardy."[21]

Clark had other priorities. "Marcus Clarkus," as he would be derisively dubbed by the press corps, craved a page in the history books, not some footnote. He wanted to be forever remembered as the liberator, if not emperor, of Rome. He'd struggled too long, made the best of a bum deal. It was payback time. He'd have his name splashed across front pages around the world, lauded as the warlord who had bagged the first Axis capital to fall to the Allies.

Truscott would never forgive Clark. Nor would many Marne men. Poised to destroy the German forces that had inflicted so much suffering on his men for over two years, Truscott instead was forced to stand aside as Clark rolled to his coronation, grinning from a jeep, crushed by adoring crowds, headed for the Capitoline and then lunch at the Excelsior Hotel. Orders were orders, even though they "prevented the destruction of the German X Army," as Truscott put it.[22] The breakout from Anzio was a Pyrrhic victory.

Rome had been declared an Open City. The Germans had left a minimal force to slow the Allies in some places but managed to do so for only a few hours. Major Keith Ware and the 15th Infantry were soon crossing the Tiber and setting up headquarters in the heart of the city, near the Villa Borghese.[23]

Umbrella pines stood, shading dry fountains. Dark-eyed girls with glossy hair were already out and about, wearing lipstick, silk stockings, and shoes with real heels. Their previous clients had left only the day before. There'd be no more making the fascist salute. No more *"Guten Abend, Mein Herr."* The Yanks with their chocolate and Chesterfields had finally come to town.

"Gawdamighty," one man cried, "they even got redheads!"[24]

Audie Murphy and his comrades in B Company set up tents in a large park. Most were in no mood to celebrate. Too many had died to get to the banks of the Tiber. In less than a month, eighteen thousand of their fellow Americans had become casualties. Three thousand lay dead, their corpses crowding makeshift graveyards in shell-holed fields, separated by mile after mile of heartbreak, all the way from the ruins of the Abbey of Monte Cassino to the malarial wadis at Anzio.

In slimy foxholes, under constant fire, Murphy and his best friend, Lattie Tipton, had imagined bacchanalian orgies and endless "I & I"—intercourse and intoxication—but in the drab park in their khaki tents, they were too exhausted, too numbed to do anything but lay their heads on bedrolls.

HE WAS SEATED in the stands of Razorback Stadium, back at his alma mater, surrounded by a crowd of eight thousand. He was not strong enough to walk for more than fifty yards or so and a wheelchair had been provided for when he wanted to take a rest.[25] His right foot was cased in spotless white plaster, his pretty young wife, Nancy, at his side, his left sleeve tucked into his tunic's waist pocket, folded neatly where he had once had an arm.

Britt had been flown in specially for the occasion from Atlanta, accompanied from the hospital by a photographer and a public relations officer. His name was called and he got to his feet and then managed to hobble out onto the field, unaided, where he stood alone. Then a small group of senior officers walked over to Captain Maurice Britt, waiting patiently on the gridiron where he'd won sporting glory as an all-American.

An honor guard from the 42nd "Rainbow Division," which had yet to be sent into combat, lined up behind Britt. Forty-eight soldiers, carrying the flags of all forty-eight states in the US, marched onto the field.

A band played the "Star-Spangled Banner." Then the 42nd Division's commander, Major General Harry Collins, placed a blue ribbon around Britt's broad neck and saluted him. Hiding the pain from his wounds, Britt returned the salute with his left hand and then limped to a microphone and told the crowd he was receiving the award on behalf of the men who had fought as hard as him but who weren't coming home. So many others had made the ultimate sacrifice. No fewer than four Arkansans who had starred with him on an all-conference 1939 team had by that June been killed in action.[26]

His voice was clear and crisp, "echoing away in the steep green hills rising beyond," noted one reporter, and carried to each corner of the stadium where he'd starred as a defensive and offensive end in one of the "runningest" teams in Arkansas history.

"I know of no happier occasion," said Britt, "than this event today for me, unless it would be the American people celebrating the end of this horrible war."[27]

It was around 4 P.M. on June 5, 1944, commencement day for the University of Arkansas.

The press gathered around as Britt hugged his wife and his mother. Then he posed with a group of Razorback football players and the university's legendary basketball coach, Glen Rose, who had taken over as football coach for the duration of the war. There were reporters from newspapers and radio stations and a Fox Movietone News cameraman, all there to witness, it was noted, "the most impressive ceremony" ever held at the stadium.[28]

Britt didn't mention that he was supposed to have received the ultimate medal in a special ceremony back in Europe, in London—a propaganda show designed to motivate the tens of thousands of Americans who were about to invade Normandy.

As Britt snapped his salute to General Collins, the first wave of paratroopers from the 101st Airborne had already blacked their faces and been fitted with parachutes in England. Earlier that morning of June 5, Allied Supreme Commander Dwight Eisenhower had finally pulled the trigger on the most important and celebrated amphibious operation in history:

"OK, we'll go."[29]

PART TWO

France

CHAPTER 8

La Belle France

WHILE CAPTAIN BRITT celebrated with his family in Arkansas, men from I Company of the 3rd Battalion of the 18th Infantry Regiment watched England slip from view as an allied armada steamed south in the moonlight, headed toward France. Among the two hundred soldiers aboard LCI-536 was a tall, gangly nineteen-year-old private called Michael Daly, weighed down by a pack, a life vest, bandoliers of ammunition, and a gas mask.

The English Channel was rough, pitching Daly's landing craft up and down as it plowed forward through the waves.

A loudspeaker blared with the voice of Allied Supreme Commander Eisenhower.

"You are about to embark upon the Great Crusade, toward which we have striven these many months. The eyes of the world are upon you. The hopes and prayers of liberty-loving people everywhere march with you. . . . Your task will not be an easy one. Your enemy is well trained, well equipped, and battle-hardened. He will fight savagely."[1]

Before dawn, the call came to get into Higgins boats. Men clambered over the side of the LCI and climbed down cargo nets. Once the men were in the boats, the waiting began again. Daly's boat circled for several interminable hours. Many men puked into specially prepared bags. Daly was luckier than most, certainly more so than the farm boys who'd never stepped onto a ship before leaving the United States. Daly had spent many heavenly days under the bright summer sun on Long Island Sound, swimming, tacking back and forth in a dinghy, getting used to the chop of high seas.

Shells screamed overhead. Then the men were on their way in, toward Omaha Beach. It was early afternoon, several hours after the first wave had landed. Daly didn't know there had been so much carnage and confusion that the top brass had considered calling the whole thing off around midmorning. The Americans' hold on Omaha was still tenuous. A concerted German counterattack could easily push the 1st Infantry Division—the "Big Red One"—back into the English Channel.

Men clutched their cellophane-wrapped rifles. They were moving steadily toward the beach, the Higgins boat bucking up and down, aiming for one of eight sections on Omaha code-named Easy Red. It was around 1:40 P.M. Having joined his unit as a replacement just a week before the invasion, Daly had not been able to train with the men beside him.[2] His nerves taut, he spotted the corpses of some of the nine hundred Americans killed that morning still bobbing up and down in the angry surf. When Daly looked ahead, he saw "just tremendous confusion, smoke, and enemy fire, which I couldn't locate. The [Germans] were searching for us. They zeroed in [on us] with [interlocking] fields of fire."[3]

Daly watched as the coxswain in his craft maneuvered between mines and beach obstacles. The ramp slammed down, and the men clambered down into the cold water. Daly had been told to get across Omaha as fast as he could. His pack was soaked, weighing him down, slowing him. Then the horrors began. A man nearby was killed, his head blown clean off. Daly kept going, dumping the pack in the surf, wading the last yards, grateful for his height—had he been several inches smaller he wouldn't have been able to keep his head above water. He would have surely drowned.[4]

Daly spotted a mine, an obstacle, a corpse floating by. Then there was a vicious snapping, a pop-pop-pop, as machine-gun bullets whipped above his head. Some men froze with fear. Daly helped a badly injured soldier. There was no sign at all of the Germans but he could see their destruction all along the beach—smoking vehicles, burned wreckage, discarded equipment. "We couldn't see the people firing at us," he recalled. "It was not a question of overcoming my fear, but of trying to control it. My father used to say there's no such thing as bravery. What people called bravery was being raised so you're more afraid of showing fear than fear itself."[5]

Daly was probably so pumped up on adrenaline that he forgot

to crouch down as bullets popped overhead. An officer told him to get down and he did so and then crawled across sand then smooth stones. There was a rise that gave some protection. Then he was up and running, following men to the E-1 exit from Easy Red. It had been secured at heavy cost. Then the battalion Daly belonged to, the last to arrive from the 18th Infantry, was ordered to push inland, up a draw, toward a village called Saint-Laurent.

Daly followed others through a minefield. Men with bangalore torpedoes inched forward and then blew holes in barbed wire. Soldiers ahead of Daly rushed the wire and then fanned out, to the left and right, enraged, hunting the snipers. Daly spotted a private, thirty years old, carrying a flamethrower. The private was moving toward a nearby field of cattails and tall grass. It hadn't been trampled. It offered protection. The private led Daly and others through it and then they were crawling forward, up and away from Omaha Beach.[6]

By evening, Daly was almost a mile inland, unwounded, no longer a boy, utterly changed, ever grateful. Others had made the ultimate sacrifice so he could escape Bloody Omaha. Then the day drew to a close. He and his platoon dug foxholes beside a hedgerow. The next morning, he was back in action, pressing with I Company farther inland. He was finally in his element, intensely alive. Over the next several days, he adapted fast, learning the sounds of the battlefield, how to move and conserve energy, when to duck, when to return fire, how to stay alive. Daly's company commander was impressed. Daly was up for the fight, aggressive, decisive, calm under pressure. He volunteered for patrols, exposing himself several times to German fire so his platoon could locate, then destroy, enemy positions.

Daly felt he had to "prove" himself in combat,[7] above all perhaps to make his father proud. He had been born into privilege, part of a tight-knit Irish Catholic family from Connecticut. His father, Paul, was a legend in the community, a highly decorated veteran of the First World War who was often referred to reverentially as the Major. During Michael's childhood, Paul had practiced law in New York City and retired on weekends to a horse farm where he trained steeplechase champions. He always rode one of the finest at the head of the annual Memorial Day parade in his hometown of Litchfield. Every Independence Day, his birthday, he held the biggest fireworks display for miles around. As the years passed, Paul's sense of himself as a soldier never left him, and even now he was serving in Italy, as a colonel with the headquarters staff of General Patch's 7th Army.

Michael Daly was serving in his father's old division, the Big Red One, commanded by General Clarence Huebner, another of Daly Sr.'s former comrades from the trenches. Back in that war to end all wars, Daly Sr. had received the United States Army's second- and third-highest awards—the Distinguished Service Cross and the Silver Star. He'd also been recommended for the Medal of Honor.

In the summer of 1942, young Michael Daly had been admitted to West Point, the institution that had produced most of the US Army's top brass in Europe, including Mark Clark and Eisenhower. From the start, he had not been a good fit. "I was a spectacular failure as a cadet," recalled Daly. "One night I was late for guard duty. I hadn't locked my rifle. I mistook the trigger for the locking mechanism and I fired a round through a building. The same night I was sitting on the running board of a car when the inspector of the guard came by. I set a record for demerits that night."[8] West Point's culture of sometimes brutal hazing and its excessive regimentation stoked his resentment. Finally, he'd had enough and quit West Point and enlisted, determined to fight as a grunt and to prove to his father—and those who had tormented him at West Point—what he was really made of.

By June 15, Daly was nearing a village called Biéville, twenty miles inland from Omaha Beach, when the 2nd Panzer Division struck back. He saw several dozen enemy soldiers charging toward him. When the Germans were two hundred yards away, he opened up with a Browning Automatic Rifle, hitting several. Others from his company caught up with him and the Germans were beaten back. In the process, Daly earned the Silver Star, his first medal.

It was probably the longest summer of Daly's life. Each morning, his company had to get up and move into the line of fire. The only escape from the horror was to "be wounded or killed." Many of the enemy soldiers were "brave and resourceful." Some "showed unbelievable cruelty." Every encounter was one Daly felt he could not "afford to lose. . . . You had to get up and go after them. For the most part, [the Germans] had better equipment, the better machine gun . . . certainly superior armor."[9]

For thirty-eight days in a row, Daly fought deeper into France, finally resting on July 14, Bastille Day, by which time the Allied advance in Normandy had slowed to a dispiriting crawl. US First

Army commander Omar Bradley developed a plan named Operation Cobra, designed to punch a hole in the Germans' lines and allow armored forces and troops to stream through. It would involve massive bombing in a narrow area of the front lines.

On July 25, Private Michael Daly waited beneath sunny skies, having moved with the rest of his battalion to a starting point for Operation Cobra. At 9:38 A.M., six hundred Allied fighter-bombers swooped, firing rockets, engines screaming as they banked and climbed. For an hour and a half, the Germans were pounded by more than two thousand bombers.[10] One German division, the Panzer Lehr, was virtually destroyed, with seven out of ten men killed. Daly's battalion then jumped off and made good progress. The breakout had begun. Within two weeks, the Battle of Normandy became a rout.

One day, as the Allies fought toward Paris, Daly shared a foxhole with a junior officer from his company. He had learned that he would receive the Silver Star. He and the officer discussed the value of combat medals.

Daly said there was just one medal he wanted—the Medal of Honor.

It was the important one his father didn't have.[11]

Five miles north of the heart of Naples lay the ancient city of Pozzuoli. In the baking July heat in 1944, it was home to more than ten thousand Marne men undergoing intense training. The night marches, done at speed, were for a reason. They were being honed to peak fitness.

Those who knew how to handle themselves, who didn't defecate when the bullets started flying, were particularly busy on the firing ranges near Pozzuoli, famous for its volcanic sand and Flavian Amphitheater, scene of gladiator fights in Roman times. Among the instructors putting replacements through their paces, showing them how best to kill, was Sergeant Audie Murphy. Even after a year of combat, he looked younger than most of his pupils.

One day, an officer called Lieutenant George W. Mohr watched as Murphy showed men how to handle various weapons.

Murphy was particularly impressive with the tommy gun.

Mohr saw Murphy give himself a fifteen-yard run-up and then sprint as fast as he could, firing a clip of thirty bullets. "He then inserted another clip, dropped to the ground, rolled over and emptied thirty more rounds," recalled Mohr.

Others weren't quite so impressed.

A jeep pulled up and a colonel got out and approached Mohr.

"What the hell are you doing—wasting ammunition?"

"No, sir, but would you like to see what Murphy did with that tommy gun?"

Mohr and the colonel walked over to several targets. "Out of the sixty rounds he fired," remembered Mohr, "I don't think he missed the targets more than four times. He was constantly in motion the whole time."[12]

Murphy was carrying his trusty carbine, not a tommy gun, as he was trucked toward the port of Naples on August 12, 1944. He and other Marne men marched past somber-faced fifty-four-year-old Lt. General Alexander Patch, commander of the 7th Army, to which the 3rd Division had been transferred that summer. Patch had grown up in the scrubland of Arizona, starred as a pole-vaulter at West Point, served with distinction in World War I, and begun this war fighting the Japanese. He was old-school, a true cavalryman, able to roll a Bull Durham cigarette with one hand. General Truscott, now serving as a corps commander under Patch, sometimes wondered why Patch couldn't be more demonstrative and articulate. Others knew only too well that once provoked "old Sandy" had a volcanic temper and a steely drive as great as any US Army commander.

Murphy and his friends were once again bound for war. But where? As boats steamed out to sea from Naples that evening of August 12, few dogfaces seemed to care. The armada carrying the 3rd Division and two others soon stretched beyond the horizon. Gamblers got down to business. These days Sergeant Audie Murphy rarely missed out on a good craps or poker game. Betting on dice or cards was his favorite distraction.

Veterans of Anzio, Salerno, and Sicily examined their hands intently. Only winning mattered.

Fold or double down?

Bet the lot?

The Italian coastline faded into the distance.

"Okay, you jokers," cried one soldier, "take your last look at Italy!"

Many couldn't be bothered. They wouldn't miss the venereal whores, the gut-rotting plonk, the stink of Naples' backstreets, the bloodied mud of Anzio.

Italy disappeared.

The sky was bright blue.

A radio played.

Men could hear Axis Sally, the German propaganda broadcaster.

There would be no surprise, Sally insisted. The Germans knew that the 3rd Division was headed their way.

They'll be ready.

Men kept gambling. They'd heard Sally say that before.

More cards were dealt. More aces.

A chaplain, new with the division, watched men gamble and relax as the sun went down.

What the hell did it take to make these boys break a sweat?

The chaplain looked at some of the men chatting away, carefully examining their cards.

"This bunch of men is awfully unexcited," the chaplain told an officer.[13]

These men were different. They were the infamous D Day dodgers, some of them participating in their fifth amphibious operation. The stalwarts, the old men, had been wading onto hostile shores since November 1942.

Sergeant Audie Murphy had seen so much violent death, so many good, God-fearing men killed, that he had little faith in the Almighty, if any. He'd always been annoyed when he'd heard men praying out loud, asking God to save them, in tight spots.

He'd wanted to shout: "Hey, why save you? There's a whole company of us out here!"

A chaplain had scolded Murphy once for not attending a service.

"You do the prayin'," Murphy had shot back, "and I'll do the shootin'."[14]

That sultry evening, a few men chose not to gamble and opted instead to stare out to sea.

There was a small boat far off in the distance.

It got closer.

A motorboat slicing through the waves until it was a hundred yards or so away.

Men screwed up their eyes.

Could it be true?

Yes, it was him.

It really was.

"It's Churchill!"

Men pressed against the rail.

"It's Churchill!"[15]

He was a short, stubby figure. His back was straight, his thinning white hair blown about by a crisp breeze.

The motorboat moved closer.

Churchill raised his right hand and gave his famous V-for-Victory sign with two fingers.

The men of the 15th Infantry Regiment cheered and waved back.

In the early hours of August 15, the Marne men prepared for war once more. Belowdecks on a ship carrying the 15th Infantry Regiment, the holds were crammed with men throwing off blankets and rising from their bunks, lit by dim blue lights. Then they formed lines, half asleep, and moved slowly, with their mess gear in hand, past the attendants who dropped pieces of meat onto their pans and poured steaming coffee into their mugs. The dogfaces were careful not to slip on the greasy decks and steps as they then made their way to the mess hall for their last breakfast before combat.

It was early morning and the seas were calm. The Marne men had finally been informed that they were part of Operation Dragoon, the invasion of southern France along the Côte d'Azur. They were dressed in woolen olive drabs, loaded down with mortar shells, gas masks, rations, and bandoliers of ammunition. They would hit enemy shores for the first time in daylight.

This would be no Anzio. The Allies had decided they were going to throw everything they could at the German defenses along the Côte d'Azur. They wouldn't be taking any chances, not like at Salerno, and they had marshaled as many landing craft and men as possible, more than a hundred fifty thousand from three combat-hardened divisions, all placed under General Truscott's command. There would in fact be more infantry battalions landed than in Normandy on June 6. The aim was to crush resistance, then chase the Germans up the Rhône Valley, linking up with General George Patton's Third Army in the heart of France.

Major Keith Ware's First Battalion would be in the first wave with Murphy's B Company, scheduled to land on the soft golden sands of Yellow Beach at 8 A.M. south of Saint-Tropez. It was after first light when Audie Murphy and Lattie Tipton heard the growl of their landing-craft motor as it pulled away from the mother ship. The skies erupted as a huge naval and aerial barrage pounded Yellow Beach and German defenses. Rockets hissed through the sky, skimming below the overcast, each landing with a mighty "cr-a-a-ck!"[16]

One man stood in a landing craft, trying to reassure greenhorns.

"Take it from me," said the soldier. "The first wave onto the beach is the best one to be in. You got a choice on the first wave! If you don't like the pillbox on the right, you move over and take the pillbox on the left. But if you gotta come in later, you get no choice. You gotta take the pillbox that the first wave passed."

Tipton and Murphy could see a thin haze of a mist above vineyards inland from crescent-shaped Yellow Beach.

The Allied destroyers that had pounded the beach lurked like ghosts behind Murphy's shoulder, holding their fire, miles out at sea.

The rocket fire ended. All that could be heard was the steady thrumming of landing-craft engines, like the "buzzing of gigantic bees."[17]

Murphy looked around the landing craft. His men were "as miserable as cats. Though the sea was relatively calm, several were seasick. Others had the lost, abstract expression of men who were relieving their bowels."[18]

Murphy told Tipton and others to sing "Beer Barrel Polka":

There's a garden, what a garden
Only happy faces bloom there
And there's never any room there
For a worry or a gloom there.

One man sang along but then stopped.

Murphy was having none of that.

They were to lift their voices and sing, like dogfaces did in the movies when they went to war.

Someone told Murphy to shut up. They were almost at the shore. That familiar gut-wrenching feeling of terror. The ramp came down and Murphy led his platoon onto Yellow Beach. It was 8 A.M.

A German machine gun rattled.

Murphy and Tipton sprinted across the beach, dived to the ground, and crawled toward cover. Then they were up on their feet and moving toward pine-clad hills through small fields and olive groves. There was little resistance and they advanced a couple of miles that morning, reaching the outskirts of an ancient hill town called Ramatuelle.

Murphy looked up and saw a few hundred yards ahead a ridge studded with boulders and large rocks, shaded by cork and plane trees.

He and Tipton came under fire from yet another machine gun.

Tipton felt searing pain. He'd been shot through his ear and blood flooded down his neck and soaked his uniform.

"Go back, Lattie," shouted Murphy. "Get back and have that ear fixed."

"You go to hell."

Tipton wiped blood from his face. He could still fight. He watched Murphy make a break for a ditch, running forty yards as bullets kicked up dirt around him.

Murphy returned sometime later, again braving German fire, and told Tipton he'd spotted the German machine gun. He'd go deal with it on his own.

"I'm going too," said Tipton.

Tipton had seen combat at Murphy's side since they'd landed in Sicily more than a year ago. Murphy was closer than any brother could be. In Italy, Tipton had been offered a promotion but turned it down, wanting to stay with Murphy.[19]

"I'm going up, Lattie," said Murphy. "Now I'm telling you again, fall back and get that ear fixed."

Murphy set off and then glanced over his shoulder. Tipton was following him. Two Germans were ahead. Murphy killed both with his carbine. He and Tipton slithered on their bellies up a slope, moving through a vineyard, ripening grapes dangling above them.

Bullets snapped overhead.

Murphy saw two Germans. One had his hands in the air. The other was waving a white flag.

"I'm going up to get them," Tipton said. "Keep me covered."

"Goddamn it! Lattie, keep down."

"They want to surrender," said Tipton. "I'm going to get them."

"Keep down!" shouted Murphy. "Don't trust them."

Crack.

"Murph . . ."

Tipton fell onto Murphy. There wasn't any sign of blood on his uniform but Tipton was dead, shot in the heart.[20] Something snapped inside Murphy. He would never be the same. The next few minutes were a blur of rage and killing. "Murph lost his head," remembered a fellow B Company soldier. "When you lose a buddy like that it's really tough."[21]

Murphy threw several grenades and killed the two Germans with the white flag, pumping bullets into them. Another German lay nearby with his jaw blown off. Blood gushed from his mouth. Murphy knew he should put the kid out of his misery. But he was done with killing Krauts for the day. He'd taken his revenge. And so he returned under the hot sun through the vines to where he'd left Tipton, then grabbed a pack and propped his dead friend's head up on it.

In Tipton's blood-soaked uniform, Murphy found a photo of Tipton's daughter, Claudean, with her pigtailed hair, soft smile . . .

Lattie's perfect little girl, all he'd had to live for.

Murphy had vowed to protect Tipton so he could hold her again. He'd failed. He slumped down to the ground, broken by grief, tears running down his cheeks, and then bawled like a baby. It was the only time anyone ever saw him cry in combat.[22] He was a boy again. He'd been abandoned again, like when his mother had died.

For his actions on Pill Box Hill in the vineyard near Rama-tuelle, Murphy would receive the Distinguished Service Cross, America's second-highest award for gallantry. He would have traded it for Lattie Tipton's life in a heartbeat.[23]

Murphy stood up and rejoined Company B, reorganizing his platoon, reloading, moving on, closer to Germany, the blue skies above, the ocean a few miles behind. "Once again I saw the war as it was," he remembered. "It was an endless series of lethal problems, some big, some small, that involved the blood and guts of men. Lattie was dead, and I was alive. It was as simple as that. The dead would lie where they had fallen; the living would move on and keep fighting. There was nothing else to do."[24]

CHAPTER 9

Blitzkrieg in Provence

OPERATION DRAGOON WAS spectacularly successful, the "best invasion I ever attended," according to *Stars and Stripes*' celebrated cartoonist Bill Mauldin.[1] Unlike at Anzio, the Allies had landed enough men and supported them with effective air cover and accurate naval bombardment. Stunned prisoners mumbled about the "bomb blanket" dropped before the landing, about the "nerve-shattering" impact of rockets, about being buried two or three times under debris and sandy soil.[2]

Lucian Truscott's VI Corps had waltzed ashore, suffering five hundred casualties with fewer than a hundred killed. "We broke a thin crust," recalled one of Major Keith Ware's fellow officers in the 3rd Division, "and behind the crust there was nothing that could stop us." By the end of August 15, D Day, the 15th Infantry Regiment had achieved all its goals. Audie Murphy and B Company snatched a few hours' rest in a fragrant pine forest.

The next day, B Company was assigned to ride in trucks and

headed north along a road skirted by hedges of pink oleander, hyacinths, and endless rows of vines laden with ripening grapes. There would be no stalling as at Anzio, no waiting around. Truscott had already spoken to his generals, making this crystal clear. They were to move as fast and far as possible. "To hell with written orders," he barked. "Let's get going."[3]

For the first time in the war, Audie Murphy and his fellow dogfaces found themselves moving at real speed, making their longest advance in the shortest time. Morale soared. Smiles returned to men's faces. Each mile closer to Germany was another nearer to home. The German 19th Army had been taken by surprise, wrong-footed, and was retreating along the Rhône Valley, retracing the legendary Route Napoléon. Many units were disorganized and panicked, leaderless. It was every man for himself.

Morale was fast collapsing among even those die-hard Germans left behind to try to stall the American advance. Desertion was common. Prisoners from several nationalities—including Russians, Poles, and North Africans—swore bitterly about arrogant officers fleeing to Germany with cases of French wine while they'd been abandoned to face the full fury of Lucian Truscott's blitzkrieg through Provence.[4]

Truscott's next objective was the town of Montélimar, famous for producing France's finest candy, a sublime mixture of honey and nuts. It nestled on the eastern banks of the Rhône and had a medieval heart of narrow winding streets—ideal territory for German snipers. As the 15th Infantry Regiment closed on the city, supporting artillery pounded key targets and roads day and night.

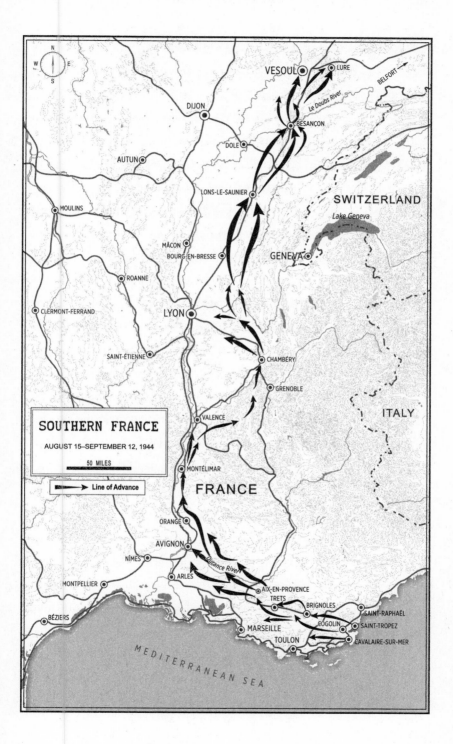

N
W   E
S

VESOUL ◉━━▶ LURE
BELFORT━▶

DIJON ◉

Le Doubs River
BESANÇON ◉

DOLE ◉

AUTUN ◉

LONS-LE-SAUNIER ◉

SWITZERLAND

Lake Geneva

MOULINS ◉

MÂCON ◉
BOURG-EN-BRESSE ◉

GENEVA ◉

ROANNE ◉

CLERMONT-FERRAND ◉

LYON ◉

CHAMBÉRY ◉

SAINT-ÉTIENNE ◉

GRENOBLE ◉

ITALY

VALENCE ◉

SOUTHERN FRANCE

AUGUST 15–SEPTEMBER 12, 1944

50 MILES

━━▶ Line of Advance

MONTÉLIMAR ◉

FRANCE

ORANGE ◉

AVIGNON ◉

Durance River

NÎMES ◉

ARLES ◉

MONTPELLIER ◉

AIX-EN-PROVENCE ◉
TRETS ◉

BRIGNOLES ◉

SAINT-RAPHAËL ◉

BÉZIERS ◉

COGOLIN ◉
SAINT-TROPEZ ◉

MARSEILLE ◉

TOULON ◉

CAVALAIRE-SUR-MER ◉

MEDITERRANEAN SEA

Supply issues quickly became apparent.[5] Thousands of shells were being fired each day, more than thirty-seven thousand on Montélimar alone in a week. Each one had to be replaced. Truckers were having to make a dusty four-hundred-seventy-mile round trip to the beaches of Provence to bring in more supplies. Keeping three infantry divisions in the fight was consuming a hundred thousand gallons of fuel a day. But nothing was going to stop Truscott from taking Montélimar as fast as possible, and he simply placed his soldiers on two-thirds rations.

"If you run out of gas," Truscott ordered, "park your vehicles and move on foot!"[6]

Montélimar finally lay in the distance, much of it in ruins. On the afternoon of August 28, Major Keith Ware's First Battalion was ordered to slice into it. Murphy's B Company led the assault.[7] On the outskirts, scouts spotted a mobile antiaircraft gun—a flak wagon—and three 88mm artillery pieces. Murphy and his platoon remained undetected and they were able to creep up on the guns, covered in camouflage netting, without the Germans getting a chance to lower the barrels and open fire.[8]

Not long after, Murphy spied an ammunition dump. He called for a bazooka, a weapon different from the carbine, with which he was unfailingly accurate. After several attempts, he hit the dump, which exploded with such deafening force that more than a hundred Germans quickly surrendered. Others fled and B Company formed a skirmish line and peppered their backs and legs with bullets, as if on a turkey shoot, and then B Company moved into what was left of Montélimar.

The fighting would be up close and personal, house to house, room to room. Murphy entered a building, a German command post, with a squad from his platoon. It took valuable seconds to see in the darkness after the bright light outside. He was carrying a tommy gun, not his beloved carbine. He could spray a room fast with far more bullets with the tommy gun.

The door to one room was closed.

Was a German behind it?

Murphy lifted his tommy gun, ready to pull the trigger.

He opened the door. Staring right back at him was a man armed with a tommy gun.

The man looked like the devil. He had red eyes and a blackened bearded face.

Murphy instinctively pulled the trigger.

Something shattered.

He'd caught sight of himself in a full-length mirror and fired at his reflection.[9]

A soldier bent over with laughter.

"That's the first time," blurted the soldier, "I ever saw a Texan beat himself to the draw."[10]

Montélimar fell three days later, with Major Ware's First Battalion earning the presidential unit citation. The 3rd Division took eight hundred prisoners and killed or wounded some five hundred Germans. There was a reason the Germans had put up stiff resistance in the city. The battle had bought precious time for many armored units to escape north. But even so there were still thousands of stragglers frantically trying to outpace the Americans. Hundreds of horse-drawn carts and artillery pieces lumbered at the rear of the panicked remnants of the German

19th Army, heading north along Route nationale 7, following the Rhône River toward Lyon.

From the air the heavily camouflaged horses looked to one observer like "moving bushes" as they trailed behind columns of troops. Spotter planes reported their position, and artillery attached to the 36th Division, one of the three in Truscott's VI Corps, went to work. In a few hellish hours, several hundred German soldiers were slaughtered. It was the worst destruction the Marne men witnessed during the war. Under the bright sun, the Germans' corpses bloated and then rotted, blanketed by flies, turning fifteen long miles of Route nationale 7 into the "Avenue of Stenches."

Bulldozers were called up to clear paths through the wreckage, leaving piles of charred crimson flesh and abandoned equipment on each side of the road. Here and there, a German truck stood miraculously undamaged, stuffed with the spoils of war: bottles of champagne and cognac, cameras, and piles of banknotes, remembered one soldier, "as thick as leaves on a tree." One of Audie Murphy's B Company comrades helped himself to an armful of "silk stockings, slips, and panties."[11]

As Major Ware and his men threaded their way along the road, they encountered horrific scenes. They would never forget the reek of mass death, the smashed tanks, debris for mile after mile, the skeletons of more than two thousand destroyed vehicles . . . all the dead young Germans, faces turned to charcoal, hair singed, so much carrion. Dozens of horses lay dying, neighing and whinnying, anguish in the big whites of their eyes.

A soft-spoken Texan in B Company saw a badly wounded horse, its guts spewing out. Audie Murphy handed him a Luger pistol taken from a badly wounded German officer. The Texan aimed the Luger at the horse's head, behind its ear, and a single shot rang out and the horse fell dead. The Texan loved horses as Murphy did. They were better than goddamned human beings, so much more deserving, the best friends a man could have. They didn't massacre one another.

The Texan wanted to hand the Luger back but Murphy told him to keep it. There were plenty more horses, and maybe some humans, that needed to be put out of their misery up ahead. A few days later, Murphy learned the Texan had been hit in the spine by a sliver of steel and paralyzed from the waist down, never to sit in a saddle again.

The Marne men kept rolling, heading north along Route nationale 7 toward the city of Besançon, a key road junction. They followed the mighty Rhône River, imperious, slowly flowing in the other direction toward the Mediterranean. Again they enjoyed the heady rush of speed and dared to hope for victory before winter as they stormed through Provence, past the fields of sunflowers and lavender, through landscape surely too beautiful to spoil with war.

Limestone villages fell one after another. Locals lined the streets. World War I veterans saluted the Yanks and children waved homemade Stars and Stripes flags and ragged Tricolors. Mademoiselles in summer frocks threw flowers and handed bottles of wine to the smirking tanned soldiers hitching rides on dusty Shermans, hulls covered with sandbags, the clanking avatars of victory. Throughout France, the Allies were also now on the move, confidence sky-high, hopes for a swift end to it all shared by both dogfaces and Allied commanders.

Major Keith Ware had been liberating Europe for a year, but it was only here, in the vine-clad Rhône Valley, on Route nationale 7, following the famous Route Napoléon, that he and his fellow Marne men felt truly appreciated.[12] There was no time to stop and enjoy the best wine in the world, the grand cru of Burgundy, but all along their route, as they headed to the northeast, the Swiss Alps soaring to their far right, Ware and his troops were cheered and applauded. The gratitude of the liberated was truly uplifting after the abject poverty and desperation of so many Italians.

The good times didn't last long. Ahead, in the lee of the Vosges Mountains, lay Besançon with its Vauban-designed fort, La Citadelle, rising above a loop in the Doubs River. Several other seventeenth-century minor forts protected the city. A good road, labeled Route 73 on Ware's tourist map, snaked eastward from Besançon toward the Third Reich, providing the main escape route for the 19th Army.[13] The Germans weren't going to give up the birthplace of Victor Hugo without a scrap. All three regiments from the 3rd Division would be thrown into what would quickly become the fiercest combat since arriving in France.[14]

B Company attacked one of the minor forts, Fort de Fontain, on September 5. "The Krauts had set up mortars and machine guns in the fort," remembered Ware. Tank destroyers and artillery pounded the fort and "with the cover of darkness" his men stormed the sole bridge leading to the fort and then cleared it.[15] The rest of the city fell three days later.[16] Ware's battalion kept going, along the winding E-23 to Vesoul, exactly four hundred miles north of Saint-Tropez. His men had covered the distance in less than a month. But there were still another five hundred before they reached Berlin, and ominously, the Germans appeared set on defending each one.[17]

On September 12, a twenty-two-year-old first lieutenant called John Tominac, a tall Pennsylvanian in I Company of the 15th Infantry Regiment, spotted a German roadblock. It was the first of many designed to slow the Marne men as they approached the Moselle River. Tominac sprinted ahead of his platoon for fifty yards and killed three Germans with his tommy gun. Then he and his platoon attacked another German strongpoint, and in a fierce firefight, they killed thirty more. A Sherman tank joined the platoon and Tominac and his men moved beside it toward a third position. There was a vicious bark as a German cannon fired on the tank, hitting it and wounding Tominac in the shoulder.[18]

The tank erupted into flames but its crew managed to get out before they were burned to death. Tominac picked himself up and then climbed up onto the tank, which was rolling slowly down a hill, out of control. Flames leapt into the air and bullets pinged off the tank but Tominac, even though badly wounded, stood on the burning tank's turret, "plainly silhouetted against the sky," according to one account, and grabbed hold of its 50mm machine gun.[19]

Tominac let rip, his fire so accurate that the Germans ahead decided to flee. Finally, he jumped clear of the tank and watched it trundle down the hill before exploding. His men gathered around. In agony, he asked a sergeant to gouge out the shrapnel from his shoulder using a penknife. Then he was back on his feet, attacking again, this time using hand grenades, forcing another thirty Germans to surrender, earning himself the Medal of Honor, adding to the 3rd Division's extraordinary medal haul, higher than that of any other infantry division in Europe.[20] Indeed, by that fall the Marne men were the most decorated American liberators, having fought longest and arguably hardest, for almost two years. Already, Tominac's fellow Marne men had earned approaching a hundred Distinguished Service Crosses and well over a thousand Silver Stars.

The weather changed for the worse. The German 19th Army newspaper, *Die Wacht*, reported that September 13 was a particularly dismal day. Men who had retreated from sun-kissed Provence found themselves drenched, shivering "on the threshold of the Reich. . . . Dense clouds hang between the mountains of the lower Vosges. The roads glisten with rain and the wind sweeps cold over the plains. . . . The thunder of the guns already echoes in the peaceful dales."[21]

Two days later, Audie Murphy's B Company encountered a roadblock.

There was a low whistle of a mortar.

This is it.

The mortar shell exploded a few yards from Murphy, throwing him to the ground.

Murphy came to and found himself beside a shell crater. He was deafened, his eyes scorching with pain. He could see his trusty carbine—broken in two. Two men lay dead nearby. Murphy looked down and saw that the heel of his boot was missing. He then reached down and felt blood. "It was only a slight wound," he recalled, "but I got the Purple Heart and spent two weeks in evacuation and convalescent hospitals before rejoining my outfit."[22]

By the time Murphy was back on the line, the German resistance had stiffened further. The leaves were turning color on
hilltops. The Marne men were heading toward the Belfort Gap,
a broad valley to the northeast that separated the Vosges Mountains from the Alps.

"As you stated the other day, the Belfort Gap is the Gateway
to Germany," Truscott wrote 7th Army commander Alexander
Patch on September 15. "It is obvious that the Boche is making
strenuous efforts to strengthen the defense of this area and that
he expects to hold that area as long as possible."

Truscott knew each week of delay could mean months of
needless attrition that winter.

"The assault on the Belfort Gap should begin at the earliest
moment. . . . As demonstrated in Italy during last winter, the
Boche can limit progress to a snail's pace and even stop it entirely, even against superior strength."

He wasn't going to see his troops trapped in mountains yet
again, not when advance patrols were just fifty miles from the
German border.

"It would seem wasteful to employ the three most veteran
divisions in the American Army in an operation where they can
be contained by a fraction of their strength and where their
demonstrated ability to maneuver is so strictly limited."[23]

Patch wasn't impressed by Truscott's letter. He didn't appreci-
ate being told what to do. He was, after all, Truscott's commanding general, not some dim-witted understudy.

Patch had to answer to his own boss, Eisenhower, who was
preoccupied with progress far to the north.

"I dread the approaching wet and cold and snow and tedious

mountain work," Truscott wrote his wife, Sarah, on September 16. "The skies weep continuously now."[24]

That evening, Patch contacted Truscott by telephone.

"I don't think that letter of yours was advisable," said Patch. "A less sensitive man than I—and I'm not sensitive at all—would see a lack of confidence shown in your leaders. I think I should tell you that it wasn't a very creditable letter."

"I wrote that letter only because it was something I believe. I don't know the full picture of course."

"I know that, but when I have something on my chest, I have to say it to that person—that's the way I am."

"So far as I am concerned, you have my complete and whole-hearted support, once the decision is made. If you think someone else can do this job better than I, it is all right with me—but I don't think you can."

"I know that."

"I have gotten into position. Everything is ready. We can't stop right now."

Patch understood. But he would have to get permission from Eisenhower before he could unleash Truscott's Corps and rush the Belfort Gap.

"I must get it approved first," said Patch, "but I'll get word to you as soon as I can."

"If I go ahead the way I'm going," replied Truscott, "I will be up against the Belfort defenses the day after tomorrow."

Patch told Truscott he would discuss matters further in person, perhaps the following night.

"In the meantime," said Patch, "don't lose any sleep over it."[25]

It was an infuriatingly glib answer and it wasn't until eleven agonizing days later, as temperatures dropped each night, that Truscott got an answer. Patch had bad news—there was no support for a big push to the Belfort Gap. It was too well defended. Eisenhower had suffered a humiliating setback during Operation Market Garden, an audacious attempt to cross the Rhine that had ended in costly failure. He didn't want any more disasters.

The Marne men were instead to reach Nazi Germany by a more northerly route, through the Vosges Mountains, soon to be pronounced *Voz-jees* by many a dogface.[26]

Truscott's troops set out beneath dirty cloud masses, crossing the fast-flowing Moselle River. "Due to the rapidly moving situation," recalled Major Keith Ware, "the only maps available to the battalion were [French] road maps."[27] They lacked fine detail but showed clearly what lay beyond the Moselle—the Vosges, which had never been crossed successfully in winter by an attacking army.

It was hard to imagine a worse place to fight. All the advantages lay with the Germans. Jagged ridgelines overlooked deep valleys pitted with peat bogs, leading to windswept moors. Giant granite tors dotted thick conifer forests at higher altitudes. The tightly bunched firs towered more than seventy feet in places, and without a compass, men could get lost after crawling beneath the lower branches for only a hundred yards. There were few roads and those that could hold tanks were narrow and twisted sharply as they snaked up and down, from one village of half-timbered homes to another. And the Vosges were famous for their atrocious weather, even for northern Europe, with cold fronts settling over them for weeks on end.

Having been promoted from major to lieutenant colonel, Ware learned that patrols had met unnerving resistance from German forces at a quarry near a village called Cleurie.[28] The hamlet lay in the lee of several three-thousand-foot mountains, forty miles due east of the city of Colmar. The Cleurie Quarry was, as Audie Murphy later described it, "a pin-point on a very large map, but in the memory of the men who fought there, it loomed like Kings Mountain in the Revolutionary War."[29] Situated at the top of a steep, thickly wooded slope, it overlooked a critical road. It could not be bypassed. The Germans had hewn two tunnels deep into the rock formation and were therefore safe from artillery and mortar fire.

Each approach to the quarry, the anchor of the 19th Army's defenses, was under sniper and machine-gun fire. Further reports from scouts confirmed the Germans had turned the quarry into a natural fortress, a granite death trap.[30] Seizing it would be the greatest challenge Lt. Colonel Ware had faced in more than four hundred days of war.

CHAPTER 10

The Quarry

A COLD RAIN fell on September 29, wreathing the Cleurie Quarry with mist. Entrances from east and west were blocked by huge stone walls erected in recent weeks by the Germans. Dozens of machine gunners and snipers waited, watching for the slightest movement as the spearhead of Ware's First Battalion approached. When men showed themselves, streams of bullets slashed through the mist, and before long, Ware's men were stopped at the southern edge of the quarry. The German fire was too intense.[1]

It was around midnight when Audie Murphy and B Company, commanded by Captain Paul Harris, tried to advance once more. Dense fog descended and they dug in close to the quarry. Harris set up his headquarters in a farmhouse, pinning up detailed maps of the quarry on a wall, about twenty-five yards behind B Company's forward positions. Germans crept forward, potato-masher grenades tucked under their belts, and quickly surrounded

Harris's command post. Bullets ricocheted off the building's walls and white tracers slashed through the darkness.

From his foxhole, Audie Murphy watched the tracer fire and then saw Germans closing on the house. He slithered out of his hole and scrambled toward the building. He'd been spotted. Bullets snapped overhead. He carried on, hurling grenades as fast as he could. Explosions ripped through nearby woods. To his relief, Murphy saw the Germans retreat back into the trees.

At battalion headquarters the following morning, Lt. Colonel Ware and others grew increasingly concerned by the holdup at the quarry, a "major thorn in the side of the Fifteenth Infantry."[2] The fight to seize it from "fanatical young Nazis" had become a "terrific contest of nerve and endurance."[3] True to form, Ware wanted to see what was going on for himself.[4] He arrived at B Company's command post with the 15th Infantry Regiment's executive officer, Lt. Colonel Michael Paulick, a twenty-nine-year-old, square-chinned son of Hungarian immigrants. A West Point graduate, Paulick had been a coal miner in Pennsylvania before the war and would end it with every award for valor except the Medal of Honor.[5]

It was another depressing day with low skies. Paulick and Ware spoke with Captain Harris, who was red-eyed with fatigue. Paulick asked Harris to pick four enlisted men to form a patrol. Then Ware and Paulick would go check out the quarry itself.

Harris didn't ask Murphy to join the patrol, even though he was the most useful soldier in B Company. Ware also would have known how helpful Murphy could be in a tight spot, ever since their days together in Sicily when he'd been Murphy's first company commander. In any case, Murphy wasn't in the mood to volunteer. He was depressed by the heavy losses from his platoon in recent days. He'd begun to forget men's names—there'd been such a high turnover.

Several men came forward to join the patrol.

Murphy didn't think Ware and Paulick should step beyond B Company's perimeter—to venture up the hill toward the quarry was to invite a vicious German response.

Paulick was under intense pressure from Truscott to clear the quarry. As for Ware, the First Battalion's canny tactician, he no doubt wanted a good look at the problem so he could solve it. That was his way of getting the job done.

Paulick and Ware set off with the patrol.

Murphy admired Ware after two years of serving under him. He wasn't about to let him get killed for no good reason. Restless, he picked up his carbine and grabbed several grenades and then followed Ware and Paulick: "I figured those gentlemen were going to run into trouble. So I tagged along, about 25 yards to their rear, to watch the stampede."

The Germans spotted the party, opened fire, and hurled grenades, taking out two men and then riddling another with machine-gun fire.

Ware and Paulick and others were pinned down, bullets popping above their heads.

Murphy called out the name of a man in the patrol and asked if he was alive.

The man shouted back.

Murphy shouted another name.

Alive.

Grenades exploded in the German position ahead. Ware and

Paulick found Murphy toting his carbine, standing beside a German machine gun. Nearby lay four dead Germans. Three terrified wounded men, their uniforms bloodied and shredded, cowered a few yards away.

Paulick was highly impressed with the young Texan. "To me the important thing," he remembered, "was Murphy's immediate grasp of the situation, his precise thinking, and his uncanny coolness in action."[6]

A German started to make a run for it.

Murphy lifted his carbine and aimed at the man's gray helmet.

The German was overweight, waddling, out of breath, "like a duck being chased by an ax-man."

Should Murphy kill him?

It felt too easy, like "killing a clown."

The clown was armed.

A single shot.

The clown fell down dead.

Murphy approached Paulick, who looked surprisingly calm, "as cool as the October morning."

"Those grenades are not a bad idea," said Paulick. "Next time I'll bring my own."[7]

Ware and Murphy went to check on the B Company soldier who'd been hit by the machine gun. The man lay in agony. Someone went to fetch a medic. Ware had plenty of time to size Murphy up. The staff sergeant was still only nineteen years old. They'd both been in combat with the 15th Infantry Regiment for the same time, what must have felt like an eternity. Murphy was as sharp as ever, utterly fearless, one hell of a fighter, "beyond doubt the finest" Ware had ever seen.[8]

A medic arrived with a litter. Then they all clambered down the deadly slope, away from the quarry, back to B Company's lines. Murphy's actions that day, quite apart from saving two senior officers' lives, would earn him the Silver Star, thanks to Paulick's recommendation. To his dying day, Ware would feel indebted.[9]

The battle continued for the quarry. Tank destroyers and artillery fired five hundred rounds of high explosive into the quarry and its tunnels. Mortar fire seeded every yard of the quarry with fragments of decapitating steel, and then before dawn on October 4, patrols from all of the First Battalion's companies attacked once more, immediately running into extraordinarily accurate sniper fire. Eighty sharpshooters, armed with the finest telescopic rifles, had been attached to each platoon of the 601st Schnelle Battalion to defend the quarry.[10]

That afternoon, under brutal stress, the 15th Infantry's regimental commander, Colonel Richard Thomas, had a heart attack and was replaced by Lt. Colonel Hallett D. Edson, a superb officer who would lead the regiment with great skill for the remainder of the war. It was getting dark on October 5, the sixth day of the siege, when the Marne men finally cleared the quarry after going "toe to toe," it was reported, as they cleared "thick nests" of snipers.[11] "That was some of the hardest fighting I ever saw," recalled Murphy. "You might go into a patch of woods with thirty men and come out with only fifteen."[12]

The 15th Infantry Regiment had been in combat since August 15 without a rest. The struggle for the quarry was over, but unnervingly, the Germans appeared as determined to fight for each ridge ahead. By October 8, 1944, three days after leaving the quarry, Murphy had advanced with Company B less than three miles. At this rate, it would take forever to reach Berlin.

It was still raining hard as Murphy led his platoon of twenty-seven men through some woods.

Snap.

A sniper.

A man behind Murphy went down and cried out in agony.

The scream was heard by German machine gunners who then opened fire. Several men in Murphy's platoon soon lay badly wounded.

Murphy knew he needed artillery support, so he grabbed a 536 radio.[13]

The Germans kept firing. Murphy dived to the ground and tried to escape the bullets. "I kept so low I must have dug a ditch down the side of a hill," he remembered. "I was cold and wet and scared and my teeth chattered so loud I was afraid I'd give myself away. I must have crawled 50 yards before I decided I could direct the artillery O.K. I called for 4.2 mortar fire, and it came. For an hour I lay there wishing I was a mole. Rifle and machine gun bullets hit as close as a foot from me, but the Nazis couldn't quite get me."[14]

The shelling worked. After-action reports listed thirty-five wounded and fifteen dead Germans. For saving his platoon, Murphy was awarded his second Silver Star in three days—an Oak-Leaf Cluster to the medal he'd won for saving Lt. Colonel Ware's life.

The only award for valor Murphy now lacked was the Medal of Honor. If he earned that highest of awards, he would equal Maurice Britt's record haul. Murphy later said he could not have cared less which medal he had pinned onto his chest. They were all worth the same. Every time he got another ribbon, he was closer to going home under what was called "the points system." "As far as I was concerned," he explained, "I just wanted to get back to Texas as soon as possible."[15]

The points system for Americans in Europe in World War II was a way of deciding who should return home first. If a dogface had three or more children under eighteen, he would be the first to be sent back at the end of the war in Europe, no matter how many medals he'd gained or how long he'd served. Murphy and almost every dogface, by contrast, needed to accumulate eighty-five points. Each man got a point for each month of military service and an additional point for every month spent overseas. Each campaign served was worth five points, so those like Ware and Murphy, who had been in combat since Sicily, had by now fought in six campaigns, meaning an automatic thirty points.

No points were given if you were married or older, and to the outrage of many infantrymen, there were no points for receiving the Combat Infantryman Badge—the average frontline grunt was treated in this sense the same as the rear-echelon shirker. Medals counted for five points, with no difference between a Bronze Star and the Medal of Honor, although receiving the Medal of Honor guaranteed by this stage of the war that a man would be pulled off the front line—the military wanted live heroes, like Maurice Britt, to bang the propaganda drum. Dead men couldn't get people to buy war bonds. The only way most infantrymen could guarantee they would stay alive, unless they were pulled off the line badly wounded, was to earn the Medal of Honor and then be notified as soon as possible of its being awarded.

Medals were one thing. Promotion was quite another. It was high time Murphy went to the next level. Murphy, however, had already told Captain Harris, B Company's commander, that he didn't want a promotion. "He didn't consider himself officer material," remembered Harris. "He was embarrassed by his lack of formal education."[16]

Murphy was summoned to see Lt. Colonel Paulick, the 15th Infantry's executive officer.

Murphy again demurred. He was happy to stay a sergeant leading a platoon.

Paulick listened patiently. He wasn't going to order Murphy to take a commission. There must be some way to get this stubborn kid with the almost unintelligible Texan drawl to change his mind?

Murphy finally said he had no problem with a new rank so long as he didn't have to do any paperwork.

That set Paulick thinking.

Why not let his adjutant do the paperwork?

Murphy liked the sound of that.

There was another issue. Enlisted men who were promoted were always sent to new outfits. Murphy had been with B Company since learning the Truscott trot in North Africa. There was no way he was going to ditch his bloodied and brutalized family when it needed him more than ever.

Paulick said he'd get a waiver. Murphy could stay with B Company.

On October 14, several days after earning his second Silver Star, Murphy was called to regimental headquarters.

Colonel Hallett Edson swore in Murphy and two other enlisted men as officers, then pinned two silver bars to each man's uniform.

"You are now gentlemen by act of Congress," said Edson. "Shave, take a bath, and get the hell back into the lines."[17]

Murphy was in fact discharged and then commissioned, spending three hours as a civilian before becoming an officer. Second Lieutenant Murphy then returned to Company B on the front lines, one of forty-eight hundred Americans holding his new rank who saw action in Europe in World War II.[18]

"You mean I've got to salute you?" asked a private who'd fought with Murphy since Sicily.

"Salute the uniform," replied Murphy.[19]

Another of Murphy's friends in B Company had joked around with him in recent weeks, telling him: "Hey Murph, if you take a commission, I hope you get your ass shot off."[20] The wisecrack was no longer quite so funny. Murphy would now stand a much greater chance of being killed or wounded. Newly commissioned as an officer, if not a gentleman, he held the most dangerous rank in the US infantry. Statistically, he could expect to last a month, perhaps a couple, but no more. At Anzio, in fifty days, his division had suffered a hundred-fifty percent losses in second lieutenants.[21]

Facts were facts. The odds were not good. Indeed, the two enlisted men commissioned with Murphy would both soon be killed.

Three days after Murphy became a shavetail, his VI Corps commander, newly promoted Lt. General Lucian Truscott, was summoned for an important meeting. It was October 17 when Truscott joined 7th Army commander Alexander Patch and then saluted Allied Supreme Commander Dwight Eisenhower in Épinal, around thirty miles from the front. Eisenhower was at first his usual charming and complimentary self. Then he dropped the small talk and got down to business.

"Lucian, I am going to relieve you from the VI Corps," he said. "You are an embarrassment to me now that you have been made a lieutenant general. All of my Corps commanders now want to be made lieutenant generals. I am going to assign you to organize the Fifteenth Army. You won't like it, because this Army is not going to be operational. It will be an administrative and training command, and you won't get into the fighting."[22]

Truscott said he would rather stay at his previous rank with his men. He had not wanted to be promoted.

Truscott asked if Patch would allow him to stay on.

Patch said he would.

Eisenhower was having none of it. He needed Truscott to set up his new army.

So it was that on October 24, 1944, arguably the greatest fighting US division commander of World War II stood before senior officers as well as enlisted men from the 3rd Division.

The 3rd Division Band played its anthem, "Dogface Soldier."

Truscott did not hide his tears as he bade his beloved Marne men goodbye. He knew he might not see them again, soldiers he'd led for two years, from Algeria to within striking distance of the Third Reich. He felt as if he were abandoning them, exhausted and dejected as so many were, at a critical juncture.

There was no doubting what the future held—another winter with yet more unfathomable tragedy. In a recent letter to his wife, Sarah, Truscott had expressed his fears—"the beast has every intention of continuing the fight to the bitter end."[23] The Fatherland was at stake. It was one thing for a German soldier to risk his life for the Führer in Italy, quite another to stop the *Amis*—those American half-breed gangsters—from conquering sacred soil: the *Heimweh*, blessed Germany.

It started to snow on the highest peaks of the Vosges a couple of days after Truscott's departure. Audie Murphy led his platoon through Montagne Forest toward a town called Saint-Dié, some thirty miles northeast of the Cleurie Quarry. It was another tough slog, another day of slithering like snakes across frosted ground at dawn and through sucking mud in the eternal drizzle. The forest stirred primeval fears. Where was the next booby trap, minefield, trip wire? What was lurking behind the next tree? The sound of a breaking twig under foot might be the last thing a dogface heard.

Making any noise could be lethal, and so it proved that day as a German sniper zeroed in on Murphy's radio operator and pulled his trigger. A bullet hit the radioman in the head, above the left eye, smashing deep into his brain, and he fell back dead.

Murphy dared not shout. But he had to expose himself to make a hand signal. He was an officer. He had to be seen to lead. He stepped into the open for just a few seconds, but long enough for the German sniper to put him in his crosshairs. Snap. The German missed but the bullet ricocheted off a tree and whacked Murphy in his right buttock.

Murphy didn't drop his carbine as he fell to the ground. He looked for the sniper. The adrenaline spiking in him numbed his pain.

A third shot rang out.

The sniper's bullet pierced Murphy's helmet lying a few feet away on the forest floor.

A movement. A camouflage cape stirring. There the sniper was, lying on the ground, hiding beneath the mottled cape.

The German lifted the cape to get a better shot to finish Murphy off.

Murphy held his carbine in his right hand and fired.

"It was his brain or nothing," Murphy later said. "That bastard would not have missed again."[24]

A bullet duly exploded in the sniper's head thirty yards from Murphy.

"Don't let anyone tell you the American soldier is soft," Murphy would later say. "When he gets mad he is as rough as any of them. I figured every Kraut I killed put me a mile or so nearer Texas."[25]

Men came over to Murphy.

The pain was now excruciating, as if a red-hot poker was stabbing his hip.

"I've been shot right in the ass."[26]

One of the men, Sergeant Albert L. Pyle, had spent twenty-two days straight in a foxhole with B Company at Anzio and considered Murphy to be closer than a brother. He watched as medics approached with a stretcher. They placed Lieutenant Murphy carefully into the litter. Murphy handed his carbine to a sergeant for good keeping. It was his lucky weapon but he wouldn't be needing it anymore.

There were two German prisoners nearby. They were made to march ahead of the litter party. "One of them was a little short Kraut and the other one was taller and I think the taller one was an artillery observer," remembered Pyle. "And Murphy had both of them walk in front of him. He wasn't bleeding very bad and he was prodding his prisoners along and he was making them carry a radio with them."

Pyle went over to Murphy.

"I hope you can stay back," said Pyle. "Good luck to you."

Murphy smiled and then gave "a baby face grin."[27]

Murphy was carried to a nearby road, where he was placed on the hood of a jeep and then driven to an aid station. Every bounce on the rutted mountain trails must have been agony. That night most of his platoon would be massacred, including the sergeant to whom Murphy had entrusted his carbine.

A medic injected Murphy with morphine. For three days, he lay on a cot in a six-man tent, feverish as his wound festered, listening to the patter of the rain and to men's cursing and groaning, before being moved toward a hospital in Besançon. A GI from the 36th Division, originally drawn from the Texas National Guard, lay in an ambulance beside Murphy as it wound its way down a narrow road and out of the Vosges Mountains. "We were held up on the road by shell fire and then deep snow," recalled the GI. Someone asked Murphy if he wanted a cigarette. "Hell no," said Murphy. "The Krauts are trying to kill me and you're trying to help them by poisoning me."[28]

From Besançon, Murphy was moved again, this time by train with its monotonous clickety-clack-clack down the Rhône Valley, past the harvested vineyards, toward blue skies and the sun, far from angry, barking howitzers. Several days later, he was admitted to the 3rd General Hospital in Aix-en-Provence, hundreds of miles to the south. His wound had become gangrenous, smelling worse than the cheapest of whores in Naples. Over the next several weeks, five pounds of rotten flesh was cut away from his buttock. He received powerful injections of penicillin every three hours. Slowly, agonizingly, the wound began to heal but he would limp for the rest of his life.

On the same ward as Murphy was a private from Tennessee called Perry Pitt. He'd been hit in the back by shrapnel and was a paraplegic. "Murphy looked like a high school kid," he remembered. "I was amazed how small he was. He found out I was a farm kid, too, and he'd hand me water so I could drink."[29]

Unable to sleep because of his wound, Murphy would wander the ward and most nights would shoot the breeze with Pitt. "He kept hobbling up the aisle on his good leg and the nurses were always making him retreat," recalled Pitt. "We used to talk about what we wanted to do when we got back. Murphy thought he might have a store. Back home I'd always wanted to have a farm."[30]

Murphy was a favorite among the nurses. He was already famous, even this far behind the lines, for his exploits, recalled Colista McCabe, who was quickly smitten—Murphy was "somebody you wanted to hug and take home with you."[31] Another nurse who grew close to Murphy was twenty-four-year-old Carolyn Price, a dark-haired beauty with a kind smile and bright eyes. "If I had to choose a candidate for the 'The Great American War Hero' from that ward of officers," she reminisced, "Murph would have been at the bottom of the list. I suppose the old maternal instinct took over and I showered him with attention."

Murphy fell head over heels in love with Price. It was his first real romance. Price was strictly professional but couldn't help but spoil the handsome officer from the cotton fields with the cheeky glint in his eye, the soft voice, the little-boy-lost charm.

Other officers became envious.

"Don't let that baby face fool you," one captain warned Price. "That's the toughest soldier in the 3rd Division."

Price knew from the captain's tone of respect that he was serious.

Murphy was a demanding patient. A doctor would examine him, but when he left the ward, Murphy would be up and about, seducing and joking, killing time, causing his wound to take longer to heal. The sunshine and peace of Provence clearly didn't suit the restless lieutenant. He couldn't lie still or relax, not for a moment. "He was obsessed with the idea," nurse Price recalled, "that he must get back to his outfit and asked each day how long it would be before he could return."[32]

Michael Daly as a West Point plebe in 1943.

Courtesy of USMA West Point Archives

DALY M J

Montgomery and Patton. The two great Allied generals bid each other farewell at Palermo Airport, Sicily, July 28, 1943. *National Archives*

Third Division commander, Lucian Truscott.
Courtesy of George C. Marshall Foundation and Library

Leaving a meeting in Italy on October 22, 1943—left to right—Commander General Dwight Eisenhower, Major General John P. Lucas, and Lt. General Mark Clark, commander of the 5th Army. *National Archives*

Armistice Day services for American dead at a cemetery near Naples, Italy, November 11, 1943. *National Archives*

Men from Maurice Britt's L Company, December 1943, scrapbook page.
Courtesy of University of Arkansas archives

Fifth Army soldiers on the march in southern Italy, spring 1944. *National Archives*

Lt. General Alexander Patch, 7th Army commander, with his son, Alexander Jr., France, 1944.
National Archives

Captain Maurice Britt after receiving the Medal of Honor, June 5, 1944.
Courtesy of University of Arkansas archives

Marne men practice using sleds before the Anzio breakout, 1944. *National Archives*

Captain Maurice salutes during the playing of the national anthem after receiving the Medal of Honor at Razorback Stadium, University of Arkansas, June 5, 1944. *Courtesy of University of Arkansas archives*

German convoy destroyed by advancing Americans in southern France, August 28, 1944.
National Archives

A 7th Army liberator is greeted in Belfort, France, late 1944. *National Archives*

Nuremberg, Germany, in ruins, 1945. *National Archives*

American tanks take to one of Hitler's famous autobahns, April 1945.
National Archives

American tanks roll through the ruins of Nuremberg, April 20, 1945.
National Archives

Lt. Colonel Keith Ware, far left, after receiving the Medal of Honor in Nuremberg, April 22, 1945.
National Archives

Audie Murphy saluting shortly after receiving the Medal of Honor in Salzburg, Austria, June 15, 1945. A still from a Signal Corps film. *National Archives*

President Truman shaking hands with a Medal of Honor recipient in a wheelchair while other recipients look on. Lt. Michael Daly sits in the second row of soldiers, third from left. *National Archives*

Photograph of President Truman posing with some of the twenty-eight recipients of the Medal of Honor who were decorated at the White House on August 23, 1945. Lt. Michael Daly sits in the second row, third from right. *National Archives*

Michael Daly receives the Medal of Honor from President Truman, August 23, 1945.
Courtesy of Deirdre Daly

Audie Murphy, 1945, US Army publicity shot. *National Archives*

Michael Daly returns to his hometown, August 24, 1945. *Courtesy of Deirdre Daly*

US Army publicity photograph of Audie Murphy on a visit to France in 1948 after receiving the Chevalier Légion d'honneur and Croix de Guerre with palm leaves.
National Archives

Audie Murphy starring in the film *The Red Badge of Courage*, released in 1951. *Courtesy of the Audie Murphy Research Foundation*

First Division commander, Keith Ware, in Vietnam, 1968. *Courtesy of Colonel Robert R. McCormick Research Center*

Michael Daly later in life. *Courtesy of Deirdre Daly*

CHAPTER 11

The Frozen Crust

GENERAL ALEXANDER PATCH, 7th Army commander, was one of the finest American leaders of World War II—the only general officer other than Lucian Truscott to command a division, a corps, and an army in the field. Yet he was virtually unknown back home. Ascetic, understated, extraordinarily self-disciplined, he cared deeply about his men, brooding over losses as he rolled endless Bull Durham cigarettes. In his pocket book, he kept a crushed flower from the slopes of Mount Vesuvius, handed to him by a girl wishing him good luck the day before his army had embarked for France that August.

The flower had faded in the long months since arriving on the Côte d'Azur. As winter set in with a vengeance in the Vosges, it was no longer a good-luck charm but a bitter reminder of the cruel fates of war. What Patch feared most had happened—his only son, Captain Alexander "Mac" Patch, had been lost on October 22 while leading an infantry company in the 79th

Division. The news that his son had been killed instantly, taking a direct hit from a tank shell, had broken his heart.

Nothing, it seemed, could assuage his grief. But then he discovered from a close friend, Colonel Paul Daly, that a West Point classmate of "Mac" was in Europe. The boy was one hell of a soldier, at a loose end. He'd be good company, might cheer Patch up a bit, distract him from his depression and loss. Patch wrote his wife, Julia, on November 6: "I've had [an aide] fly over to England [and] pick up Michael [Daly] and bring him here, as I did Mac—the boy is magnificent—6 feet 3 inches tall and a lovely looking & attractive Kid."[1]

There would have been much to discuss over a first dinner in Épinal at Patch's 7th Army HQ. Young Daly had been wounded near Aachen on September 6, hit in the leg by a piece of mortar shrapnel. He'd then gone back to England to recover from the wound. That was when Patch had sent for him.

Michael Daly remembered "Mac" as a handsome and popular first classman at West Point who had sought him out and welcomed him to the academy. "Mac" had been back in action a few days before being killed. He'd only just recovered from being badly wounded that summer.

Patch had buried his only son in Épinal.

He had stood for a long time over his son's grave.

Then three words.

"So long, son."

At least "Mac" was, as his father put it, no longer "cold and wet and hungry."[2]

Patch had told his wife: "You, and only you, know how deeply hurt I am. . . . It is our private, strictly private grief."[3]

Patch received delayed letters from his wife back in the US. In one letter, Patch's wife begged him to take their only son out of combat. He had not. "You [told] me in those letters," Patch replied to his wife, "to please not let him get back to his outfit too soon. And I could hardly stand it, knowing I had done that. I shall never be able to forgive myself. . . . As I write, the tears are falling from my eyes."[4]

Michael Daly no doubt reminded the commanding general of his own son. He was a substitute of sorts. He joined Patch for dinners with the top brass, including General Patton, who swore heartily over each course. Daly spoke only when asked a question.

Daly's father was not at the dinners. He was back in combat, leading the 398th Infantry Regiment, which Patch had wanted him to knock into shape. And as he had in World War I, Colonel Paul Daly led from the front, earning the Silver Star, risking body and soul while his son made small talk with generals and drove Patch to meetings. The younger Daly, a hothead behind the wheel, was far more worrisome than the occasional German bombing of Épinal. One day that dreary November, Michael drove so fast that he lost control of a jeep and almost killed himself and Patch.[5]

In the end, the odds caught up with even the luckiest soldier. On December 17, 1944, Colonel Paul Daly was wounded in the thigh by a mortar, the same weapon that had injured his son earlier that fall. To his great frustration, he was sent back to the States to recuperate. His son meanwhile felt increasingly restless. He didn't want to see out the war as an unreliable chauffeur, making polite comments at dinner as generals cursed the Hun. Patch knew it, and the day after learning that Colonel Daly had been badly injured, he promoted Michael Daly to second lieu-tenant and arranged for him to return to frontline duty. "He asked what kind of assignment I'd like," Michael remembered. "He implied I could be his aide. I said I wanted to re-join the infantry."[6]

A FINE ERMINE coated the upper branches of the towering fir trees in the Vosges Mountains. Men from the 15th Infantry Reg-iment hugged one another in their foxholes to share body heat, hoping they didn't fall asleep and freeze to death. It was the harshest winter in forty years. Day after day the wind blew down from the Arctic, whipping up shards of ice that blinded eyes and pierced weatherworn faces.

These were days of immense suffering for hundreds of thou-sands of infantrymen all along the Western Front, which stretched from the North Sea to the Alps. Dwight Eisenhower, like Alexander Patch, agonized over their plight. As supreme commander, he knew only too well that some men in the 3rd Division, such as Lt. Colonel Keith Ware and Lieutenant Audie Murphy, were trying to survive their second winter of war.

The folks back in America would never understand how ter-rible the conditions were for their loved ones. In a letter to Ernie Pyle, America's most widely read correspondent, Eisenhower confessed in December 1944: "I get so fighting mad because of the general lack of appreciation of real heroism—which is the uncomplaining acceptance of unendurable conditions—that I become completely inarticulate."[7]

The unendurable was relentless. As the Battle of the Bulge

raged two hundred miles to the north, that December the 3rd Division was thrown into the maw yet again, ordered to clear an area of formidable German resistance, the Colmar Pocket—in Audie Murphy's words: "a huge and dangerous bridgehead thrusting west of the Rhine like an iron fist."[8]

The Pocket stretched twenty miles to the west of the Rhine and thirty miles south of Colmar to the city of Mulhouse, in total some eight hundred fifty square miles that Eisenhower believed was a "sore" that had to be "cleaned up" at all costs.[9] Clear the Pocket and the Marne men would have a straight shot at the Rhine. Then they'd be able to plunge deep into the heart of the Third Reich. More than twenty-five thousand Wehrmacht troops, including veterans of the 19th Army, occupied the Pocket. They were, it was noted, "filled with a new hope," inspired by the shock success of their comrades in the Ardennes, where the Allies had been caught off guard and plunged into crisis.[10] Many villages and towns had been turned into fortresses along the Pocket's hundred-thirty-mile-long perimeter. One of these was called Sigolsheim. It lay directly in the path of Lt. Colonel Ware's battalion.

Ware had reached his twenty-ninth birthday on November 23, 1944. He had led Lieutenant Audie Murphy and others for more than five hundred days of war, an exhausting length of time for any soldier. At some point, he would surely reach his limit. A man could take only so much. An army psychiatrist had concluded that most men could last around two hundred days before "becoming ineffective."[11] Just seven percent made it to two hundred without being wounded or killed. "There aren't any iron men," another psychiatrist stressed. "The strongest personality, subjected to sufficient stress over a sufficient length of time, is going to disintegrate."[12] Ware and Murphy had yet to disintegrate but they had spent far longer than two hundred days in combat. Each was, as Murphy put it, a "fugitive from the law of averages."[13]

Allied bombing and artillery fire had flattened Sigolsheim. Timber-framed homes and medieval buildings had collapsed into piles of rubble that stretched for hundreds of yards. Ware's men began to probe the smoldering outskirts early on December 23. Then the Germans, "men of high physical ability and arrogant morale," it was noted, struck like a coiled snake, attacking from strongpoints in the center and from high ground overlooking the town, marked on Ware's map as Hill 351.[14]

On Christmas Day 1944, Ware met with Lieutenant George Mohr. He'd fought at Anzio, and after returning at Thanksgiving from being wounded, he had been chosen by Ware to replace B Company's former commander, who'd lost the respect of B Company's junior officers. In Mohr, Ware knew he had a "take charge person" who would inspire confidence.[15] He told Mohr to attack Hill 351 and join forces with C Company. It was not what Mohr wanted to hear on Christ's birthday. It was too dangerous, said Mohr, to move from their positions, which were under German observation, "during daylight hours."

Instead, Mohr would jump off under the cover of darkness at 5 A.M. the next morning. The cloak of night proved to be scant protection. Mohr and B Company came under intense fire when they set out for Hill 351, which turned out to be held by seasoned SS troops. It was as if, remembered one soldier, "the gates of hell broke loose—the hillside was flooded with wave after wave of fire that devoured everything in its path."[16] Those who dared lift their heads above the ground could glimpse Germany. The Rhine Valley lay in the distance and the vast Black Forest lurked beyond. "Each time we moved," remembered Mohr, "a rain of fire fell on the men. As we pressed forward, we encountered fire from half a dozen machine guns, which had excellent field of fire; they dominated our approach to the crest."[17]

So often in Italy and France, Hitler's most loyal soldiers had fought until they were surrounded or about to be killed and had then surrendered with a barked *"Kamerad! Kamerad!"* But not here, in sight of their homeland. They had known Hitler only as a savior of Germany. They had been indoctrinated with Nazism since early childhood. They were not going to drop their machine pistols and MG-42 machine guns when the enemy stood on the threshold of the Third Reich. Their tenacity was unnerving. One SS soldier that morning kept firing his machine gun even though one of his buttocks had been shot off. Others had gaping wounds yet kept pressing their triggers to their last breath as they defended what would be known as *"Blutbuckel,"* Bloody Hill.[18]

Vineyards surrounded the hill, and as dogfaces climbed through the brittle vines, linked by wire, one of Mohr's best young officers was hit in the chest. Others fell, killed or wounded as they neared German positions. B Company risked being wiped out. At his command post, Mohr asked twenty-three-year-old Private William Weinberg to take a message to Ware at battalion headquarters. "I was to tell Lt. Colonel Ware our situation and to ask for tanks and GIs who could be assigned to help us," remembered Weinberg, who'd joined B Company as a replacement that fall. "He showed me his map of the area. I stared at it and memorized it."[19]

Getting to Ware without being killed would be a formidable challenge. Weinberg set out after dark, armed with a carbine, with another soldier who brought along a German machine pistol. They ran as fast as they could through straight rows of vines. A machine gun snarled. Weinberg knew from the "loud crack" of bullets that the German gunner had spotted him: "The shots sounded like a small rapid fire cannon aimed at us."

Weinberg kept running. He could not zigzag. The straight rows of vines meant he had to keep sprinting. Out of breath, petrified, Weinberg dived to the ground and clawed his way through several rows of thick vines, hoping the gunner would lose sight of him. The gunner could still see Weinberg but had to shift his aim when Weinberg crawled through the sticks and wires holding up vines. Then the bullets came whistling once more. Weinberg lay gasping, panting, then heard the clomp of hobnailed boots—a German patrol getting closer, just three rows of vines away.

Weinberg lay as flat as he could, one arm curled around his helmet, heart beating loudly, looking away, not wanting to see the Germans as they killed him . . . but then they moved on. He got to his feet again and scurried toward Ware's battalion command post, a manor house on the edge of a village called Mittelwihr, half a mile to the northeast of Hill 351. Weinberg was glad he had played cowboys and Indians as a boy; he had learned to avoid stepping on twigs and to grasp branches so they would make no sound as he brushed past. Finally, Ware's command post was in sight. A tank stood close by, silhouetted by the bright starlight.

"GI," shouted Weinberg.

"Who'zat?"

Weinberg entered the manor house around 8 P.M., pushing through heavy blackout blankets. Ware was seated at a table with other First Battalion senior officers. Ware recognized Weinberg, who had been a runner between B Company and battalion headquarters. Weinberg showed Ware on a map where B Company was stranded, badly outnumbered, pinned down by SS troops, without water or food, having to scavenge morsels of rations from dead comrades. They needed all the help they could get.

Ware reacted instantly, telling the officers around the table to gather every man available, "all the clerks, cooks, drivers," and to call up armored support. Then Ware asked Weinberg if he could lead the way back to B Company's positions. Weinberg nodded, prodded the map, and suggested the best route for a tank.

They'd set out before dawn, said Ware. Did Weinberg need anything?

"Food."

Greasy vegetable soup and coffee would have to do. Weinberg then wrapped himself in a blanket and tried to catch some sleep curled up on the floor. Before dawn breakfast was served—fresh bread and powdered eggs and milk. The skies began to lighten as Ware led his rescue party of some twenty-five men toward Hill 351, Weinberg showing the way to the driver of a tank loaded with cooks, clerks, and jeep drivers from battalion headquarters. "The responsibility of leading the hastily improvised task force and fear of frying in the tank," recalled Weinberg, "was almost overwhelming. The tank was such a large target."[20]

Ware followed in a jeep behind the Sherman from the 756th Tank Battalion, a large white star emblazoned on its muddied front. In the tank's turret beside Weinberg sat a sergeant called Simon Bramblett. Weinberg showed Bramblett where B Company's positions were. He then jumped down from the tank, pointed out the command post for B Company, and took cover as fast as he could. The Germans had surely spotted them and heard the growl of the tank.

Weinberg saw Ware and two other officers calmly get out of their jeep and look around. Weinberg shouted for them to get the hell down but they ignored him.[21]

Mohr and other officers from B Company joined Ware beside the tank and discussed tactics. Weinberg then saw Ware reconnoiter in front of the tank, out in the open in broad daylight, a clear target, examining the terrain for several minutes. Weinberg then cowered down in a foxhole, hoping he'd not be the first to get shot when the Germans inevitably opened fire.

Ware walked back toward Weinberg.

"Let's go," shouted Ware.

The Germans appeared to take their cue from Ware and mortar shells hissed through the air. Men dived into foxholes. B Company commander Mohr shouted for men to get to their feet and out of their holes. None did so. Weinberg watched as Ware, exasperated, "went around from hole to hole kicking the asses of the guys who [were lying] as flat as they could get. Ware was a big man. He had a big kick. The guys came out. Not sheepishly, but grim, realistically facing immediate death."[22]

Bramblett's tank hopefully would make all the difference against the SS men who had pinned down what was left of

B Company. But Ware also needed as many soldiers as possible to help clear Hill 351. In the words of the division's official history, he had decided "that a vigorous display of personal leadership was necessary to invigorate the troops with an offensive spirit that had been dampened by the extremely heavy losses that had been sustained, the icy-cold weather, and the continuous fighting."

Ware led the way, braving volleys of machine-gun bullets and mortar fire, moving up the hill to other B Company positions where traumatized survivors still cowered, many frozen with terror. Ware exhorted. He cajoled. They had to attack. If they stayed put amid the twisted vines, they would die.

"Follow me!" shouted Ware.[23]

Ware grabbed a Browning Automatic Rifle, the most powerful gun he could fire while moving, from the arms of a man nearby. Then he started to run up the hill, a hundred fifty yards ahead of his rescue party, following a dirt trail. Ten men followed. Bramblett's tank clanked forward. Bramblett watched carefully as Ware clambered up through the vines. If Ware laid down heavy tracer fire on a position, Bramblett knew to blast it with everything he had.

One soldier saw Ware as he came under "terrific enemy fire, consisting of artillery, mortar, machine gun, machine pistol and rifle fire . . . a shell burst so close to him he seemed to have been enveloped in a sheet of flame, but he emerged from this inferno and still kept irresistibly moving toward the enemy."[24] Bullets ripped into the ground at his feet and ricocheted off rocks a few inches away.

As Ware neared an SS machine gun, he lifted the BAR and

squeezed the trigger, hitting two soldiers. He then fired tracers into the machine-gun nest. There was an angry bark from Bartlett's tank and then an explosion and the machine-gun nest was destroyed. Ware was a man possessed. He kept moving, closing on another machine-gun position. Germans had their hands in the air. No need to kill them.

There was no more ammunition left in the BAR and so Ware grabbed an M-1 rifle from a wounded man and kept firing. In less than thirty minutes, he and Bartlett's tank destroyed four machine-gun positions. Five of the ten who had attacked with him were wounded, some seriously. The commander of D Company, Captain Vernon L. Rankin, had supported Ware's rampage by directing mortar fire on SS positions. He believed Ware had "personally killed five Germans and captured about twenty others." Ware himself had been hit in the hand by shrapnel and was bleeding but refused to be treated. The battle for Bloody Hill had yet to be won.[25] Some SS diehards still clung to their positions.

Ware returned to his battalion headquarters by jeep and contacted B Company commander, Lieutenant Mohr, ordering him to make a final attack to clear the last resistance. But before Mohr could do so, he was badly wounded in the hip by a sniper. "I immediately asked a private to come up and cut open my canteen so I could put ice on the wound," recalled Mohr. "It was so cold that day that my drinking water was frozen. Then the scariest thing happened. A shell came into our foxhole and hit the private right in the chest. I looked down on my leg and there were parts of his brains sitting there. We lost a lot of good men that day; it was one hell of a fight."[26]

Private Weinberg found Mohr lying down, bleeding profusely. A medic cut Mohr's trousers and stopped the blood and tried to wrap the wound in bandages. Mohr had been hit by shrapnel that had also gouged his holster and belt. Weinberg asked Mohr if he could take the holster—Mohr wouldn't need it: He'd gotten a million-dollar wound, serious enough to be sent home. Mohr tried to smile and then simply nodded and Weinberg cleaned blood from the holster, strapped it to his side, and then slipped a valued prize, a Luger, into it. "I felt honored that he gave it to me," remembered Weinberg. "It was a symbol of his short but effective leadership of B Company."[27]

Artillery support was called in before a final assault by what was left of Ware's First Battalion. The last SS holdouts began to flee in panic and terror around 3 P.M. as mortars dropped on their positions, seeding the hilltop with flying shards of shrapnel. Then Ware's men moved in to mop up any survivors. Private Richard Byham, who had witnessed Ware's heroics earlier that day, was told to try to take prisoners if he could. They might provide useful intelligence. "Thirty-seven of the enemy surrendered," he remembered. "I was told later that many of the Germans occupying the trenches at the top escaped to Sigolsheim below the hill."[28]

It was reported that around one hundred fifty "crack SS troops were put to flight."[29] Hill 351 had finally been taken. Darkness fell. B Company's survivors, twenty from two hundred, clustered in a cave near the summit, recalled one of them, "worn old men," bearded, aching at each joint, covered in sores and rashes, hair matted and crusted, "Neanderthals with guns, without spears."[30]

The skies were clear. Smoke drifted lazily into the black night from burning buildings in the valley below. Men had been too focused, too traumatized, too tense to cry that day. Numbed, they didn't even have the strength to pick the pockets of the German dead. "Most of the guys slept fitfully because there was a tangle of arms and legs," recalled Weinberg. "Everyone stunk. German blankets blacked out the entrance. It was a group of pained, aching guys, none enjoying their survival, all sure they were going to die soon. The cave was our death row cell."[31]

The bodies of dozens of young Americans littered the barren slopes and crushed vineyards. B Company, which Ware had first commanded in Sicily, had lost all its officers, including its commander, Lieutenant Mohr. Half of B Company had been killed or wounded.

Lt. Colonel Ware, acting commander of the First Battalion, would receive the Congressional Medal of Honor for his actions at Sigolsheim, the ninth man and the highest-ranking from the 15th Infantry Regiment to receive the medal in World War II.[32] "Lt. Colonel Ware was directly responsible for the taking of Hill 351," it was reported, "hitherto thought to be impregnable, against overwhelming odds, despite being wounded in the hand at the outset."[33] Unlike other recipients of the Medal of Honor, Ware wasn't about to be sent home so he could go bowling, a prewar passion, or be given a soft job far from danger. His experience and leadership were far too valuable. His time was far from up.

Hill 351 had been seized but the town of Sigolsheim remained infested with the enemy, hiding among its rubble and in the shells of buildings. It still had to be liberated, cleansed of the SS.

Later that night of December 26, Ware's First Battalion joined forces with the Second Battalion. The next morning Typhoons swooped down from the skies and pummeled strongpoints, but still Hitler's most loyal held out. "In all its long combat record," it was noted, "never had the regiment encountered such bitter die-hard resistance."[34] There was no option but to fight from one ruin to another.[35]

Yet again, the Marne men were stunned by the ferocity of the SS defense. "It was not unusual to see a German standing completely exposed in the center of the street," remembered one soldier, "firing a bazooka or sometimes only a rifle at our tanks as the armor relentlessly mowed him down or the doughboys took pot shots at him."[36] According to one account, the SS "attacked tanks with rifles, several standing up in the middle of the street until run over and crushed beneath the treads." It was indeed the most fanatical resistance the regiment had faced in more than four hundred days of combat, worse even than in Cisterna during the breakout from Anzio.

Lt. Colonel Ware had shown the way the day before. Now, on December 27, another officer from the 15th "Can Do" Regiment—a lieutenant called Eli Whiteley, a graduate of Texas A&M—stepped up and went far beyond the call of duty. Like Ware, Whiteley was bespectacled and soft-spoken. He had turned thirty-one on December 10, making him among the oldest platoon leaders in the regiment, having been drafted as he was studying for a master's degree in Texas. After several days in combat, his and other platoons in L Company had been reduced to a handful of men.

As Whiteley headed toward a schoolhouse in the heart of

Sigolsheim, where an SS major had set up a command post, he came under machine-gun fire. He attacked a building alone, cleared it, moved on to another house and then yet another, killing the SS wherever they lurked. Then his luck ran out. He was wounded in the shoulder and arm. Still he fought on, throwing smoke and fragmentation grenades with his good arm to clear a path ahead. Whiteley ordered the survivors of his platoon to follow him, telling one of his men to bring up a bazooka that he then fired with his good hand, smashing open a large hole in the side of a building that Whiteley then charged through.

With his carbine under his good arm, Whiteley ran into a room and shot five SS soldiers dead, forcing twelve more to give up. His rampage continued. Adrenaline coursing through him, he seemed to have almost superhuman stamina. He had gone "gun crazy" as he continued to stalk the SS amid the piles of singed bricks and broken stones. Then a piece of shrapnel blinded him in one eye. Blood streamed down his face but Whiteley still wasn't going to quit. He was bleeding so badly, however, that he was finally persuaded to be treated by a medic and so his killing spree ended. For his actions that long day in Sigolsheim, he would be awarded the Medal of Honor. According to his citation, like Lt. Colonel Ware, he had "cracked the core of enemy resistance in a vital area."[37]

There wasn't much left of Sigolsheim by the time the last of the SS were defeated. Trees had been stripped of branches, trunks shredded. For hundreds of yards not a single building had a roof. Walls that still stood were pockmarked with bullet holes. The streets were strewn with the enormous waste of war: discarded rifles and smashed Panzerfausts, scatterings of spent bullets, pieces of broken furniture and abandoned carts used as roadblocks.

The next day, December 28, 1944, a tall second lieutenant joined Lt. Colonel Ware's First Battalion, headquartered in the shattered outskirts. Michael Daly had arrived to take over command of the first platoon of A Company. He would rather have finished the war with his old unit—the First Division—but because of atrocious weather and intense fighting, he'd been unable to reach it, despite trying three times. And so now he was reporting for duty in Lt. Colonel Ware's battered battalion instead.

Daly's new unit, A Company, reputedly led the 15th Infantry Regiment in total medals. And his battalion commander, Ware, was clearly an exceptional leader, his hand patched up after his heroics on Bloody Hill. Indeed, Ware was revered by all his junior officers. Here was a warrior Daly could truly look up to, of the same ilk as his own father. The fact that Ware had survived combat for so long greatly enhanced his authority. For old-timers, having convinced themselves irrationally that they'd escape death or serious wounding, Ware was in fact a talismanic figure, just like Audie Murphy. "It was easy for any GI to talk to [Ware]," recalled Private Weinberg, who had witnessed Ware's rampage on Hill 351. "He was bright and daring. I doubt if he had any education beyond high school, if that. But he was quick to grasp a situation, understand it and deal with it."[38]

One stalwart in A Company, Sergeant Troy Cox, was surprised by how young Daly appeared. He was nothing but a lanky boy. Cox did not know that Daly had seen his fair share of combat—he had, after all, earned a battlefield commission, being promoted straight from lowly private to the officer class, a rare progression. And he had won the Silver Star.[39]

The skinny kid had not joined any old tribe.

Did he have the right stuff as a leader . . . like Lt. Colonel Ware?

Would he choke . . . piss his new pants when the killing and dying began again?

Would he waste their lives?

CHAPTER 12

———————————

At All Costs

It snowed in the Vosges Mountains on New Year's Eve. The singed ruins of Sigolsheim disappeared beneath a fresh coat of white. In their foxholes, Lt. Colonel Ware's men shivered and swore. Firing mechanisms, water pipes, and engines iced up. It was a struggle to clear roads and even to lay barbed wire defenses around dugouts. For those spending night after night in rock-hard frozen foxholes—or "ice-boxes," as the men had taken to calling them—the weather was as dangerous as the Germans, if not more so. The landscape "resembled an immense city of the dead," remembered French general Jean de Lattre de Tassigny, "from which emerged the skeletons of trees, haunted by croaking clouds of crows."[1]

In the first two weeks of January, there was patrolling and the odd German probe into Lt. Colonel Keith Ware's lines but no major confrontation. It was as if the weather had frozen the war.[2] It was so dark some nights that his men couldn't see their hands.[3]

When there was dense cloud cover and no moon, they had to hold on to the shoulder of the soldier in front on patrols.[4] The slightest sound—a snapping twig, a sudden gust of wind—was enough to make a man jump in terror. Ware's men could not see the enemy, nor the booby traps, the mines, the trip wires, and they were forced to rely on their intuition and their sense of smell. The Boche really did reek of sauerkraut, as the Italians had smelled of garlic and onions. Sometimes, the nighttime jaunts would be horrifically fatal, leaving those who survived with recurring nightmares for decades. One night, a skillful SS soldier heard Ware's men moving along a forest trail and, emerging from a heavily camouflaged lair, silently killed a soldier and then took his place in the patrol before leading it into an ambush.[5]

Lieutenant Audie Murphy rejoined Ware's First Battalion on January 14, 1945, one of the coldest days in living memory.[6] It was a stark contrast between the balmy climes of Provence and the Colmar Pocket, where men left behind patches of their hair, frozen to the ground, when they stirred each morning. When they checked their feet, many hoped to see signs of trench foot—"a legitimate, approved way of getting out of combat," recalled B Company's Private William Weinberg. "Most of us would gladly have given a few toes to get out of the lines. It was better than a million dollar wound."[7]

Murphy wasn't looking for an easy way out, and he rubbed his toes as often as possible, changing socks whenever he could, trying to make sure he didn't get his leather boots wet. Still, he suffered more than most in the appalling conditions. A platoon sergeant, Tom Rocco, recalled helping Murphy remove his boots after one patrol: "Taking his stockings off was like peeling his skin away. We were all jumpy, disgusted, and discouraged. But when we looked at Murphy, limping on his aching feet, we would have been ashamed not to follow."[8]

Word was that the Marne men would be going back into combat. They were going to close the Colmar Pocket. But before that could happen, replacements had to be brought in to fill the ranks. One morning, Lieutenant Murphy visited a depot to collect recruits to his 3rd platoon in B Company. The greenhorns had arrived from the Channel port of Le Havre in freezing boxcars, the bolts sealing them inside "white with frost," according to one man.

Murphy told a sergeant he needed eighteen men from Texas.

The sergeant examined a list of the new arrivals.

"Lieutenant, I only have sixteen Texans."

"OK, give me those sixteen and give me two more."

The sergeant did so, adding one man from Oklahoma and another from Tennessee. The soldier from Oklahoma turned out to be a Native American. Murphy was delighted. From experience, he knew the Oklahoman could be trusted to fight.

Murphy led his new men to B Company's headquarters, on the banks of the Ill River, a western tributary of the Rhine. They lined up. Snow fell, dusting their new uniforms. Artillery could be heard in the distance, an ominous booming. The replacements hadn't heard the sounds of war before. "We were wondering what in the world was going to happen to us," remembered one man. "Fresh recruits from the States with . . . really inadequate training."

Murphy could see the fear on their faces.

"Look, you're gonna join one of the best outfits in the United States Army. You're gonna find that these are gonna be some of your closest friends."

The replacements listened carefully.

"Now there'll be times when you'll be scared to death. I'm always scared when we're up front. Don't be ashamed of it. There'll be times you'll want to cry. There's nothing wrong with that."[9]

Murphy's recruits trained for a few days, "all in awe," recalled one private, of their platoon leader—a "living artifact in their midst." Every old-timer had a fantastic story about Murph. He was at his best when "shooting to kill." He always "seemed to be looking for a fight." He rarely picked on the weak or rode a man, not like some officers. He never bragged, never bullshitted. "There were no reservations," remembered one man from B Company. "You could count on him."[10]

The medieval city of Colmar, famous for its white wine merchants and canals, still had to be pried from Nazi hands. And to reach Colmar, the 3rd Division needed to cross the Ill River. Lt. Colonel Ware's First Battalion was to jump off on January 22. Men painted tanks and trucks white while others tied together sheets and sewed together pillowcases seized from local homes, and then donned the ill-fitting "spook suits" to provide a modicum of camouflage against the snow. Letters home were brief, scribbled with blue fingers as men mumbled last prayers, their stale breath frosting the air.

It was bone-numbingly cold when Ware, Murphy, and Daly awoke on D Day, January 22, 1945. Angry winds swept down from the Vosges, freezing men's exposed faces. Several feet of snow blanketed the landscape. The mercury in thermometers showed 14 degrees Fahrenheit. There were fewer than a dozen men in each of Ware's line companies who'd been with his battalion since the ill-fated Anzio invasion, exactly a year ago to the day.

Daly led his platoon in A Company to its jumping-off area near the Ill. That evening, he crossed a footbridge and headed south, tasked with protecting the 3rd Division's rear along with the rest of the 15th Regiment. All went well at first. By the next afternoon, men from the 30th Infantry Regiment were probing the outskirts of the villages of Riedwihr and Holtzwihr, two miles east of the Ill. But they lacked armored support. As a first Sherman, hastily splashed with white camouflage paint, crossed over the Ill, near a hamlet called Maison Rouge, a wooden bridge collapsed. "With a sudden rasping and unexpected silencing of the motor roar," recalled an officer, the tank dropped "like an elevator . . . through jagged ends of planks and beams it could be seen sitting tilted but upright in the swift current."[11]

There were no other bridges that could support tanks. Until engineers built a new pontoon bridge, the 30th Infantry Regiment would be seriously vulnerable, "exposed on both flanks as it stuck out like two fingers into German-held territory," it was reported.[12] Tragically, the enemy struck back with perfect timing. A dozen Panzers stormed into the stranded men's positions. Chaos and panic ensued. Dogfaces turned and fled. Three hundred fifty from one battalion of the 30th Infantry Regiment were taken prisoner, a stunning defeat. Most companies lost a third of their men. Two were destroyed. Those who managed to get back across the Ill were, said one survivor, a pathetic sight, a "disorganized mob. . . . Combat jackets were drenched, and the cheesecloth of the white camouflage capes were freezing into weird drapery."[13]

Terrified men, teeth chattering, eyes glazed, pants soiled, had to be yanked from ditches and from wooded areas. They had the "pained, blank, gray look of combat trauma," noted one soldier, and they mumbled about indestructible Panzers being everywhere, blasting men to hamburger as they clanked inexorably forward, trailing wraiths of black exhaust.[14] Many were no longer fit for combat, in dire need of "mental-conditioning," but were given new weapons and hot chow and told to be ready to wreak revenge—to "bowl the Krauts over for good"—the next morning.[15]

On January 24, Lieutenant Michael Daly pushed six hundred yards into the woods but his platoon was low on ammunition and he called a halt. There were the ominous sounds of Panzers approaching and tracks squealing and then the barking of their 88mm guns. Shells burst in treetops, sending lethal splinters flying. Daly ordered his men to retreat, and even though some were wounded, they all reached the eastern banks of the Ill in good order and waded across, shivering from exposure, ice crusting their wet uniforms.

That night, few men slept as they huddled together in hastily dug foxholes. "You kept awake, if you could," remembered one private, "and listened carefully to any movement, a step, a scraping sound, the rustle of leaves."[16] Tanks blasted at one another and the battle continued for nearby villages. Eight soldiers had been killed in the last twenty-four hours in A Company alone. So many had been wounded that Daly's men and C Company were later that night merged. They still numbered only seventy men. There should have been more than four hundred from both companies at full strength.

Early the next morning, engineers completed a bridge, under enemy fire, north of the collapsed wooden edifice at Maison Rouge. Shermans and tank destroyers crossed and the 15th Regiment attacked once more. That evening, Michael Daly closed on a German position, killed a machine gunner with his carbine. Then he went ahead of his men, hunting the enemy deep into some woods. His men caught up with him and then took several dozen prisoners. His "inspiring and aggressive leadership" earned him a second Silver Star.[17] He had shown he could "fight ruthlessly without losing his head."[18] The skinny new lieutenant had the right stuff.

Lt. Colonel Keith Ware's battalion attacked the next day, January 26, toward the village of Holtzwihr. That very morning, Murphy had been promoted to B Company commander.[19] "We had started with six officers [four days before]," he remembered. "I was the only one remaining."[20]

Murphy led the thirty men left in B Company toward Holtzwihr and then stopped near a wooded area a few miles from the village. His men took up positions while they waited for fresh ammunition to be brought up to them.[21] Then Murphy heard the roaring engines and clanking tracks of six German Tiger tanks, gears grinding. They quickly smashed through B Company's forward positions. Other companies in Lt. Colonel Keith Ware's First Battalion were hit hard.[22]

Around 2 P.M., Murphy ordered B Company to pull back five hundred yards. He stayed behind at a command post with a forward artillery observer and a radio. Then Murphy spotted some two hundred Germans wearing white camouflage as they began to cross a field, headed his way. As the enemy closed on them, the forward artillery observer tried to contact battalion headquarters. He looked terrified. Murphy didn't trust him, didn't want the radio falling into German hands.

Murphy told him to get going. He'd call in artillery support himself. German shells exploded nearby, gouging the frozen ground, sending shards of rock and shrapnel flying in all directions. One shell hit a tank destroyer and it burst into flames. Several men escaped from it and then fled to the rear.[23]

Murphy broke cover and sprinted to the tank destroyer and climbed up. The corpse of an American officer lay sprawled close to the mounted machine gun. Murphy pulled the dead man off the turret and laid him down in the snow. Then he climbed back up. A cloud of black smoke hid him from the enemy. He opened fire with the .50 caliber, spraying bullets at oncoming Germans.

The noise of battle smothered that of the machine gun. None of the soldiers attacking seemed to have spotted him. In any case, who in their right mind would jump onto a burning vehicle, a smoking time bomb filled with ammunition? "I was pretty well hidden by the turret," recalled Murphy. "The flames made it hot, but that felt good after being cold for so long. I had a good supply of ammunition and kept firing. I was scared but too busy to worry."

A young officer watched in awe as Murphy stood "completely exposed and silhouetted against the background of bare trees with a fire under him that threatened to blow the destroyer to bits if it reached the gasoline and ammunition. . . . His clothing was torn and riddled by flying shell fragments and bits of rock. Bullets ricocheted off the tank destroyer as the enemy concentrated the full fury of his fire on this one-man strongpoint." He killed or wounded dozens. Some fell dead only a few yards away from his position.

There was a lull in the German attack and Murphy caught his breath and examined a map. He'd been on the tank for more than thirty minutes. But then yet more Germans, having spotted him, charged forward. In between bursts from the gun, Murphy shouted into his radio, reporting his position and directing artillery fire.

Murphy later recalled that a German shell slammed into the tank destroyer but somehow he kept his balance, stunned but able to shoot.

"Are you still alive?" asked a sergeant on the radio at headquarters.

Murphy looked down.

The flames were leaping higher from the burning tank destroyer.

The sergeant was still on the radio asking questions.

Where were the tanks?

Was Murphy there?

Were the tanks closer?

Murphy came to his senses.

"Hold the phone," Murphy said, "and I'll let you talk to one of the bastards."

Murphy spotted a dozen Germans in a ditch and turned the gun on them. He could see everything clearly. There was no fog, no confusion, no blurring amid the violence—everything was sharply defined. It was as if the machine gun was a part of him, dealing death wherever he looked.

There was a searing pain in his thigh. Blood seeped through his uniform.

Murphy kept his finger on the trigger, firing until he ran out of ammunition:

"I had been on the tank turret for an hour," he recalled. "So I dropped over the side and sat down in the snow."

How come I'm not dead?[24]

Murphy limped away to rejoin his men and then led several of them back toward the tank destroyer and together they beat off what was left of the enemy force. Murphy finally hobbled to an aid station to get his leg seen to.

Well, another Purple Heart Cluster.

Murphy returned to the battlefield and found a group of survivors from B Company squatted around a brass lamp-stove, eating scraps of food, heating coffee. In the distance, the tank destroyer still smoldered. Dead soldiers, American and German, dotted woods nearby. A GI said the lousy Germans had bayoneted prisoners. Men who had earlier turned and run drifted back.[25] Later that afternoon, Typhoons roared toward Holtz-wihr. For once, the weather gods conspired to help the Marne men. There had been thick cloud cover all day but the skies cleared minutes before another German attack was due to begin. The Typhoons screamed into action, their rockets ripping through the air, causing the Germans to pull back. Then the clouds closed in again.

Ware, Daly, and hundreds of others might have been killed, wounded, or captured, had it not been for "Audie Murphy's Wild Man Stand," as a division historian would label it.[26] Ware would later recommend Murphy for the Medal of Honor. No man he had commanded deserved it more. In some rare instances, as was the case that day with Murphy, one single soldier's actions could change the course of an entire battle. "The heroism of one man, Second Lieutenant AUDIE L. MURPHY," stressed Ware, "was primarily responsible" for saving his battalion.[27]

The light faded as dogfaces dug foxholes along the bank of a canal. Some of Murphy's men were so thirsty, they risked their necks to go fetch water. Stiff corpses of soldiers were jammed against one another in the canal. Men had had to push the dead gently aside so they could fill their canteens.[28]

PART THREE

Germany

CHAPTER 13

"Murphy Crowds Britt"

BACK IN THE US that winter, Captain Maurice "Footsie" Britt was studying for a law degree at the University of Arkansas. He'd been medically discharged, returning to the "permanent rank of Mister," and had been awarded the Distinguished Service Cross, thanks to testimony provided by men in L Company who had wanted to see him recognized for his actions at Anzio when he had lost his arm.[1] He himself "couldn't plumb remember" a single thing that had happened. His mind had been numb. He'd been too focused on staying alive, killing the enemy before he and his men were slaughtered.[2]

"It was who could spit the most lead first and fastest," Britt said.[3]

In a special ceremony on the steps of the New York Public Library on Fifth Avenue, on the third anniversary of the attack on Pearl Harbor, in front of a crowd of ten thousand, Major General Fred Walker had pinned the Distinguished Service Cross to

Britt's uniform beside the Silver Star and the Medal of Honor.[4] He had thereby become the first American in history to gain every medal for valor in a single war, making him, according to *The Arkansas Traveler*, "the most bemedaled hero in WWII."

Britt could only pick up the newspaper with one hand to read about himself, and he was still in a great deal of pain. His home state's newspaper had concluded: "Men of the Third Division, who have seen twelve of their comrades win the Congressional Medal of Honor—more than any other fighting unit in the US Army—think records back up their contention that Captain Britt is the Number One hero of this war or any other war."[5]

Britt's twenty-one-year-old wife, Nancy, the dimpled "Queen of Freshmen" who had met Footsie at a sorority dance, was described in another story as being "dazed by it all—for along with marrying a football star, she got herself a hero—the number one military hero of World War II, to be exact." She was surprised, she said, by her husband's war record. He had never told her what had really happened in Italy.

"I didn't have any idea," she added. "All I got was a geography lesson—about how beautiful the Italian countryside was. He did tell me he got the Purple Heart, and casually mentioned he was sending 'something else' along with it, which he hoped I'd like. The something else was the Silver Star."[6]

Then came the standard reflex of the blessed, the stock response of so many decorated survivors, of most recipients of the Medal of Honor down the ages. Others had done far more. Their heroism had not been witnessed. He had been incredibly lucky.

"We lost some good men who deserved the Medal of Honor more than I did," stressed Britt. "The army does its best to award medals justly, but obviously, in the confusion of battle, it is impossible to weigh the merits of individual soldiers. How can you measure bravery?"

Britt acknowledged that his years on the gridiron had served him in good stead, and he was careful to give credit to the junior officers and noncoms who had served under him: "In my own case, I always wanted to be up front, perhaps because my football training made me accustomed to rough, bodily contacts."[7]

Britt had dutifully played his role as returning war hero since arriving back in the United States the previous spring. He had lectured young officers, toured bases, promoted war bonds, all while trying to recover from terrible wounds. There was a hint that winter in New York, however, that the fame and adulation were perhaps a burden, embarrassing, more and more tiresome. He was starting to chafe, certainly, at being called a "one man army."[8]

"There's no such thing as a one-man team," he corrected one journalist. "You know that in football. I accepted the Medal of Honor in the name of my company."[9]

The journalist watched Britt flick ash from his cigarette.

"I haven't been able to enjoy anything much here," added Britt, "thinking of the boys still over there."[10]

It was Britt's duty to play the jocular superhero. Selling war bonds mattered. Reminding jaded Americans of the sacrifice of so many infantrymen was vital. But Britt, who had majored in journalism before being called up, also knew what a good story he was and how he was being played. He was no fool, having received one of the highest grade point averages on record as a freshman at the University of Arkansas.

The army's public relations officers and the press were eager to splash his name across front pages. He had a good voice and sounded great on the radio. As one reporter noted in a memo to an editor, Britt "sorta looks, acts and is being built up as the Sergeant York of the European war."[11] York had received the Medal of Honor and become the most celebrated American hero of World War I overnight following a *Saturday Evening Post* profile in which he'd detailed how he'd killed twenty-five soldiers and taken 132 prisoners, his actions guided by God in the last days of a holy crusade to defeat the Boche.

Britt's actions at Mount Rotondo in November 1943 were as fantastic as York's during the Meuse-Argonne offensive in 1918. York had received the Medal of Honor but no other American award for valor and had none of Britt's charisma, wit, and looks. Britt had it all, including a distinguished record as a professional athlete. Of the many candidates to become World War II's answer to York, he was clearly the standout.

Others who had notched up big firsts and garnered glory had fizzled, burned out, including Sergeant Charles "Commando" Kelly, the first enlisted man to receive the Medal of Honor in the European Theater, who had hit the bottle and "turned sour," as one reporter lamented.[12] Kelly had been dubbed a "one man army" like Britt, but he and others were no longer as reliable or as useful to the war effort as Britt, who had earned every award for valor as "a soldier's officer" and was photogenic to boot, especially when he appeared in public with his adorable young wife.[13] There could surely be no doughboy more handsome, more supernaturally courageous than Footsie Britt in World War II.

Britt would have to be this war's Alvin York, whether he liked it or not. He was caught in a hero's cage, unable to create a new life for himself so long as the war raged and no other American beat his record haul of medals. But how could he dare complain? He was alive, after all, a star. Yet he'd never asked to be a hero, to receive any medal. He'd simply done his duty, been part of a superb team, run the offensive for a bunch of athletes in green, quarterbacking his men.

That winter, Britt bore other wounds, less visible than the missing limb. His father's death and his family's ensuing poverty had scarred his youth. He'd promised his mother, in a heart-wrenching letter on Mother's Day 1940, before the war had broken out, that even though penniless he would one day ease her burden so she could do "other things than always striving to make [her] pennies meet." But now, on a captain's wage, he would have finally been able to make up for the "years of unhappiness" she had suffered since his father had died.[14]

For the time being, Britt would continue to play the propaganda game but he would at least set some of the rules. He had, after all, "TRADED HIS RIGHT ARM FOR TEN MEDALS," as one headline blared.[15]

One reporter in New York had noted astutely that Britt refused to "discuss his own heroism or his disability."

"A tank shell hit me, that's all," said Britt.

He'd use the spotlight as the "ARMY'S NO. 1 HERO" to highlight others—"ordinary Americans, civilians turned soldiers."[16] The vast majority of men receiving the Medal of Honor in World War II belonged to the infantry but the American public was fixated on marines and the glamour boys in the air corps with their nice blue uniforms.

"The boys who do the tough fighting are the doughboys," stressed Britt.

A press relations officer accompanying Britt in New York asked him what branch of service he would join if he had a chance to serve again.

"Public relations," said Britt.[17]

ANOTHER OFFICER FROM Britt's division—another warrior who always wanted to be up front—stood that January 28 on a field in France in front of 3rd Division general John "Iron Mike" O'Daniel. Lieutenant Michael Daly did not know that O'Daniel was doing his best to hide a broken heart—like General Patch, he'd lost his only son the previous fall.

Daly could see the scar from a bayonet wound on O'Daniel's haggard face—"features that might have been carved out with an axe," as one French general had described his rough-hewn visage.[18] Five-foot-six-inch O'Daniel had fought in North Africa, and he had been with the division since November 1943.

O'Daniel pinned an Oak-Leaf Cluster to Daly's uniform.

It was his second Silver Star.

Was Daly "ready to go back in there" and get it all "over with"?

Daly did not snap back a "yes, sir!"

His answer could barely be heard.

"I think so."[19]

Daly returned to the front lines. One day, Lt. Colonel Keith Ware turned up at A Company's command post, unexpected.

Ware then led Daly and the rest of A Company through heavy snow but unfortunately in the wrong direction. Realizing his mistake, Ware turned around, and Daly and the others found themselves wearily retracing their footsteps and then digging in before spending another night in brutally cold conditions in the Colmar Pocket, by now referred to by some Marne men as the "frozen crust."[20]

On such nights, Daly drew strength from prayer and memory. His father had told him so many true stories about courage and endurance. A favorite tale was how Paul Daly had one night been patrolling in No Man's Land, trying to get through curls of barbed wire. There had been no moon, nothing but inky darkness. Paul Daly had lost his way. He'd failed to find a gap in the wire. Then it had started to get light. The Germans would soon spot him and a sniper would then kill him. Paul Daly had prayed to the "Blessed Lady" and she had answered him. Suddenly, high above, was a shining star. He'd crawled toward it and then found a gap in the wire.

There were so many other memories savored by Michael Daly as he waited for the wan light of yet another dawn. Father and son had often played at war in a garden with a long regal lawn. "Every June 18 was Waterloo," recalled Daly. "We dug trenches in the soil and put our soldiers and artillery in place and my father would shout, 'French cavalry on the right!'"[21] Then there was that night before the war when his father had heard an intruder in his home. He'd grabbed a sword with an ivory handle and swiped the invader across the leg, drawing blood. But he'd then bandaged him up and even fed him.

The stories inspired. But it was devout prayer that probably helped more than anything to save Daly from a breakdown. Not even a dozen Hail Marys could salve the grief, however, when he saw young men die in front of him, teenagers whose lives he was responsible for, whose parents would want to understand why they had not come home.

One night, a young replacement, a private, was hit by mortar fire. He had a terrible back wound but it was impossible to get him to an aid station until daylight. The death of the private affected Daly more than any other in the war. The kid had died and there'd been nothing he could do, not a goddamn thing.

The battle for the Colmar Pocket intensified. On February 5, the 15th Infantry Regiment was ordered to seize bridges across the Rhine near Neuf-Brisach, a fortified town built in the early 1700s to defend the border between France and the Holy Roman Empire.[22] Once the bridges were in American hands, the Germans beating a hasty retreat from what remained of the Colmar Pocket would be trapped.

There had been a brief respite from the cold. Snow and ice had melted. After slogging across a field, Daly led his men along a muddy road but then spotted a stone house surrounded by barbed wire and manned by at least two dozen German soldiers. Machine guns snarled. Daly and his men dropped to the dirt, bullets snapping above their heads. He ordered his men to withdraw along a ditch, out of the line of fire. He'd be a decoy, drawing the bullets toward him. Daly stood in the middle of the road, pulled out his pistol, and fired. For as long as thirty minutes, he was a target. Bullets zipped around him, lashing the road at his feet as his men scurried to safety.

The Germans still held the house, and so Daly and around sixty men from A Company were sent back to seize it, thankfully accompanied by a Sherman tank that blasted a hole in a wall. A Company's commander was hit by a grenade as he tried to get inside, leaving Daly to lead the company in a final assault, grappling with a German outside the house and, first to the draw, shooting him dead with his Colt .45 at point-blank range.

For his actions that February 5, Daly would receive a third Silver Star. If he continued to earn ribbons at this clip, he might even catch up with his fellow Marne man Captain Maurice Britt. One thing was certain—he was as capable in combat as his father. "Here was this gangly guy," recalled Major Burton Barr, an assistant battalion commander, "always where you could see him, not hiding his height, an easy target, as though he believed wherever he stood would protect him. He never told you about himself, but men wanted to follow him."[23]

The next day, the Americans seized the fortress town of Neuf-Brisach, and the Colmar Pocket was finally closed. After seventeen days of combat, the 3rd Division had won, it was noted, "one of the most smashing victories of the war" but at the cost of more than forty-five hundred casualties. The German 19th Army, by contrast, was virtually destroyed. It had fought long and hard since August 15 but was no more. Only a fraction escaped east of the Rhine into the Fatherland.[24]

The Marne men took a well-deserved rest before returning to the fray. The sun reappeared, and dogfaces basked in its faint rays as they waited for the shower wagons to turn up—tankers with burners to heat water. In the open air, they undressed for the first time in weeks. Their ribs showed. Under each man's chin there was a dark patch, marking where he'd left his collar open. Their teeth were loose from malnutrition and their gums were bleeding. Old-timers like Murphy and Daly had multiple scars, red slashes across their ghostly white bodies. When they shaved off their beards, soldiers couldn't recognize one another.

No one was trying to kill them. They could enjoy a fortnight of hot chow, real hamburgers with Jell-O for dessert, and hopefully plenty of intoxication and fornication—"Zig Zag"—in the nearest city of Nancy, famous already for *"beaucoup femmes."* Word was a GI could get laid for almost nothing—a Lucky Strike cigarette, a Hershey bar. That's all it took with the "vagabond girls."[25] The Marne men had spent 188 days "in continuous contact with the enemy," as the official record put it, and they were more than ready to let off steam. They understood only too well that Germany still lay ahead, across the swirling Rhine. Many were convinced they would be killed before Hitler was defeated. It made no sense to think otherwise.

There was no sign of any weakening in the Germans' desire to defend their homeland, despite terror bombing and heavy defeats on all fronts.[26] Allied Supreme Commander Dwight Eisenhower felt it necessary to remind his soldiers, in a specially printed message, that they were not about to enter Germany as liberators but as victors. It was time to be merciless, to show the Krauts who was master. "Do not keep smiling. Never offer a cigarette . . . nor offer him your hand. Germans will respect you as long as they see you as a successor to Hitler, who never offered them *his* hand."[27] Germans were not to be trusted. The Germans viewed "fair play" as "cowardice." "The only way to get along with the Germans is to make them respect you, to make them feel the hand of the master."[28]

ON THE WESTERN borders of the Third Reich, the snows finally began to melt. On March 5, 1945, it was Lieutenant Audie Murphy's turn to look directly into the scarred face of General O'Daniel—they were almost the same height. O'Daniel presented Murphy with two medals—the Silver Star for his actions at the Cleurie Quarry and the Distinguished Service Cross for his heroism at Ramatuelle the previous August, when he'd lost his best friend, Lattie Tipton.

Murphy found time that same day to write to a sister, telling her he was going to send a trophy back to the States—a rifle he'd taken from a sniper he'd killed. He'd been having a good time in Nancy, where fashions were slow to change—European women were "wearing the same Brassiers" he'd unfastened with nimble fingers in 1943 and 1944. He told his sister about his medals. Each was worth five points. If he could only bag the "Cong. Medal of honor" then he would be sent back to Texas.

"Boy, if I get that I will soon be coming home."

The only thing any of the medals had ever meant to him was "another five points toward coming home."[29]

But where was home? With his sister? Where would he settle? Could he? For the first time in a long time, he dared to imagine a life after fighting and it made him feel uneasy, empty inside. "On the medals . . . they were supposed to give you five points each toward a total for going home," he would later say. "I had 100 points more than necessary, but no home to go to."[30]

———

To BREAK INTO Germany, the 15th Infantry Regiment would have to cross what the Germans called the West Wall—known to GIs as the Siegfried Line. "The attack will be pressed with ruthless vigor," ordered O'Daniel, the 3rd Division commander. "All men will be brought to the highest offensive spirit prior to the jump-off. Bayonets will be sharpened."[31] Having whetted his blade, Audie Murphy would lead B Company, jumping off from a small town in France called Bining, south of the German city of Saarbrücken. Michael Daly's A Company was to be the actual spearhead of the First Battalion advance.

Night became day as countless batteries of American search-lights reflected off heavy cloud cover, casting an eerie glow on Daly and his men as they checked weapons, loaded up on phos-phorus grenades, and tested radios. At 1 A.M. on March 15, Daly and A Company moved out. An advance platoon in A Company entered Hornbach, the first village in Germany to be seized by the 15th Infantry Regiment. Then Daly and his men ap-proached the vaunted Siegfried Line, cast into stark relief by the searchlights—the "world's most carefully planned and embel-lished system of fortifications."[32]

There were five rows of tank traps. Beyond were rolling hills with no cover—the Germans had stripped away any trees—until another line of defenses, dozens of pillboxes. The Siegfried Line was indeed daunting, four hundred miles long and in places more than ten miles deep, studded with thousands of strong-points and mile after mile of concrete obstacles, the famous Dragon's Teeth.

Facing Daly and his battalion were excellent German troops, men of the 17th SS Panzergrenadier Division—some five hundred strong and highly motivated. This was doubly troubling, given that even the least capable soldier, firing from a pillbox with thick walls, could mow down a platoon in a few seconds.[33]

Daly's A Company jumped off toward the Siegfried Line's first defenses at 5:45 A.M. on March 18 under cover of darkness. They were given plenty of backup—nine battalions of artillery, hopefully enough to stun German defenders and destroy strongpoints. Near a village called Heidelbingerhof, a respected sergeant who had fought since July 1943 with A Company was killed. The sergeant was due to return to the US the next day. Some men had asked A Company's commander to let the sergeant stay back. Now he lay dead. It was infuriating.

The sergeant was quickly forgotten as A Company was pinned down by machine-gun fire in the actual Dragon's Teeth. Earlier, Daly's company commander and another officer had lost their nerve and run back the way they had come. Daly now took over and led an attack on a pillbox. But the Germans fought ferociously and that afternoon Daly had to order his men to retreat.

Artillery fire landed all around with increasing fury and accuracy. A German observer was clearly directing fire, zeroing in on A Company. One of the unit's finest soldiers, Pfc. Gordon D. Olson, realized A Company could be slaughtered and laid down covering fire with his BAR, drawing the enemy's attention, buying time for others.

A mortar shell exploded thirty feet away, knocking Olson to the ground.

Olson got back up and aimed at the slits of the nearest pill-boxes, emptying several magazines. A bullet ripped off his ear. Blood poured down his neck. Enraged by Olson's defiance, three German riflemen ran from a trench and set up a machine gun and fired at him. A bullet ripped into his leg but Olson stayed on his feet and killed all three with his BAR. His ammunition was low and he timed his shots to save bullets. Finally, he collapsed and died from blood loss. Meanwhile, other men had managed to find cover. Olson had sacrificed himself to save them. The last man to pull back and join them was Lieutenant Michael Daly.[34]

That same morning, Audie Murphy's B Company also ran into serious problems and like A Company was pinned down. Murphy was not with his men in the front lines, however, having been notified on March 10 that he was being considered for the Medal of Honor. A press report that day had in fact announced that Audie Murphy, the 3rd Division's undisputed star, was "SWEATING APPROVAL OF A MEDAL OF HONOR" and had been relieved of his command of B Company.[35]

Murphy had then been assigned to Lt. Colonel Ware's battalion headquarters as a liaison officer on March 11, a week earlier. It was there that Murphy now learned B Company was stranded and risked being destroyed. He dropped whatever he was doing, jumped into a jeep, and sped to the front, where he eventually came across a platoon from B Company, shell-shocked, frozen with fear, in a trench that led toward a bunker.

Murphy quickly had them straightened out and ready to move. He then ordered a private to fetch a bazooka and get close enough to blast open the entrance to the bunker.

"Let's go up there and hammer on that Siegfried Line," ordered Murphy.

Dragon's Teeth surrounded them. They could not operate with tanks among the concrete obstacles. It was an infantry job.

"Shoot that door with that bazooka," said Murphy.

There was a loud explosion. Smoke billowed from the door.

The private was blown back by the blast.

Murphy picked up the private.

"Shoot it again," he snapped. "They're still in there."

The private fired again and this time he saw a "little bright spot" on the thick metal door.

There was the sound of banging on the door.

The door started to open.

"Comrade!" cried a German. "Comrade!"

The Germans wanted to give up.

It turned out there had been so much smoke caused by the bazooka that the Germans thought the Americans were using poison gas.

A group of terrified Germans soon gathered outside the bunker.

"Murphy, what do you want to do with these prisoners?"

"Hell, send them out there where we come from. Run them off."

Out of view of Murphy, one of the Germans picked up a rifle lying nearby and blew his brains out, preferring to end his own life rather than be killed by an American.

Murphy moved with his men down into the bunker. They had been spotted and before long shells were landing close by with a relentless fury, sending shock waves. Someone closed the door to the bunker and they climbed down flights of steps to ride out the shelling. A soldier pulled out some candles. They waited. The electric exhaust system had broken down and they were four stories underground. The air was thin and foul. In one corner of the room, there was an "old blacksmith blower" and they took turns running the blower by hand. It brought in fresh air and blew out the stale through a vent.

A GI looked down and saw water around his feet. Perhaps the Germans were trying to flood them out. Murphy and his men climbed up to the floor above, away from the water. But soon enough the dirty slosh had filled the bottom floor and kept rising toward them.

No one wanted to drown in an underground tomb.

They moved to a floor above.

"Gas, gas, gas!" yelled a soldier.

A private sniffed the air.

"There must be a sack of carbide up there," said the private.

Water had seeped into a storeroom and had wet a supply of carbide, used for portable lamps. That was why the air smelled of gas. The men found the carbide and took it to the bunker entrance and threw it out. Then the shelling stopped. There was a strange silence. The private and Murphy left the bunker and looked around. The private saw a "desolate, vacated battlefield. Nothing. Nobody at all."[36]

The next day, Michael Daly pushed his men forward. Tanks supported A Company and softened up defenses, forcing many Germans to withdraw, but not all—some of the imposing concrete pillboxes were still manned. Each one had to be secured. As men closed on each of them, they shouted as loud as they could, demanding surrender. If there was no reply, they blew doors open with bazookas and then lobbed phosphorus grenades downstairs, smoking out the last defenders, pieces of phosphorus scorching through limbs in a few seconds.

It was grueling work. But thanks to air strikes and massive artillery fire, the 3rd Division made steady progress and by March 20 had pushed through the fabled Siegfried Line, Nazi Germany's last defensive bulwark. In doing so, the 15th Infantry Regiment had lost forty-five men killed and almost two hundred wounded.[37] A Company's Michael Daly had earned himself a Bronze Star. "We really gained a good leader in Lieutenant Daly," remembered one sergeant. "Through his leadership, I believe many lives were saved. I was probably one of them."[38]

HAVING CROSSED THE Siegfried Line, the Marne men were able to rest for a fortnight. There was time to read mail from home and to catch up on news of the Allies' progress. A front-page headline in their division's newspaper, *Front Line*, declared:

"MURPHY CROWDS BRITT'S RECORD."[39]

The accompanying report detailed how Audie Murphy, if his Medal of Honor recommendation was approved, would be in "the same class" as Captain Maurice Britt, equaling the record haul of medals of "Footsie Won 'Em All."[40] Was it possible that

Murphy might then even surpass Britt? Or would another man emerge at the eleventh hour to steal both men's glory?

The medal count mattered to the headline writers as well as to the top brass. Combat decorations boosted morale. That was the view of General George C. Marshall, army chief of staff, who had been vexed by accusations that the army was handing out too many medals. "No one who understands the effect of the prompt bestowal of a bit of ribbon would ever feel that our awards have been excessive," Marshall had stated the previous July, by which time ninety-five men, in all branches of service, had been awarded the Medal of Honor. Almost half of those Medal of Honor recipients had been killed.[41] After three years of total war around the globe, as many men had received the Medal of Honor as from 1917 to 1918. Too few warriors were being recognized, not too many.

Infantrymen so close to the end, by far the most likely to die, needed all the inspiration they could get. "All of us know what the medals are for," noted one soldier. "They encourage a man to risk his neck another time and make others want to do the same, and wars are won by men who risk their necks."[42]

Two Marne men who were more than willing to "risk their necks" met by chance late that March on a training field. The Marne men were back in intensive training, refining their street-fighting tactics.[43] Murphy came across Lieutenant Michael Daly. The big push across the Rhine was up next and the latest green recruits clearly needed all the help they could get. Murphy saw a chickenshit major chew Daly out for not doing things by the book. Daly protested and then Murphy stepped in and told the major he'd best listen to Daly. Unlike the major, Daly had seen more than enough action to know what the hell he was doing.

Before returning to combat, Daly and Murphy received three-day passes to Paris: one last chance to truly let go before the final deadly race to the finish line. Murphy liked Paris a lot more than Rome and bought his sister Corinne some fancy perfume when he wasn't trying to find a craps or poker game. Like Murphy, Daly headed to the Place Pigalle, famous for its bars and brothels.

Daly spent his last morning in Paris in the Church of the Madeleine, near the Place de la Concorde. He later remembered walking up the front steps into the awe-inspiring building. He then looked around, passing through pews. There were gold chandeliers above. Light streamed down from a cupola. And there at the back of the church was a high altar. Above the altar was a white marble statue of St. Mary of Magdalene being lifted to the heavens by three winged angels, her eyes closed, hands outstretched in the ecstasy of supplication. She was magnificent to behold and Daly later said he very much identified with her. She had once been a sinner but she had shown great remorse. In this war, he too had found redemption. He had also atoned for his sins. God had answered Daly's prayers so far, ever since he'd crossed Bloody Omaha. That was why he'd beaten the odds. He'd also made himself and his father proud. Not far from a statue of Joan of Arc, he sat down and prayed devoutly.[44] The patron saint of France didn't look at him. She held her sword up, clasped with both hands, her helmeted head raised, eyes fixed on the heavens.

Daly walked back through the church toward the massive bronze doors at the entrance.

The Ten Commandments could be seen magnificently depicted in the bronze.

NON OCCIDES. . . .

YOU SHALL NOT KILL. . . .

He walked down steps, the Place de la Concorde ahead of him. Then he got in a car and headed east to meet his fate, no doubt at high speed, passing through towns toward the Rhine. When Daly arrived back at his regiment, he assumed the greatest responsibility of his life. A Company's previous commander had turned and run at the Siegfried Line. It needed a new leader. Aged twenty, Daly found himself in charge of two hundred men. Now he had to guide them to the heart of the Third Reich.

CHAPTER 14

The Heart of Darkness

It was past dusk on March 25 when engineers pulled sections of pontoon bridges to the western bank of the Rhine River midway between the cities of Worms and Mannheim. The last major natural barrier for the Allies had first been crossed two weeks earlier to the north, at Remagen. Now Patch's 7th Army approached the waters of the longest river in Germany.

Early the next morning, at 1:52 A.M., the 3rd Division's supporting artillery opened up. In thirty-eight minutes, ten thousand rounds were fired, a constant thunder. Then men from the 30th and 7th Infantry Regiments began to row across, the sky a lurid red from fires set by the barrage. Some boats were hit by enemy mortar fire and sank with men forced to swim, powder smoke burning their nostrils, bright moonlight greeting them on the eastern side of the river.

Almost twenty-four hours later, after midnight on March 27, Lieutenant Michael Daly led A Company into thick woods two miles east of the Rhine.[1] His regiment had been held in reserve the night before, when the rest of the division had crossed, but was now its spearhead. When Daly and his men left the woods, they came across one of Hitler's famed autobahns, an impressive strip of concrete leading to the village of Hüttenfeld, four miles to the east of the Rhine.[2] Later that morning, Daly's company climbed into trucks and onto tanks and started down one of Hitler's vaunted freeways.

Not since the previous September had the Marne men moved so fast. Wherever the Allies had crossed the Rhine, they were rolling toward victory. Hitler's armies were collapsing, in the east and the west. The dam had finally burst.[3] POW cages were filling with tens of thousands of bedraggled Wehrmacht soldiers. Some liberators were so eager to chase what was left of the enemy that they became maniacal. "We didn't even stop to piss," recalled one American tanker. "Individual soldiers would squeeze into the turrets and urinate down the sides of the tanks. Sometimes two men were back to back, their cocks bent over a metallic ridge. An odd phenomenon, as if the tanks themselves were running with yellow sweat."[4]

There were roadblocks but tanks blew through them. Before long, the Germans themselves were calling the pathetic obstructions "61-minute roadblocks. . . . It will take the Americans sixty-one minutes to get past them. They will look at them and laugh for sixty minutes and then tear them down in one."[5]

The end was nigh. On April 2, Hitler ordered that cities in what was left of the Third Reich were to be fiercely defended. "No doubt he believed implicitly," recalled Kesselring, commander of German forces on the Western Front, "that every German would make the last sacrifice."[6] That same day, Audie Murphy found time to write to his sister. He'd been taken off the lines and was a liaison officer, coming across Lt. Colonel Ware and other senior officers at headquarters. He was waiting for the war to end, he told his sister, and he'd learned that he would receive the Medal of Honor. There was no other medal he could gain as an infantryman. "Since that is all the Medals they have to offer," Murphy quipped, "I'll have to take it easy for a while, ha, ha."[7]

Nuremberg lay ahead, the symbolic heart of the Third Reich, where Hitler had held his famous rallies in the 1930s, and which drew the Americans "magnetically," according to Kesselring.[8] Three US infantry divisions were within striking distance and each of their commanders wanted to be first.

It was impossible to relax. Even stalwarts were jittery, knowing the war was almost over. In the words of one veteran: "To die at this stage—with the door at the end of the passage, the door into the rose garden, already in sight, ajar—would be awful."[9] After enduring so much, survival was all that mattered. "Hope and fear walk hand in hand," noted Audie Murphy. "We can see the end . . . always in a man's mind is that one lead pill, that one splinter of steel that can lose him the race with the finish line in sight."[10]

Finally, Lt. Colonel Keith Ware's battalion arrived on the outskirts of Nuremberg. Before him lay endless rubble and ruin, trees blasted from their roots. Throughout the war, the city had drawn Allied bombers like a lodestar. A particularly devastating raid had occurred on January 2, 1945. Under a rising moon, the RAF had dropped a million incendiary devices, burning countless half-timbered buildings to the ground. The famous Nazi

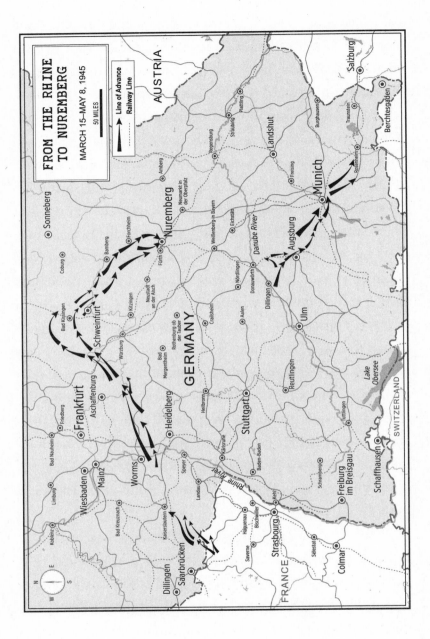

FROM THE RHINE
TO NUREMBERG

MARCH 15–MAY 8, 1945

50 MILES

Line of Advance
Railway Line

rally grounds had first been hit in late 1940, one of the earliest targets for the British seeking to avenge the Blitz. The day before Ware and his battalion reached the outskirts, Kesselring himself had passed through and been caught in a bombing raid. "Fighting in the streets," he recalled, "tragic and unnecessary as it was, could hardly cause any more destruction."[11] Ninety-five percent of the "intellectual center of Nazism" had been laid waste.[12]

NUREMBERG WAS THE last great prize for the US Army in Germany. The Bavarian city also loomed large in the minds of the Nazis. It was, after all, Hitler's favorite metropolis, "the most German" in the Third Reich, according to the Führer, who was now holed up in his bunker in Berlin, drug addled, raging at providence and betrayal.

The Nazi commander of Nuremberg, forty-nine-year-old *Gauleiter* Karl Holz, a World War I veteran, now chose to disobey Kesselring, who had ordered that the city be defended beyond its outskirts, not in its central streets. That would have been excessively bloody. But Holz could not have cared less. He was hell-bent on defending every block, every square yard of the city, particularly its medieval heart, and he was ready to fight dirty. He had arranged for a hundred fifty antiaircraft guns to be aimed at the Americans, who were fast approaching from the north and from the southeast: the 3rd Division and the 45th Division, both under the command of General Alexander Patch. Around eighty of the devastating guns were in the 3rd Division's assigned sector.

Holz had also vowed to lead five thousand defenders to the bitter end, promising in a missive to Hitler that he "would rather stay in the most German of all cities under all circumstances and die fighting than abandon it."

A police chief in Nuremberg had seen the futility of the situation. He had begged Holz to save lives by surrendering.

"*Gauleiter*, the defense of Nuremberg is crazy," the police chief had argued. "It can't be held."

Holz had erupted with rage.

"I'll have you arrested for not carrying out the Führer's orders. I'm reporting this immediately."

Thousands of Germans in what remained of the Third Reich had been summarily hanged by "flying courts" in recent weeks. Holz had even shot to death a senior city official for refusing to carry out his order, triggered by the code word "Puma," to destroy all bridges and the city's waterworks and essential services. Holz and his kind were particularly fond of the term "rabid dog" to describe their latest shooting victim. Of course, those who opposed total Götterdämmerung were always to be killed "out of hand."[13]

At dawn on April 17, Ware's battalion struck from the northeast and managed to capture almost fifty 88mm guns. The SS lurked in the skeletons of buildings, armed with Panzerfausts, high-powered telescopic sniper rifles, and the MG-42 machine guns that could fire well over a thousand rounds per minute.[14] That morning, A Company's Michael Daly was as aggressive as ever, exposing himself to enemy mortar and machine-gun fire. "The rubble was very extensive," he recalled. "A lot of large buildings had been completely knocked down. You had to dislodge the enemy in a piecemeal way, because they used the rubble as cover. You had to get in pretty close to be effective."[15]

There was to be no holding back, no easing up for Daly: "You don't win unless you occupy."[16] More than ever, he wanted to save his men. They deserved to go home. He'd take the big chances: "When the war was winding down, you felt strongly the necessity of doing everything you could to protect the people who were still alive."[17]

That first morning on the outskirts of Nuremberg, April 17, the Marne men made steady progress, darting from one ruined building to another, alert for snipers, hugging crumbling walls, avoiding bunching, not dropping their heads, stepping over singed beams and broken furniture. It was said that civilians had been armed and were hiding in spider holes, under orders to let the Americans pass by before shooting them in the back.[18]

Germans wearing SS uniforms were in fact lying in wait for A Company and would probably have killed many of Daly's men, had it not been for twenty-seven-year-old Lieutenant Francis Burke, who'd grown up in the rough-and-tumble of Hell's Kitchen in New York. That morning, Burke was scouting ahead of A Company, looking for the best route for the First Battalion's motor pool, when he saw dozens of Germans. He warned men in A Company and then grabbed a machine gun and let rip, taking out a German squad and quickly coming under answering fire. Spotting yet more of the enemy in some ruins, he borrowed an M-1 rifle from one of Daly's men and ran a hundred yards as bullets flew. Finding shelter behind an abandoned tank, he continued his killing spree but was then hit by a sniper lurking in a basement twenty yards away.

In the cauldron of combat, truly exceptional soldiers are capable of seemingly superhuman feats. So it was with Burke that day. Even though wounded, he managed to get to a window of the basement and fire a full M-1 clip inside, reload and drop down through the window, consumed with vengeance, hell-bent on shooting the sniper. His M-1 jammed and he went to find another, returning with a fresh rifle and more grenades. Spotting the sniper, he pulled the pins from two grenades, held one in each hand, ran forward, and threw the grenades as the German tossed one at him.

All three grenades exploded, killing the German and leaving Burke badly dazed. A German armed with a machine pistol ran at him. Burke killed him with three "calmly delivered shots," according to his Medal of Honor citation. For another couple of hours, he fought with Daly's A Company and eventually shot dead eight more of the enemy, bringing his tally for the day to thirty-two.[19] Then he had his wound treated. The German counterattack against Daly's men had been blunted and the First Battalion was able to push farther into Nuremberg. "We knew the war would be over soon," recalled Daly. "The Germans in Nuremberg were very dedicated. They wanted to bring down as many Americans as they could before the end of the war. We'd run into a hornets' nest. I did the best I could to try to protect my company."[20]

Daly did not sleep that night. Perhaps he was too jacked up on adrenaline. Perhaps he wanted to stay awake, ever vigilant for enemy infiltration. It was still cold and dark at 5 A.M. the next morning when Daly gave the orders to his bleary-eyed platoon sergeants and junior officers to move out. They were to head due south again, along the Bayreuther Strasse, a main road that led toward the medieval heart of the gutted city.

Up ahead were French volunteers and many Romanian Germans of the 17th SS Panzergrenadier Division. They weren't the schoolboys and old men to be found in the *Volkssturm*, the ragtag militia Hitler had assembled to resist invasion. They were professional killers, especially those belonging to the 38th SS Regiment, which in the next forty-eight hours would be wiped out—such was the savage intensity of the battle to come. SS stalwarts with twin lightning bolts etched on their helmets, they had no thoughts of tomorrow. All that mattered was stopping the Americans from the *"Sturm"* Division, as the Marne men were known. They clipped magazines into their machine pistols, draped themselves in MG-42 machine-gun belts, and stuffed potato-masher grenades into their pockets. Others hid in ruins, listening, waiting for Daly and his men to stroll into their telescopic sights.

Daly had lost a great deal of weight since arriving at Omaha Beach ten months before. Rake thin, he moved ahead of A Company toward the center of the "City of the Movement," the last citadel of National Socialism, his long, slim fingers gripping his carbine.

Gauleiter Holz was meanwhile busy shoring up morale and defenses within the city center's walls, sending a message to his beloved Führer in his bunker in Berlin: "The final struggle for the town of the Party rallies has begun . . . soldiers are fighting bravely, and the population is proud and strong. . . . In these hours, my heart beats more than ever in Love and Faith for the wonderful German Reich and its people. The National Socialist idea shall win and conquer all diabolical schemes."[21]

The final denouement had come. The last hours of Nazi rule.

"Everyone stays in Nuremberg," ordered Holz, "and will die if necessary."[22]

Message sent, Holz led a group of fanatics, many of them mere teenagers, toward the city's main train station, toward Michael Daly and A Company.

The steady growl of a Sherman, following behind A Company, was both reassuring and unnerving, a loud signal to the enemy as it clanked behind Daly, ready to lay down the heavy stuff if needed. An SS soldier had a scout in his crosshairs, aiming for the center of his body. Then he pressed his trigger, killed the young American, adjusted his aim, and fired again. Another scout was dead. Out of sight of Daly, the sniper emerged into the open, hands in the air. A lieutenant grabbed the sniper, pulled him into a nearby building, then riddled him with tommy gun bullets.[23]

The lieutenant would never say a word about the execution to Daly. Drilling a prisoner, even if he was a Nazi, with .45 slugs . . . tearing a man who had surrendered apart like a pathetic rag doll . . . after he'd given up . . . that wasn't Daly's way of war. He'd always made it plain—no killing prisoners, no matter how evil.

Daly had, in the meantime, decided to become the point for his lead platoon.

No one protested.

He'd be the tip of the spear.

He began to move farther down Bayreuther Strasse. It was overcast, a chilly day. Explosions ripped the air as US artillery landed farther ahead, in the heart of the city. Daly sprinted from cover to cover, one pile of broken masonry to another.

A machine gun snarled. The bullets came from a water tower. Daly lifted his carbine, aimed, and pulled the trigger. The machine gun went silent. D Company followed and Daly reached the twisted wreckage of what remained of the Nordost Railway Station. There was a destroyed railroad bridge that spanned the Bayreuther Strasse. Daly began to climb up a low embankment. Railroad cars. Ruins. A square off to his left. A German machine gun opened up again and this time his men were caught out in the open, bullets ripping into several, killing and wounding. The German fire was unrelenting. Daly realized his company could be slaughtered. With bullets riddling the earth between his feet, he sprinted across railroad tracks toward the German machine gun.

The Germans could see him coming for them, a lanky young American with a death wish. Bullets again smashed into the pavement at Daly's feet. He found cover. Then he jumped up and fired again, hitting a German. Two more Germans showed themselves. Finger to trigger. Daly took two more lives. There were more Germans in the distance. A small group, maybe half a dozen. One was armed with a Panzerfaust. They wanted to take out the Sherman accompanying A Company.

A sergeant saw Daly signal for him and the rest of A Company to halt. Daly moved on alone to the ruins of a house and spotted three Germans moving toward him. He'd been seen. Bullets holed the wall beside Daly. Eddies of white plaster dust lifted into the sky. Then a shell from the Panzerfaust exploded into a wall of the house. Then another.[24] He could see Germans clearly. Daly aimed his carbine and killed each one.[25]

Daly knew there was a large park farther to the south, a few hundred yards ahead. He led the way again, carbine reloaded, ready for more. There was the park. Smashed trees lying on the churned ground, a field of debris and litter. Two more Germans only ten yards away, one firing a machine gun. A sergeant, a hell of a good man, fell dead. Daly grabbed his M-1 rifle and killed the main gunner. Another bullet hit the other German, who fell, wounded, but then jumped up and fired at Daly. One more slug from the M-1. The German breathed no more, the last of the fifteen Daly killed that day.

Daly had led his men far ahead of all other units in the division.[26] Several were in awe. They'd witnessed the miraculous and they knew it. Had it not been for the "long-tall boy," how many of them would still be alive? "There was no fear in him," one remembered. He'd "smashed a path" to the core of evil. "His heroism towered above the courage of those around him."[27] According to a senior officer in Daly's battalion: "During two days and nights of bitter hand-to-hand fighting, he served as first scout of the company, taking all the major risks himself and fearlessly disregarding deadly enemy fire."[28]

For his actions that day, April 18, 1945, Daly would receive the Medal of Honor. It was one of the last awarded in the European Theater.[29] The very last would go to Texan fighter pilot, Raymond Knight, flying a P-47 in Italy on April 24.

That afternoon, encountering intense American fire, Holz and his fanatics pulled back to within the thick twenty-foot-high walls around the medieval center of the city. When the Marne men used a 155mm howitzer, the largest artillery piece they possessed, to blow a hole in the wall, it made little impact. It would be down to the infantry yet again—up to Daly and his men in A Company. They'd have to finish the job tomorrow.

That night, Daly hunkered down in the park he'd helped clear earlier, a few hundred yards from the high wall around the heart of Nuremberg. Again, he did not sleep.[30] Early the next morning, he led his men once more along the shattered Bayreuther Strasse to the medieval center of the city, where the last SS diehards lurked.

Finally, he neared the wall itself.

German sniper fire was intense.

From his new headquarters inside a police station within the city's walls, Holz ranted and raved at the last SS stalwarts under his command. They were to kill as many Americans as they possibly could.

Daly stepped to the base of the wall. It towered above him, several feet thick. Beside Daly was twenty-eight-year-old Major Burton Barr, a thin-lipped Arizonan much admired by Audie Murphy, Keith Ware, and Daly himself. "We'd just come through a park, getting ready to attack the old city," Barr remembered. "As usual, A Company was to lead the attack. [Daly] was leaning on my shoulder, talking to me."[31]

The wall had to be breached. That was the order from higher up.

Daly had been in battle for long enough to trust his instincts. Climbing over would be risky but he wasn't going to ask any of his men to go first.

Burton Barr stood on a pile of rubble beside the wall.

If Barr gave him a leg up, Daly would be able to reach up and pull himself over the top of the wall.

As he started to climb over, exposing himself, there was the whack of a sniper round.

One of Holz's men had spotted him.

The bullet clipped his ear and then tore through Daly's face, from right to left, breaking his upper and lower jaw, passing through his palate.

Daly spun around and then fell back, down the pile of rubble, and began to choke on his own blood. His men spotted him. He'd finally bought it. Such a shame, so close to the end of the war, to lose the best officer they'd ever had. But Daly was not dead, not yet. And he was damned if he was going to bleed out among the broken bricks and dust of Hitler's favorite city.

Barr looked over at Daly. "He took a pencil out of his pocket and stuck it down his throat to keep his windpipe open," recalled Barr, "did it as calmly as can be."[32]

The pencil worked. It was a primitive form of tracheostomy, preventing his tongue from spasming, partly clearing his windpipe so he could breathe.[33] But Daly could not stop himself from choking for long. He was drowning in his own blood. A sergeant ran to Daly's side, knelt down, and reached quickly into Daly's throat with his fingers and cleared it of blood and mucus.

Medics arrived and placed Daly on the hood of a jeep, which then headed to the nearest aid station, the 10th Field Hospital. Daly pulled his tongue as far out of his mouth as he could, trying to breathe. "I thought I was finished," he would recall. "I'd seen enough face wounds. I remembered to be still. But it was like there was a pillow over my face. I knew I was suffocating."[34]

Daly was carried from the jeep into an aid station. Other men in critical condition were being treated, some for bullet wounds inflicted by snipers. A priest arrived and gave Daly last rites, absolving him of his most recent sins. Daly was ready to meet his Maker. Meanwhile, what remained of A Company had gotten through the wall. They had found a gate and rushed it, opting not to climb over like Daly.

There was a visitor to Daly's bedside later that April 19: 7th Army commander Alexander Patch. The general was disturbed by what he saw. "It was a dreadful sight," he recalled. "He had a tube in his throat, could not speak, and was receiving a blood transfusion. I walked to his bed and looked at him, and through one partly opened eye I felt he recognized me so I held out my hand and he took it. . . . When I left that evening, the doctor could not tell me whether he would pull through."[35]

Patch had, of course, lost his own son only six months before. He'd wanted young Michael to see out the war as his aide, far from combat, but had allowed him to return to the front lines, just as he'd permitted his own son to do the same.

The next morning, April 20, Lieutenant Daly was taken for surgery. The operation went well and he returned to his bed in the 10th Field Hospital with his face heavily bandaged but finally able to breathe properly. It was Adolf Hitler's fifty-sixth birthday. In Berlin, a gaunt Führer emerged from his bunker, fifty feet beneath the ground, to present some Hitler Youth teenagers with a few medals and then shuffled back to his subterranean lair. "His complexion was sallow," remembered one of his inner circle, "his face swollen, his uniform, which had been scrupulously neat, was neglected and stained by the food he had eaten with a shaking hand."[36]

The last great battle by Americans for a German city was

almost over. It was 10 A.M. when a scout from the 7th Infantry Regiment met up with a dogface from the 30th Regiment in the Adolf Hitler Platz, at the heart of the city. Only Holz's band of hard-core SS and some fifty policemen were still holding out. Holz didn't last long. That afternoon he was shot in the jugular vein as he tried to escape from the police station, where he'd decided to make his final stand. Holz did not die instantly. He was left to bleed to death in a pool of his own blood as his men surrendered to a tall, well-built American officer who spoke fluent German.

The officer had the good grace to congratulate the last defenders of Nuremberg for their fighting spirit.

"Du hast tapfer gekämpft, Jungs."[37]

"You fought bravely, boys."

All of Nuremberg was finally in American hands. At 6:30 that evening, in the Adolf Hitler Platz, the Marne men formed up to mark a historic moment, arguably the finest in their history, to be celebrated down the ages like their forefathers' determined defense of the Marne in 1918, which had earned them their name. Here they were, at the end of an epic odyssey of combat and liberation, arguably the finest US infantry division of World War II.

Each regiment from the division provided a platoon for the celebratory procession. Tanks and other vehicles lined up. A heavy silence descended. There was the stench of decaying flesh. Hundreds of rotting corpses of Germans lay beneath the mounds of rubble surrounding the square. Some soldiers had set up a flagpole and then the Stars and Stripes was raised in the center of the square at the heart of the Third Reich.

The 3rd Division Band played the national anthem.

Major General "Iron Mike" O'Daniel stepped forward.

"Again the 3rd Division has taken its objective," said O'Daniel.

As with Alexander Patch, he had lost his only son the previous fall, killed near Arnhem while fighting with the 505th Parachute Infantry Regiment. O'Daniel himself was by now one of his division's most decorated veterans, with only the Medal of Honor eluding him. "We are standing at the site of the stronghold of Nazi resistance in our zone," said O'Daniel. "Through your feats of arms, you have smashed fifty heavy antiaircraft guns, captured four thousand prisoners, and driven the Hun from every house and castle and bunker in our part of Nürnberg. I congratulate you upon your superior performance."[38]

A few German civilians, impressed by the military pomp, gazed at the Stars and Stripes as it flew at half-mast to honor President Roosevelt, who had died on April 12.

The division band started playing "Dogface Soldier."

> *I wouldn't give a bean*
> *To be a fancy-pants marine.*
> *I'd rather be a*
> *Dogface soldier like I am.*

TWO DAYS LATER, on April 22, five of Michael Daly's fellow warriors from the 3rd Division stood on concrete steps overlooking the vast Zeppelin Field, the site of the Nuremberg rallies. Three of the men belonged to Maurice Britt's 30th Infantry Regiment. Two others were from the 15th "Can Do" Infantry Regiment:

Lieutenant John J. Tominac and none other than twenty-nine-year-old Lt. Colonel Keith L. Ware. It would be the first time in US history that five men received the Medal of Honor on a battlefield.

A massive swastika, looming above the stadium, had been covered in sheets and primed with two hundred pounds of TNT explosives. The 10th Engineer Combat Battalion, which had set the charges, was intent on sending a message that would be seen around the world on newsreels. It was a bright sunny day. Spring had truly arrived in Bavaria. Ware stood, wearing sunglasses, beside the four other men on the steps of the main stand of the Zeppelin Stadium. Audie Murphy might well have been watching, given that these days he belonged to the 15th Infantry Regiment's headquarters staff, many of whom were present.

Ware was first in line. He was a rarity. Just one other officer remained in action who had joined the 15th Infantry Regiment in the US before it had shipped out to Europe—a captain called Henry Auld, Lieutenant Audie Murphy's immediate superior.

General Patch approached the men.

Ware stood staring straight ahead, his eyes hidden by his sunglasses, arms ramrod straight at his side. Sheets were pulled off the swastika thirty yards away. Patch placed the Medal of Honor around Ware's neck—the cue to blow up the massive swastika. Cameras rolled as lumps of concrete flew through the air. One piece almost ripped off the arm of a chaplain who was standing watching a hundred yards away.[39] "Christ, there were rocks all over that stadium," remembered one officer. "Two hundred pounds—that's a hell of a lot of TNT."[40]

Patch went down the line, hanging a medal around the neck of each man. There were no smiles, only grim pride. So many of these men's friends had not made it this far, had been killed so close to the end. Patch himself was lucky to be there. Four days earlier, he had been flying toward Nuremberg when a German fighter had intercepted his small spotter plane. Thankfully, his pilot had evaded the German. Patch would die of pneumonia in a matter of months, short of his fifty-sixth birthday, having sacrificed everything, including his health, for victory over evil.

The following day, Lieutenant Michael Daly was flown to Paris and then sent to England. In surgery, a passage had been made from his ear to his palate, and to amuse other GIs, he sometimes stretched out his cheek and spat through his ear.[41]

On April 30, with a few days left of the war, the 15th Infantry Regiment organized into task forces that pushed past Munich and mopped up resistance farther south. One of the task forces was called Task Force Ware.[42] The Germans were surrendering in entire units, not piecemeal. In rapid succession, Ware seized several towns before pivoting, as a late-spring snow fell, to the southeast, headed toward Salzburg. The Alps loomed in all their jagged white magnificence on the horizon.

Although Hitler's Alpine retreat near Berchtesgaden was beyond the zone of the 3rd Division, troops from the 7th Infantry Regiment actually liberated it, sent by O'Daniel to claim one final honor. The Marne men had, after all, fought longest and hardest and lost more men, all the way to Hitler's famous Alpine lair. They found a smoldering ruin and then raised the Stars and Stripes. They were at long last at the end of an extraordinary journey, starting in Fedala in French Morocco—twenty-two months of killing and dying with thirty-five thousand battle casualties, more than any other US division in Europe.[43]

Early on May 7, 1945, an American sergeant called Louis Graziano watched fifty-four-year-old General Alfred Jodl enter a crowded classroom in a three-story redbrick building in the city of Reims, capital of the Champagne region in France.[44] It was 2:41 A.M. when the steely-faced Jodl signed formal surrender documents with a Parker pen. Then Graziano and other American personnel escorted Jodl along a corridor to where Allied Supreme Commander Dwight Eisenhower was waiting. Graziano watched Jodl walk into a classroom, click his heels, and salute Eisenhower, who had refused to ever shake the hands of a Nazi and wasn't about to start doing so.[45]

Jodl was dismissed.

Later that morning, Eisenhower sent the following message to Washington:

"THE MISSION OF THIS ALLIED FORCE WAS FULFILLED."[46]

The war in Europe, after the loss of nineteen million civilians, was over.

The 3rd Division had been involved in five amphibious landings—the most of any unit in the European Theater. It had logged 635 days in combat.

"It's amazing to think it's over," said one man. "I feel a little let down."

Field Marshal Kesselring—former commander of German forces on the Western Front—surrendered on May 9 to the

Americans. A reporter for the *Chicago Tribune* had a question for him.

"What was the best American division faced by troops under your command on either the Italian or Western Fronts?"

He answered without hesitation.

The Marne men.[47]

PART FOUR

Peace

CHAPTER 15

No Peace Within

MICHAEL DALY WAS not in Salzburg, Austria, with the 15th Infantry Regiment when the news arrived of the formal German surrender on May 7, 1945. He was in a hospital in England with a nerve-damaged throat, his face wrapped in bandages, when he heard a radio report. There was no elation. He was "just glad" it was all over.[1] Daly's comrade Audie Murphy was not in Salzburg either. On Victory in Europe Day, May 8, 1945, he was in a hotel room in Cannes, on the French Riviera, toying with a gun, admiring "the cold, blue glint of its steel," when he heard bells pealing, signaling that the fighting had ended. "There is VE-Day without," he noted, "but no peace within."[2]

Murphy had survived but he didn't feel like celebrating. His best friend, Lattie Tipton, should have seen this day. So many had longed for the end. So few had reached it. His muscles were stiff with stress, so he soaked in a hot bath. Finally, with the bright Riviera light flooding through a window, Murphy started to relax, later saying his blood pressure dropped and never spiked again. Nothing—not even a beautiful actress or a race-winning horse—would ever truly excite him as much as war. He was twenty-one but felt like an old man.

Murphy had never felt so tired. He fell asleep as crowds filled the streets below his hotel room. When he awoke, it was as if he'd been released from a death sentence. Someone was playing the song "Lili Marleen." The killing and dying were finally over, at least in Europe, and for that reason alone, it was the best day of Audie Murphy's war. "I will find the kind of girl of whom I once dreamed," he vowed. "I will learn to look at life through un-cynical eyes, to have faith, to know love. I will learn to work in peace as in war. And finally—finally, like countless others, I will learn to live again."[3]

Murphy had already learned he would receive the Medal of Honor in Salzburg and returned on May 20 to Lt. Colonel Ware's headquarters. Ware and others had provided recommendations that Murphy be awarded the medal. Recognition of Murphy's exceptional heroism was only fitting—it was in fact a moral imperative. He personified so many Marne men's heroism. So many of those warriors had died, their acts never recorded.[4] They might not have had such resilience but they had, at times, been equally courageous as Murphy.[5]

On Memorial Day, May 30, the man who had led the 3rd Division through much of the war stood in a graveyard at Anzio Nettuno. His heavy-boned face was creased with emotion. He turned his back on the dignitaries and press gathered close by. Instead he spoke to the more than seven thousand Americans who lay in eternal peace in the soil they had died to liberate.

The cartoonist Bill Mauldin, famous as the originator of "Willie and Joe," based on characters under Lucian Truscott's command, had witnessed Truscott's incisive leadership many times. Truscott had in fact kept one of Mauldin's cartoons next to his desk during the Battle of Anzio, admiring its pithy honesty. Two of his beloved Marne men were shown in a foxhole at Anzio, one telling the other: "Th' hell this ain't the' most important hole in th' world."[6] Now Mauldin watched as fifty-year-old Truscott—like so many of his men a "redneck from nowhere," as he called himself—addressed the many gravestones.[7]

Mauldin believed the gesture—turning to face his dead men—was the "most moving" he had ever seen or would see: "He apologized to the dead men for their presence here. He said everybody tells leaders it is not their fault that men get killed in war, but that every leader knows in his heart that this is not altogether true. He said he hoped anybody here through any mistake of his would forgive him, but he realized that was asking a hell of a lot under the circumstances. . . . He promised that if in the future he ran into anybody, especially old men, who thought death in battle was glorious, he would straighten them out."[8]

The war had marked Truscott indelibly. His health had been damaged by the unending stress, the countless nerve-steadying swigs of booze, the daily heartbreak, all the chain-smoked cigarettes. He sensed, correctly, that his finest hours were behind him. Already his best aides were leaving. He had loved ones at home, a doting and beautiful wife, but the family he had spent the last three years with was disbanding, falling apart.

In the end, the center did not hold. Truscott sinned. Painfully aware of his fading powers, physical and military, he strayed.

There was a brief lapse that spring, a few weeks of infatuation with forty-two-year-old Clare Boothe Luce, the famous congresswoman and wife of the founder of *Life* magazine. She had a spellbinding gaze, quick wit, and considerable sexual energy. His affair with her peeled away the years, made him feel like the virile cavalryman of his youth. He fell hard for her "warm red lips . . . heavenly blue eyes . . . a companionship so perfect to erase dull care, and pain, and time, and reality . . ."[9]

It could not last, and a few weeks after his visit to Anzio Nettuno, Truscott returned to the United States and to his wife, Sarah, to whom he had written so often in the three years he'd been at war. His place in history was secure. He had arguably been the greatest US fighting general of World War II, enormously admired by both his men and his peers.

Back in Austria, Lt. Colonel Keith Ware opted to stay on in Europe and perform occupation duties. He had no wife or children to hurry back to. At some point late that spring, if not before, he decided to devote the rest of his life to the US Army. It would be his salvation, his balm. Ambition burned within him. His calling was to lead men in battle. He'd proved to be damn good at it. An unremarkable draftee three years before, he had become one of the most respected and decorated officers to ever wear a blue-and-white patch on his shoulder. There was no way Lt. Colonel Ware, dog tag number 0-1388333, was going to return to his former job in a California department store, pushing paper dutifully from nine to five.[10] Making life-and-death decisions had been a heavy responsibility but one he had shouldered with ever-greater pride.

Ware's finest soldier, Audie Murphy, was often to be found

late that spring at a headquarters in Salzburg—the elegant Villa Trapp, a twenty-two-room manse, notable for its light yellow stucco and the many rolls of barbed wire around its perimeter. It had once been the home of the von Trapp family, who would become the subject of the smash hit 1965 Broadway musical and movie *The Sound of Music*. Ware and Murphy were the only two surviving men who had served with Company B on the first day that the Allies had begun to liberate Europe.

Another recipient of the Medal of Honor often to be seen at the headquarters was twenty-three-year-old Lieutenant John Tominac. He'd been summoned one day that spring and had arrived at "Himmler's estate," as he called it, bang on time. The von Trapp mansion seemed to be empty. Bored, Tominac decided to take a look around. On the second floor, where the SS had planned the liquidation of millions, he went in search of a bathroom.

Tominac hung his tommy gun on a doorknob and sat down to defecate.

Before he could empty his bowels, there was a loud gunshot.

He lunged for his gun.

His trousers were around his ankles.

Had Himmler's SS returned?

Was the bathroom booby-trapped?

After chasing Nazis across Europe, Tominac wasn't ready to die with his underpants down. He pulled up his trousers in a flash, flushed the toilet, and crept out of the bathroom, tommy gun raised.

There were a couple more gunshots.

He kept close to a wall and made his way carefully toward a staircase.

Tominac came across a large room where Himmler had once gathered his most trusted men. At its center was a thirty-foot-long mahogany table. The room was otherwise empty except for "a young, boyish looking" officer who had his boots on the table. "In his right hand he held a .45 caliber pistol," remembered Tominac, "which he was using to take pot shots at a large portrait of Adolph Hitler that was hanging on the opposite wall. Needless to say, I breathed a sigh of relief and was happy to meet for the first time 2nd Lt. Audie Murphy of Company B, 15th Infantry. This seemed to be Audie's unique way of celebrating [the end of the war]."[11]

Another officer, Colonel Henry Bodson, arrived at Himmler's former summer residence that May and was delighted to find a "festive air."

Bodson had known both Murphy and his fellow colonel Keith Ware for over a year. One evening, Murphy and others pulled out bottles of booze, stowed away for a special occasion. Men were soon getting drunk in the room where Himmler had planned his mass murder of the Jews. Before long, the schnapps and white wine were running low. Bodson was worried they might run dry. But then, recalled Bodson, "Audie Murphy and a few of the other staff officers came through as only the 'Can Do' regiment could. In they charged with several cases of champagne, real champagne."

"Here it is, drink up!" they shouted. "This is brought to you straight from the Eagle's Nest at Berchtesgaden with the compliments of the host, Adolph Hitler."

Bodson remembered "a resounding cheer in the headquarters. The party took on renewed vigor and went on and on and on."[12]

While Murphy knocked back champagne, the War Department Bureau of Public Relations went into overdrive. Here was a hero straight out of central casting, the perfect face of victory in Europe. Unlike Maurice Britt, Murphy had all his limbs and showed no outward scars. And he was movie-star handsome. On May 24, a two-page press release about Murphy, full of superlatives, was sent to news outlets, reporters, and radio correspondents throughout Europe. Here, at last, was World War II's Alvin York, seemingly heaven-sent.

The media was more than eager to take the bait.

The folks back home couldn't get enough of the glory stuff. It was time to celebrate their heroes as never before.

On May 27, a story appeared in the newspaper *Stars and Stripes*, the main news source for GIs throughout liberated Europe:

"MURPHY TIES BRITT'S RECORD."

Reporter Vic Dallaire breathlessly recounted how, while Murphy had been "relaxing on the Riviera beaches which he helped win last summer," a message had arrived at 3rd Division headquarters in Austria that the Texan had finally been approved for the Medal of Honor. This meant he "automatically went into a tie with the legendary Capt. Maurice 'Footsie' Britt, of the Third, as the most decorated soldier of this or any other war."[13]

The 3rd Division's newspaper, called *Front Line*, showed a photograph of General "Iron Mike" O'Daniel, pistol holstered at his waist, shaking Murphy's hand.

A headline declared:

"SECOND MAN SO HONORED IN US ARMY."

Then came a detailed report:

> A 21 year old Texan who rose from buck private to company commander in 30 months of combat with the veteran Third Division has been awarded the Congressional Medal of Honor and has thus become the second man of his division and the second man in the U.S. army to win the nation's every existing individual medal for valor.
>
> He is 1st Lt. Audie L. Murphy, Farmersville, Tex., who added the Medal of Honor to his Bronze Star, Silver Star and Distinguished Service Cross to join the legendary Capt. Maurice L. Britt as the army's most decorated men. Murphy is the 29th member of the Third Division to win the CMH, which gives the famous "Marne" Division more than one-fourth of all Medals of Honor won by the ground forces.[14]

WHEN THE ACTUAL awards were finally tallied, Murphy was found to be the most decorated, with two Silver Stars and three Bronze Stars, whereas Britt could boast one of each, although

Britt had earned four Purple Hearts to Murphy's three. Britt had, it was reported, starred in his "greatest game" and had received "the greatest title"—the Medal of Honor—but had not ultimately gained the accolade of most decorated warrior.[15]

Lieutenant Michael Daly had received an extraordinary three Silver Stars, as many as Murphy's and Britt's combined, but lacked the Distinguished Service Cross. Lt. Colonel Keith Ware had also received every award for valor except the Distinguished Service Cross—that one elusive medal would come more than two decades later. Britt, Ware, Murphy, and Daly had all far exceeded eighty-five points—the magic number required for soldiers to be allowed to return home.

Audie Murphy was told he had a choice. He could receive his Medal of Honor in Washington at the White House from President Harry Truman, or he could get the award in the European Theater itself. He chose to receive it in Europe, in front of some of his fellow Marne men.

On the afternoon of June 2, 1945, Murphy arrived at an airfield near Salzburg and was soon standing on a raised wooden stage.

Facing him was Lt. General Alexander Patch, commander of the US 7th Army, the close friend of Michael Daly's father. It was a sunny day. Generals and US senators stood close by on the platform.

Patch placed the blue ribbon of the award around Murphy's neck.

"Are you as nervous as I am?" asked Patch.

"I'm afraid I'm more so, sir," replied Murphy, the twenty-ninth man from the 3rd Division to receive the medal up to that date.

Patch smiled at the boy before him and then laughed. It was

one of the few truly joyous moments for the 7th Army commander during the entire war.

Patch turned to a table nearby and picked up another medal.
Then he pinned the Legion of Merit above Murphy's left pocket.
It was for "exceptionally meritorious conduct" and "outstanding
services" in France and Italy, from January 22, 1944, to February
18, 1945.[16]

Murphy showed no sign of the trauma that lay deep within.
He had a single white bar on the front of his helmet, the division
patch on his shoulder, a cheeky grin on his face.

"Lieutenant Murphy's personal bravery," Patch said, "his skill
in imparting his own knowledge of enemy tactics to his men,
and his voluntary assumption of hazardous patrols and missions
have benefited his unit to an immeasurable degree."[17]

Murphy then shook hands with no fewer than nine US senators, who had arrived in Salzburg that morning.

Also watching the ceremony was General "Iron Mike"
O'Daniel.

O'Daniel addressed his dogfaces, praising them for seizing
more territory than any other US division, reminding them that
Kesselring had said the Marne men were the best.

They had never given the Germans a rest.

Then the division band played "Dogface Soldier."

I'm just a Dogface Soldier,
With a rifle on my shoulder,
And I eat raw meat for breakfast every day.
So feed me ammunition,

Keep me in Third Division,
Your Dogface Soldier's A-okay.[18]

AFTER THE CEREMONY, a reporter asked Murphy what had made him courageous.

"Wanting to go back to Texas," said Murphy, "lack of sleep, anger, disgust, discomfort and hate—those things won me my medals, and they've won many other medals for many other guys."[19]

Murphy's fate was forever sealed. He would carry the burden of officially being World War II's gutsiest American—the most decorated of the sixteen million who had worn a uniform during the greatest conflict of modern times. He had in fact become the most decorated American soldier in history.

One of the reporters in Salzburg sent a story back to *Life* magazine, and within a few weeks, Audie Murphy would grace its cover, making him a nationwide star.[20] In more than two years of combat, he had fought in seven campaigns, in every theater of the war in Europe, and killed some two hundred forty enemy soldiers, an average of more than twenty per month.[21]

Murphy could return to the US or stay on in Europe to carry out occupation duties—as a captain, a jump in rank. Texas called too loudly. He wanted to go home. On June 10, 1945, Murphy flew to Paris and the next day crossed the Atlantic. He arrived in Texas three days later along with dozens of other veterans and several generals. The hip wound still irked Murphy as he limped down the steps from a C-54 plane at San Antonio airfield. He was the last to leave the plane, so shy he didn't even tell the welcoming party his name.

A crowd of two hundred fifty thousand lined the route to downtown San Antonio. Girls threw flowers. Petals drifted from the heavens. Everyone seemed to be smiling. As Murphy's party of elite, highly decorated soldiers passed the Alamo, several of the veterans spotted "genuine cowboys lolling around." "The welcome had all the color of a New Orleans Mardi Gras celebration and the glamor of a New York ticker tape parade," it was reported. "Roofs and windows of all the downtown buildings, as well as the streets, were jammed with spectators."[22]

Among the dignitaries assembled in San Antonio were thirteen generals, including Lucian Truscott and Alexander Patch, the true top brass, and other stars such as Jim Gavin, commander of the 82nd Airborne, and twenty-five-year-old Lt. Colonel James Minor, the youngest commander of a regiment in the war, with a Distinguished Service Cross and a Silver Star to his name.

A scrum of reporters surrounded Murphy at 4:30 P.M. at a press conference. One newsman noted that Murphy was "a big hit. His youth, pleasant personality, and bashful modesty drew people around him wherever he went."[23]

Reporters scrupulously wrote down Murphy's awards: the Medal of Honor, the Distinguished Service Cross, the Legion of Merit, two Silver Stars, the Bronze Star, the Croix de Guerre with palm leaves, and the Croix de Guerre with Silver Star.

"You have two clusters on your Purple Heart?"

"Yes," said Murphy, and then explained he'd gotten shot in the hip by a sniper and been wounded by shrapnel.

"I'd like to know every detail about how you won the Medal of Honor," a female reporter said.

"There wasn't much to it."[24]

The journalists looked at the medals on his chest.

"I wouldn't part with any one of them for anything," he said. "But in spite of that, they weren't worth what I went through. My birth certificate says I'm 21 years old, but I'm actually much older. You'll understand when you know more about the last few years of my life."

What did he plan to do?

"All I want to do is loaf and fish and sleep and see my friends. . . . I have 146 points toward a discharge, but if the army has something for me to do that will help them, the army comes first. I won't be sent into combat again unless I request it. And I won't. I'm not a fighting man. From here on, I want to like everybody."[25]

There was dinner in a banquet hall that night at 9:30 P.M.

Truscott and Patch and other top brass ate heartily.

There was a place of honor for Murphy.

At the end of the banquet—"a stuffed squab, chicken-under-glass affair"—a toastmaster stood up.[26]

Murphy was described as having won "every medal in the book."[27]

Heads turned. People raised themselves from their seats, ready to give Murphy a standing ovation.

There was no sign of the Texan.

According to one account, Murphy had left the banquet early, returned to the St. Anthony Hotel, limped across the Oriental carpets in the spacious lobby, past the Italian marble, Corinthian columns, and gold chandeliers, and stepped into an elevator. A pretty young woman operated the elevator. Making fast work of the ride to his floor, Murphy invited her to join him in his air-conditioned room with its mahogany moldings. Then he apparently sweet-talked her into bed. When he'd finished making love, Murphy was said to have topped off his first night back in America with a steak dinner. Then he fell into a deep sleep.[28]

A reporter from the Associated Press drove the next day with Murphy from San Antonio to north Texas. Murphy looked happy to be home as he gazed at well-fed cattle and the fields of corn and cotton.

"You can't realize how swell this is until you've been away," said Murphy. "Over there was a helluva thing. You got mad and tired and disgusted and you didn't care what happened to you. Bravery is determination to do a job that you know has to be done. And if you throw in discomforts and lack of sleep and anger, it's easier to be brave. Coldness and wetness and disgust have gotten medals for lots of soldiers."

Murphy pointed to a field nearby.

"This is enough for me."[29]

CHAPTER 16

Coming Home

WASHINGTON WAS UNBEARABLY humid. Eight days before, the Japanese had surrendered after the dropping of the atomic bombs on Hiroshima and Nagasaki. Lieutenant Michael Daly was still recovering from his severe face wounds but had been able to travel to the White House where, on August 23, 1945, he waited with other soldiers to receive the Medal of Honor.

Daly looked around the East Room of the White House, crowded with soldiers, generals, and the press. George C. Marshall, army chief of staff, entered the room and then began to shake the hand of each man. At 10 A.M. music played. The soldiers all stood up.

All hail the commander in chief.

Here came President Truman, all business, dressed in a light suit, the most powerful man on the planet.

A general arranged medals on a table.

Daly's name was called and he got to his feet and walked to

the center of the room, tall and thin and pale, his body covered in scars beneath his uniform. And then Truman was leaning in and hanging the medal from around his neck. There it was, dangling from a light blue ribbon . . . the ultimate prize—the award that General Patton, no less, once said he'd trade his soul for.

The thirty-third president of the United States adjusted the light blue ribbon on the medal. Cameras flashed. Daly was among the youngest of this batch of Medal of Honor recipients—a record twenty-eight in uniform.[1] Two men had their legs missing. Twenty-four had fought in the European Theater of Operations.[2] They hailed from nineteen states. There were three captains, five lieutenants, four privates, and sixteen sergeants.

Truman told Daly he'd rather have earned the medal than become president.

The flash of a camera. The resulting photo showed Daly with his eyes closed, as if he was being blessed—as if a priest, not a Missouri politician, was giving him a benediction.

From the ribbon at his neck there dangled the gold medal.

The medal had five points.

One word was clear to see.

VALOR.

Then Truman made a mistake. He saluted Daly. He should have waited for Daly to salute first. Daly returned to his seat and watched as Truman stepped to a microphone to say a few words. The men assembled here, said the president, loved peace but had adjusted themselves to the rigors and demands of war.

The widely seen newsreel and photos of the event showed the young officer then sitting in a back row, quiet and unsmiling, as Truman continued to address the assembled heroes. Two men were in wheelchairs. Twenty-eight-year-old Pfc. Silvestre S. Herrera from Arizona had seized a German position after losing his feet in a minefield, dragging himself onward with his hands. The other soldier, sitting a few yards in front, was Sergeant Ralph G. Neppel, twenty-one, from Glidden, Iowa. He'd stopped a tank after losing a leg and then killed twenty Germans.

The ceremonies were over after an hour and fifteen minutes. Reporters approached.

Daly was asked about the medal.

"Sometimes," he said, "things like this are harder to go through than battles."

Daly also told reporters that he had simply been "lucky." As with Lieutenant Audie Murphy and Lt. Colonel Keith Ware and so many others from his regiment, he was distinctly uncomfortable talking about his own record. The press should write instead about "the guys who didn't come." They were the ones "who deserve the medals."[3]

The following evening, he was back home in Connecticut, seated in an open-top car beside his father, Paul, riding in a motorcade.[4] Both had been seriously wounded in Europe. Both knew the price of victory. Father and son stared at the cheering crowds as rain poured down. Only one of them wore the Medal of Honor around his neck. Michael Daly wished that his father, who had twice been recommended for the medal in World War I, now wore the ultimate prize.[5] The medal already weighed heavy and set him apart from others, creating an even greater separation from those who had not experienced combat. He had been deified, it seemed, ordained as different from all the other young men who had come home. Already there was perhaps a fear that he might fail to live up to the expectations associated with being a public hero. Gone was the energizing mission, the all-consuming commitment to others he'd discovered in combat, in the bloodied rubble of Nazi Germany, leading scared young Americans.

In Fairfield, Daly walked into a packed Roger Ludlowe High School and onto a stage. He stood, painfully thin and bashful, before a thousand people who cheered him and clapped during a three-minute standing ovation. Several dignitaries lauded him. One said he was an example of the best of American manhood. Another compared him to his father—he was "a chip off the old block," as courageous.[6]

A priest asked God to bless him.

Because of his damaged throat, Daly had difficulty raising his voice but he managed to be gracious.

"I can't talk very well," said Daly, "but I want to say that this is the swellest thing that ever happened to me. A heck of a lot sweller than getting the medal from the President."[7]

On VJ Day, September 2, 1945, Daly spoke at a party held in his honor and again deflected attention from himself, placing it instead on other soldiers, adding once more that he had been darn lucky. A fortnight later, on September 15, he marked a major milestone—his twenty-first birthday. Daly's father ordered Daly's twelve-year-old brother, Gilroy, to drive father and son to popular watering holes in town. Daly Sr. dropped a fistful of dollars on each bar and bought each punter a round.

"This is on Michael!"[8]

Michael wasn't shy about knocking back a drink or two when others began to toast him, Fairfield's most famous World War II veteran. He had an Irishman's thirst. Over the next few months, like many returning veterans, he drank to excess. He liked to rough it up after too many beers, taking on anyone looking for a brawl. He didn't want to go back to West Point—he still resented the place. But he felt far too old, even though twenty-one, to attend some other college.[9] Daly had made it home but he was adrift, aimless without the sense of responsibility that came with holding other men's lives in his hands.

THE SUN SHONE as Audie Murphy climbed down the steps of a plane in Los Angeles on September 27, 1945. That day, he had been formally discharged from the US Army with the rank of first lieutenant. There to greet Murphy was none other than the legendary actor Jimmy Cagney, who had read about the young soldier that July in *Life* magazine.

Cagney wanted to help the handsome boy on the cover by bringing him to Hollywood and had sent an invite by telegram with the promise that all his expenses would be paid. "I knew Murphy only from his photographs," recalled then forty-five-year-old Cagney. "In reality he was terribly thin. His color was bluish gray. I had reserved a hotel room for him. But he looked so sick that I was afraid to leave him alone. I took him home and gave him my bed. This was after a three-month rest from combat. The war had taken a horrible toll on his nerves."[10]

Cagney allowed Murphy to stay in his guesthouse, and to pay his way Murphy did some yard work. He started to exercise, boxing at a local gym, slowly putting on weight, regaining color in his cheeks thanks to the California sunshine. Cagney proved to be extraordinarily generous, offering Murphy a film contract for $150 a week—a fortune to Murphy—if he agreed to go to acting school and lose his Texas drawl. Before long, he had learned to smile again. He was in Hollywood after all, where everyone sooner or later learned to fake it to make it.

MAJOR GENERAL KEITH Ware, the new commander of the military district of Washington, looked less than pleased. A pretty nineteen-year-old called Joyce had sent the major general an eviction notice, and here he was, in her office, in 1946, waving it in the air.

"Who sent me this?" asked thirty-one-year-old Ware.

Ware had stayed too long in his current digs. Joyce said she had a long list of men who needed to be housed. Regulations were regulations. In that case, Ware politely asked, could she help him find a new place? There was something familiar about him. She was sure she'd seen his face before. As luck would have it, she learned that a major was looking to share a two-bedroom apartment and arranged for Ware to move in as quickly as possible. To show his gratitude, Ware asked Joyce out on a date. Before long they were seeing each other regularly and then fell madly in love.

Joyce and Ware were married on May 3, 1947. About a year later, remembered Joyce, she looked through photographs Ware's mother had sent. One showed him lined up with four other Medal of Honor recipients in Nuremberg in April 1945. Joyce realized why Ware's face had been familiar when she first met him. She'd actually seen him on the big screen in a newsreel about the liberation of the city: "I'd gone to the movies with a girlfriend. The newsreel showed Keith and the four other men. Keith had on a pair of sunglasses and the others didn't. I told my friend: 'You know, the first guy there, with the sunglasses on, he's cute. I wish he didn't have those sunglasses on.' So, when I saw the photograph his mother had sent of him in Nuremberg . . . well, my heart stopped."

Oh, my God, destiny.[11]

Ware had been deeply affected by the war. Like many of his fellow veterans, she noticed, he liked a good stiff drink. "He had nightmares and I knew it was about the war," she remembered. "He'd be saying 'shoot this and go there,' things like that. His arms would move. I got pregnant five months after we were married. One night, he had a nightmare and he flung his arm and it almost hit my stomach."

She was lying on her back.

He had almost hit their unborn child. . . .

Oh, God, if he'd hit my stomach . . . what would it have done to me . . . ?

Joyce told Ware what had happened in his sleep. He began to open up about the war, the loss, the violence, all the pain. He couldn't bear the thought of hurting the two people he loved most.

EVENTUALLY, THE NIGHTMARES went away. But not for Ware's good friend Audie Murphy. By 1947, as Ware settled into married life, Murphy was struggling to find work. The contract he'd signed with James Cagney had expired and Murphy found

himself at a loose end, without income or, it seemed, any pros-
pects. These were hard days, living on unemployment, sleeping
in a dingy room above a Hollywood boxing gym.

To kill time, Murphy would put on the gloves and take on all
comers, wanting to work out his aggression and boredom. The
film director Budd Boetticher, himself a keen pugilist, remembered Murphy vividly during this period: "This young man, who
weighed about a hundred and forty-five, with a baby face, was
the only one who wanted to box with me and he would try to lick
me every day and I'd have to belt him once in a while to keep
him in line."

Around the same time that Murphy met Boetticher, he
started dating a young actress named Wanda Hendrix, and she
urged him to stay in Hollywood and make a go of it. He shouldn't
quit and go back to Texas. Sure enough, his luck changed. Murphy met a journalist who fed the notorious columnist Hedda
Hopper gossip stories. His name was David "Spec" McClure, he
was also a World War II veteran, and the two bonded. Through
McClure and his connections such as Hopper, Murphy got a bit
part in a romantic comedy, *Texas, Brooklyn and Heaven*, and
featured in another 1948 movie called *Beyond Glory*, set at West
Point. It starred Donna Reed and Alan Ladd. He had to say eight
words, remembered Murphy, "seven more than I could handle."[12] Then he was cast in the lead role in the B movie *Bad Boy*
and impressed executives enough to get hired by Universal International to star in another movie, *The Kid from Texas*.

Murphy found time in 1948, between movies, to return to
Europe for the first time since the war, a guest of the French
government. His friend "Spec" McClure accompanied him. On

the way to a reception in the village of Ramatuelle, near Saint-Tropez, Murphy told his driver to pull up. He jogged through a vineyard to a drainage ditch and then made his way up Pill Box Hill toward a cork tree. He was back where he had earned the Distinguished Service Cross, where his best friend, Lattie Tipton, had been senselessly killed. He found the spot where Tipton had breathed his last.

Nearby was a mound, and at one end, there was a cross. "Spec" McClure watched as Murphy "took off his army cap, held it over his heart, and stared silently at the grave. I never saw [Audie] humble himself except in the presence of the dead. I think he grieved all his life for the friends he'd lost in combat."[13]

The people he'd set free were as poor as Murphy remembered, their pain and memories still fresh. In Alsace, he explored the Colmar Pocket. He'd never seen the landscape without a thick crust of snow and ice. In the village of Holtzwihr, near where Murphy had earned the Medal of Honor, he was greeted by a large crowd and the town's mayor, who was wearing a shabby old black coat. Murphy would never forget the look of joy on the faces of the children singing Alsatian folk songs in his honor. It was all too much and the tears came streaming.[14]

Murphy returned to the US and his fledgling Hollywood career. He married Wanda Hendrix on February 8, 1949. The union was rocky from the start. According to Hendrix, Murphy still had nightmares about combat and slept with a pistol under his pillow—hardly an aphrodisiac. There was one name he'd call out over and over.

Lattie.

Waking from horrific dreams, he grabbed for his pistol and

one night blew a light switch to smithereens. There was so much buried trauma. A mirror and a clock on a wall were perfectly holed. He was ever the ace shot. It was a brave woman who shared a bed with him. "The big thing in his life was his guns," claimed Wanda Hendrix. "He cleaned them every day and caressed them for hours. . . . There were times he held me at gunpoint for no reason at all. Then he would turn around and put the gun in his own mouth. I finally told him one night to go ahead and shoot. He put the gun away and turned all white."[15]

Murphy and Wanda Hendrix divorced in 1951. She claimed she'd been so traumatized by Murphy during their marriage that she had become mentally and physically ill. "I was in no shape to get married," Murphy himself later admitted. "I had nightmares about the war—men running and shooting and hollering and then my gun would fall apart when I tried to pull the trigger."[16]

Murphy couldn't be without a woman and remarried, this time taking Pamela Archer, a young air hostess from Dallas, as his bride—just four days after his divorce from Wanda was finalized. Good fortune followed. The prestigious director John Huston chose Murphy, much to the displeasure of studio bosses, to play the lead in an adaptation of Stephen Crane's classic *The Red Badge of Courage*. When Huston met with Murphy the first day on set, he asked Murphy if he was excited. There was an awkward silence before Murphy answered honestly: "Well, after the war and all, there's not too much left that really excites me."[17]

Huston found the response unsettling. He was, however, able to coax a fine performance from the man whom he would later describe as a "gentle-eyed, little killer." During filming, Murphy befriended another World War II veteran, cartoonist and writer Bill Mauldin, who had a role in the movie. Several times in the script, Mauldin's character goaded Stephen Crane's young soldier Henry Fleming, played by Murphy. "There's something mighty incongruous about saying, 'Whatsa matter, ya skeered?' to a scrappy character," remembered Mauldin, "who had in real life clobbered a fair-sized portion of the German Army. The script was even harder on poor Murph. Every time I sneered the awful taunt at him, the back of his neck turned dull red and his hands began to curl into fists. After several unsuccessful retakes, he whirled on me and said, 'Listen, you rear-echelon ink-slinger, I know we're only play-acting, but you don't have to say that like you meant it!'"[18]

In 1955, Murphy starred in *To Hell and Back*, an adaptation of a bestselling autobiography ghostwritten by his friend "Spec" McClure. Murphy initially refused to appear as himself, not wanting fellow veterans to think he was cashing in on his war experiences, saying the actor Tony Curtis would do a better job. But he was finally persuaded to take the role and so began a surreal experience, reliving the most intense moments of his life, actually acting them out, such as when his mother died and his best friend, Lattie Tipton, was killed.

The film's director, Jesse Hibbs, recalled that Murphy "didn't seem to think about acting. There was a primitive alertness about him. He reacted to every explosion and every sound of machine-gun fire instinctively."[19] When it came to reenacting Tipton's death, Murphy had to dig deep and filming was delayed until he was able to find the courage to relive the trauma. The film concluded with a scene of Murphy receiving the Medal of

Honor, an ending that he despised and wanted to cut. Hibbs barely persuaded Murphy to keep it.

The film reconnected Murphy with arguably the man he respected more than any other in his life—Lt. Colonel Keith Ware, his former commanding officer. Murphy contacted Ware, then teaching at West Point, and asked him to become the technical consultant on the film, relishing the prospect of going to war once again with the soft-spoken gentleman whose life he had so gladly saved in October 1944. Sadly, Ware had to decline the offer because he could not leave his duties at West Point, where he was a much-valued instructor in psychology and leadership. Of more value to both men was the rekindling of their relationship.

Although Ware could not find the time to help Murphy with the film, he kept abreast of developments. At one point, Murphy told Ware he'd had to change the way he walked. He'd always had the gait of a stalker, even before he'd learned how to hunt as a boy, and of course he had limped after the war because of his hip injury. To please studio chiefs, he'd had to straighten his back and walk upright, head held high.[20]

The film ended up being a smash hit, making Murphy more than $400,000, a large sum in the 1950s. Although Murphy gambled and spent too freely, he managed to save enough to buy a horse ranch outside Los Angeles and devoted more and more of his time to it. He bought a plane and became an excellent pilot. He was perhaps at his happiest when flying from Hollywood to his ranch to be with his horses. At the height of his success, he stressed in one interview that he'd not starred as himself out of vanity or to glamorize violence. He hated what war had done to his generation, so much so that he'd wanted to give away all his medals when he'd returned to the US in 1945. "War is a nasty business," he believed, "to be avoided if possible, and to be gotten over with as soon as possible. It's not the sort of job that deserves medals."[21]

ON THE EAST Coast, Murphy's regimental comrade, Michael Daly, had struggled since the war to find a clear direction. After one particularly wild night on the town, he was arrested for fighting and forced to cool off behind bars. Then everything changed. There was one Sunday in 1957 when the Smith family came to visit the Daly clan. The Smiths brought a strikingly attractive thirty-six-year-old woman called Margaret Miller with them. She had been divorced for six years and had two young children and a glamorous past, having appeared as an actress on Broadway.[22]

Miller's divorce had been hard on her. She wasn't looking for another husband. Even so, Daly and she were quickly smitten with each other. But they had to wait until Miller's marriage was dissolved before being able to wed in the Roman Catholic Church, which was what Daly wanted to please his parents. They finally did on January 31, 1959, and then spent a year in Ireland, living simply in a spartan cottage in a small village called Glen of the Downs in County Wicklow.[23] A daughter called Deirdre was born during the yearlong honeymoon, much of it spent roaming nearby hills and along the banks of the Three Trouts River, which flowed into the whitecapped Irish Sea a few miles to the east.

The war was never to be discussed and Daly's memories were

locked away like the many medals he had stowed in a velvet-lined case. It was not until the early 1960s, when he got involved with a local hospital, St. Vincent's, volunteering and then raising funds, that he found a "cause greater than self," as he described it, a true sense of purpose to his life. Through devoting himself to the patients and staff of the hospital—run by a Roman Catholic order of nuns in nearby Bridgeport—Daly rediscovered a spirit of service. He would eventually serve on the hospital's board for more than thirty years, becoming its "conscience." Above all, he cared about the poorest patients and those who were terminally ill, comforting them, often attending their funerals.[24] In combat, there had rarely been time to mourn, to show love other than by risking his life to save his men. At last, he could say goodbye.

KEITH WARE, DALY's former battalion commander, was promoted to a one star and sent to the Pentagon in 1964. The *New York Times* reported: "Brig. Gen. Keith L. Ware, a Medal of Honor winner, has been chosen as deputy chief of information for the Army."[25] Ware did a rare interview upon his appointment, telling the *Army Times* that the famous movie star Audie Murphy had been one of his men during World War II and, he stressed, the "finest soldier [he'd] ever seen . . . because of his outstanding leadership ability, even old pros followed his commands."[26]

Ware had patiently risen through the ranks, an ever-dutiful "workaholic," according to his wife, Joyce. He had earned a degree from George Washington University and his teaching position at West Point had only increased his pedigree. The army had become his essence. When President Eisenhower asked him to become his senior military adviser in the 1950s, Ware refused, protesting that he hated politics, but the real reason was that he wanted to rise further in the ranks.[27] Finally, after two years at the Pentagon, he made history. In 1966, he became a major general—the first and to date only draftee ever to rise from private to general officer.[28]

MAURICE BRITT, LIKE Keith Ware, enjoyed considerable success after the war. He too had found a sense of purpose. He had returned to Arkansas, to the town of Fort Smith, and worked in a furniture manufacturing business, the Mitchell Company, which his wife's father owned. He became the doting father of five children.[29] In the early sixties, increasingly involved in Democratic politics, Britt started his own company, making aluminum products. Sadly, his first marriage did not survive, and after divorcing, he remarried in 1966. That same year he joined the Republican Party, dismayed by the segregationist views held by many Arkansas Democrats, and he was elected lieutenant governor of Arkansas, appealing to new Black voters.[30]

On assuming office, Britt received a congratulatory message from the only man who had topped his medal count in World War II.

"Is there anything you can't do?" asked Audie Murphy.

"I ain't no movie star yet," replied Britt.[31]

Thanks to Murphy, Britt had escaped the curse of celebrity. Because of Murphy the media had mostly left Britt alone.

Although he still suffered from his wounds, Britt had come to terms with the loss of his arm and felt no bitterness.

AUDIE MURPHY COULD never escape his demons. In 1967, the year after Britt was first elected to office, Murphy told an *Esquire* reporter: "To become an executioner, somebody cold and analytical, to be trained to kill, and then to return to civilian life and be alone in the crowd—it takes an awful long time to get over it. Fear and depression come over you. It's been twenty-odd years already, and the doctors say the effect of all this on my generation won't reach its peak until 1970. So, I guess I got three years to go."

Murphy was by then living on Toluca Road in Hollywood, in a large brick-and-shingle house. In Murphy's garden, there were bushes of roses actually named after him—Audie Murphy roses, not far from a flagpole.

Esquire reporter Thomas Morgan had been sent to Los Angeles to write a profile of Murphy and duly spent several days with him. Naturally, Morgan asked about his medals. Murphy said he didn't have his full set—he'd given a few to kids in the neighborhood. Besides, he didn't like wearing them in public anymore, didn't want anyone making a fuss about his record. He'd been invited to President Kennedy's inauguration in 1960, as all Medal of Honor recipients had been, but had declined.

Murphy had a small potbelly, haunted blue eyes, red-brown hair starting to turn gray. He loved to play pool in his garage for four-dollar stakes.

"We don't entertain often, that's for sure," said Murphy. "Tell you the truth, I've never gotten along with Hollywood people and they don't get along with me."

Murphy didn't seem to care about stardom one iota.

He'd made a lot of money . . . but so what?

"If I hadn't been in the movies, I might have been a farmer." He laughed, then added: "A happy farmer!"

Why hadn't Murphy stayed in the army?

"Wasn't my decision," Murphy claimed. "West Point turned me down because too much of my right hip was gone. I can't swim because of it. I've got other ailments besides. Fifty percent disability—shrapnel in my legs, a nervous stomach, regular headaches. So listen, I didn't want to be an actor. It was simply the best offer that came along."

The nightmares had never gone away. He'd been addicted to pills and gone cold turkey by locking himself in a hotel room and sweating it out: "I stayed in there for five days, having withdrawal pains like a junkie. I had convulsions. But I quit. I stopped the pills and I quit gambling. The past year I feel like I've been starting my life all over again. I've been sleeping lately—most nights anyway. But I won't take any more pills. Not one."

As a soldier, living in hell, Murphy had been at his best.

"There's this to say about combat," he stressed. "It brings out the best in men. It's gory and it's unfortunate, but most people in combat stand a little taller."

He'd loved being a part of Company B, 15th Infantry Regiment, 3rd Division: "You trust the man on your left and on your right with your life, while, as a civilian, you might not trust either of them with ten cents."[32]

Morgan concluded that Murphy was "more than the war hero

of our time. He was a casualty—so much of his spirit, in fact, had
been killed in action."[33]

The start of a new decade, Murphy's sixth, did not augur well.
In a bizarre episode in May 1970, he became involved in a violent
altercation with a dog trainer that led to serious charges of assault. As ever, Murphy had been carrying a gun.

A new headline appeared:

"AUDIE MURPHY HELD FOR ASSAULT; WAR HERO MURPHY: I DIDN'T HAVE A GUN."[34]

Murphy was acquitted of all charges.

"Audie, did you shoot at that guy?" asked a reporter.

"If I had," drawled Murphy, "do you think I would have
missed?"[35]

OF THE MARNE men who had been among the most decorated
of World War II—Murphy, Britt, Ware, and Daly—one had remained in uniform, and by 1967, he yearned to lead men again
in combat. It was in Major General Keith Ware's bones. Scheduled to go to Germany to take command of a division, instead
he paid a visit to the silver-haired chief of staff of the United
States Army, General Harold K. Johnson, in the Pentagon.[36]
Johnson was a canny tactician and a keen admirer of Ware—he
too had commanded a battalion of the 3rd Division, in his case
in the Korean War, and he was increasingly frustrated that the
government was asking the US military to wage a war in Vietnam without full mobilization of resources.

Not long after Ware's meeting with Johnson, Ware's wife, Joyce, received a call from Johnson, a survivor of the infamous Bataan Death March in World War II.

"Joyce, Keith and I had a talk," said Johnson. "Keith wants to go to Vietnam and not to Germany."

Germany was, of course, a much safer option.

Joyce simply had to say the word and Johnson would send Ware to Europe.

Vietnam was a lousy place, best avoided. The Communist forces, Johnson believed, had a distinct advantage—they decided when to engage the US troops, choosing the terrain and tactics, avoiding pitched battles. A new approach was needed—massive support for counterinsurgency to pacify the country. But President Lyndon Johnson made a key decision—he decided not to mobilize the US Army's reserves. This was not going to be a full-out all-or-nothing conflict like World War II. It was clear to General Johnson that the White House was not committed to victory in Southeast Asia.

Joyce Ware knew where her husband belonged. He arrived in Vietnam in early January 1968, just before his new enemy launched a massive surprise attack on US and South Vietnamese forces, the Tet Offensive. Thirty-five battalions of Vietcong fighters targeted Saigon, and for several days, it looked as if the capital of South Vietnam might fall.

As deputy commander of II Field Force, Ware was ordered to fly by helicopter with a group of senior officers to take command of all US forces fighting in the city. If the US military lost control of Saigon, the repercussions would be catastrophic. The American people's support for the conflict, already dipping, would erode far faster. If the Green Machine, as the US military in Vietnam was dubbed, could not hold the capital of South Vietnam against a bunch of ill-equipped Communist peasants, then what chance was there of winning the war?

Lt. Colonel William Schroeder, Ware's operations officer, took off for Saigon with Ware on the morning of February 1, 1968. "General Ware was a very impressive individual," he recalled. "He never got excited, never raised his voice, never wore his rank on his sleeve like so many of them did. He was a good, soft-spoken soldier, and his calm demeanor instilled a lot of confidence."

Ware and Schroeder were headed to an army compound in central Saigon, near a street called Le Van Duyet. "During the approach we could see groups of Viet Cong running right down Le Van Duyet," remembered Schroeder. The Huey carrying Ware and Schroeder touched down close to the army compound. Ware was wearing a backpack radio, and he jumped down from the Huey and then hopped into a jeep. "There was an overweight US Air Force master sergeant at the wheel," remembered Schroeder. "He was sweating blood, and shouting, 'Let's get the hell out of here!' It was a little hairy. We were taking small-arms fire from the roofs of the apartment-type buildings around the compound. We made a mad dash around barrels that protected the entrance from a suicide attack . . . through it all the general was as cool as a cucumber."[37]

By 11 A.M. that morning, Task Force Ware was up and running. Ware's men seized Phu Tho Racetrack later that afternoon after fierce combat. It was a vital objective—the only place in Saigon where several helicopters could land at once. Ware reinforced his troops and, on February 3, deployed elements of several units, including the 101st Airborne and the 1st Division, to secure the city. The heavy lifting done, he ordered his task force on February 5 to pull out of Saigon to make way for the ARVN—South Vietnamese forces—who had asked to be given the honor of clearing the capital of the last remaining Vietcong. It made for good publicity in both Vietnam and back in the US and saved American lives.

By March 7, 1968, Saigon was back under control. Ware's superb leadership under extreme pressure had been noted on high and he was rewarded with command of the 1st Infantry Division. It was a great honor for Ware to take over such a storied fighting force. The Big Red One had received sixteen Congressional Medals of Honor in World War II compared to the Marne men's forty but it had been and still was a proud division.

Ware was back in his element. He wore sunglasses similar to those he had carried that sunny day in April 1945 in Nuremberg when the light blue ribbon was placed around his neck. He was at the sharp end again, visiting the front lines to encourage his men and see for himself what needed to be done. On March 20, 1968, a fortnight after Saigon had been secured, Ware arrived at an outpost near Thu Duc, close to the Saigon River, and pinned medals to the chests of four men from the 18th Infantry Regiment. "He was a true inspiration for all soldiers," remembered one of the decorated men. "Leaving, his Huey conked out in mid-air and his pilot brought it back down on auto-rotate. He had an incredible military history and lived it to its fullest."[38] Another soldier recalled Ware carrying "a case of mason jars, each one filled with a grenade with the pin pulled out, and [he] would fly over us during a firefight and lob these glass jars with perfect aim at the enemy positions."[39]

Ware's superiors arranged for him to be promoted to lieutenant general, even sending three-star flags to his headquarters.[40] There was no telling how far he would then rise after he'd been promoted. Many believed he had the experience and demeanor to become a future army chief of staff.

Early on Friday, September 13, 1968, during the Battle of Lộc Ninh, Ware again boarded a Huey, intent on visiting the front lines. He took along his pet dog, King, a white German shepherd, a gift from men who fought with his division's long-range reconnaissance patrol.[41] Later that morning, he landed near Lộc Ninh inside Cambodia and then conferred with his field commanders, issuing crisp, precise orders.

There was "heavy action" in the area. At 12:52 P.M., shortly after taking off in bad weather with cloud cover at seven hundred feet, his helicopter was hit by intense enemy machine-gun fire.[42]

Ted Englemann was a young radio operator working at a nearby base camp. He listened carefully to messages coming over the radio.

"Danger 6 is down."[43]

Danger 6 was the call sign for Ware—for the commanding general of the Big Red One.

Ware's helicopter had gone down in thick jungle.

Were there any survivors?

There were more messages, more calls. It turned out that no one had lived—fifty-two-year-old Ware, three senior officers, four crew, and the white German shepherd King, were all dead.

Engelmann would never forget September 13, 1968: "I felt responsible for Ware's death. Basically, nobody dies on my watch. That's what I was thinking. Right? And especially not a general—damn right. Especially not Maj. Gen. Keith Ware. It would have been bad enough if some private had been blown away, but you know—the major general of the division. Holy mackerel. That sort of stuff doesn't happen."[44] But it did. And he would carry the guilt for almost twenty years, finding the memories especially painful every September 13.[45]

Ware was buried in Arlington National Cemetery, the highest-ranking army general killed in Vietnam—the only soldier to receive the Medal of Honor, since World War I, who was killed in a later war.[46] President Johnson attended his funeral. Ware was posthumously awarded the Distinguished Service Cross in October 1968, meaning he had finally matched his fellow Marne men Maurice Britt and Audie Murphy in receiving the Bronze Star, Silver Star, DSC, and Medal of Honor.[47]

AMONG THOSE MOST saddened by the news of Ware's death were his former comrades from World War II, notably Audie Murphy, who reportedly took "the news report of Ware's death very hard."[48] For Murphy, Ware was perhaps a last link to a more vibrant, ironically innocent time. Murphy was still able to center himself at times—when he had to play his old self, the dutiful soldier, ever bound by honor to his brothers-in-arms. He refused to appear in cigarette and alcohol commercials, ever aware that as the most decorated soldier in US history he should try to set a good example. "The war floats through my mind like flotsam and jetsam," Murphy told one reporter. "It is no big thing. But when the war was on, somebody had to fight it. Hitler was not playing marbles. People seem to forget that these days."[49]

In 1970, as protests about the Vietnam War tore America apart, Murphy worried that his two teenage sons would be drafted and sent to Vietnam, a war he could no longer support. "It's not right to ask young men to risk their lives in wars they can't win," he told an interviewer. "I'll tell you what bothers me. What if my sons try to live up to my image? What if people expect it of them? I've talked to them about it. I want them to be whatever they are. I don't want them to try to be what I was. I don't want dead heroes for sons."[50]

On May 28, 1971, a blue-and-white twin-engine plane— painted in the colors of the 3rd Division—took off from Atlanta and flew toward Martinsville in Virginia. Murphy was on the plane. Friends felt Murphy was about to make a comeback. He'd flown to Virginia hopeful of beginning a new business venture. An associate had told him he'd be richer than Croesus.

There was a problem. The pilot called ground control in Roanoke and reported that he was going to land in twenty minutes because of rough weather. He never did, crashing instead into a mountain near Roanoke.[51] There were no survivors. Murphy's mangled corpse was identified due to a nine-inch scar—caused by that damned German sniper's bullet in Alsace a quarter century before.

There was a memorial service on June 4 in Los Angeles. Six recipients of the Medal of Honor attended. The big names in

Hollywood couldn't be bothered to turn up. They weren't his type anyway. Wanda Hendrix, Murphy's first wife, was there to grieve. She had never stopped loving him. In tears, she told the press: "He was a great soldier. No one can ever take that away from him. May he rest in peace."[52]

Murphy's funeral was held on June 7 at Arlington National Cemetery. General O'Daniel, who had led the 3rd Division to victory in World War II, was there to mourn his finest soldier, to watch Murphy be buried not far from the Ampitheater of the Tomb of the Unknown Soldier. There were forty other Marne men, all there to pay their respects. General William Westmoreland, who had commanded US forces in Vietnam from 1964 until the year Keith Ware was killed, came to say goodbye. World War II veteran George H. W. Bush, then ambassador to the United Nations, was at the gravesite. So too were Audie's second wife and his two sons.

Several soldiers played the 3rd Division anthem, "Dogface Soldier":

> *I wouldn't trade my old OD's*
> *For all the navy's dungarees*
> *For I'm the walking pride*
> *Of Uncle Sam.*
>
> *On army posters that I read*
> *It says "Be All That You Can"*
> *So they're tearing me down*
> *To build me over again.*[53]

———

WORLD WAR II's most decorated soldier, who had defied all odds on the battlefield, was finally laid to rest. There was precious little commemoration on television. America was tired of war. People seemed to have forgotten what he had defeated, what he had risked his life so many times to end—Nazism and all its attendant evils. Murphy's friend Bill Mauldin perhaps summed him up best in *Life* magazine: "In him we all recognized the straight, raw stuff, uncut and fiery as the day it left the still. Nobody wanted to be in his shoes, but nobody wanted to be unlike him, either."[54]

LIKE AUDIE MURPHY, Michael Daly stayed close to his former comrades. A decade after the war, Daly was invited back to France by the American Battle Monuments Commission, and he joined other recipients of the Medal of Honor in the recently completed Rhone American Cemetery in Provence. *National Geographic* magazine reported that there were 861 markers in the smallest of the six "overseas military shrines" dedicated to America's World War II fallen, consecrated in 1956.

Draguignan was a sad place. The previous winter it had been so cold that two hundred olive trees had been killed. "The memorial stood in perhaps the loveliest natural setting of all," noted a reporter. "Removal of the trees, cut down at ground level, left a pathetic emptiness."[55]

The sun shone as Daly met with fellow Marne man Robert Maxwell, who had received the Medal of Honor for his actions near Besançon in September 1944. The two were photographed amid perfect rows of white crosses. Both understood the pressures that came with receiving the Medal of Honor. They were held to a higher standard than other veterans. But they hadn't chosen to earn the ultimate prize. They didn't want to be put on a pedestal, didn't want to be lionized or treated as special in any way. "Anybody would have done what I did," Daly later insisted.[56]

Daly felt a heavy "responsibility" because of the honors he'd received. He had pushed his luck to the very limit in combat, spending so much time "out front." He knew how blessed he'd been to beat the odds, to come home: "There are an awful lot of things done in war that people do not see and I always felt that the real heroes were killed in action in the infantry, people who took the most chances. Without that type of soldier, you never win a battle. Somebody has to attack. The medal I wear is in their memory."[57]

The war cast a long shadow. Daly's first child, his daughter Deirdre, noticed how much it preoccupied her father at times.[58] "I used to wonder why my father looked back so much, even more as he got older," she recalled. Then one summer, when she was the same age as her father on D Day, she hitchhiked from Paris to Omaha Beach. Soaked to the skin by a heavy rain, she slept in a greenhouse in a garden not far from the crashing waves and then walked Bloody Omaha the next morning, thinking of her father wading ashore in Easy Red sector. It was a pilgrimage, a quest to comprehend why his time in combat had mattered so much. "Now I understand," she later explained. "It's probably the one time in life when you are willing to sacrifice everything for the guy alongside you. You never have that again. You forget the carnage and sadness and you remember one thing—you had a cause greater than self."[59]

Michael Daly's father had certainly understood the sanctity of that cause, having served with honor and great courage in two world wars. Paul Daly passed away on June 10, 1974, aged eighty-two. According to one report: "There was a three-day Irish wake for the Colonel who was laid out in his living room in uniform with a flag draped by the coffin. It was a diverse group of mourners who cried and laughed and ate and drank—horseplayers and Democrats and veterans. Friends said that the Colonel would finally get to ask Napoleon why he had blundered at Waterloo."[60]

Aged fifty-eight, Michael Daly returned to Europe one last time in 1982 to visit those serving in his old unit—A Company of the legendary 15th Infantry Regiment of the 3rd Division—based not far from Nuremberg, where Daly had been badly injured on April 19, 1945. He noted that the suite he was allocated on the army base was named after good old Audie Murphy, B Company commander in the Battle of the Colmar Pocket. That first evening back in Germany, his sleep was fitful as lost warriors in the 15th Infantry Regiment came back to him—the ones who had not beaten the odds. More than sixteen hundred men from his regiment had given their lives in World War II. Yet he was glad the "faces had come back" for he'd begun to fear that when the "memories dimmed he would become a stranger to himself."[61]

Dawn. So many times in the war, this had been the worst time, waiting in the cold and darkness to go into battle, praying, wondering if he'd live to see another day. Before it was light,

Daly got up and dressed. He crossed a field and stood beside some memorials. The sun began to rise. He was remembering the long days of combat, in the Colmar Pocket, in Normandy, in Nuremberg.

The following evening, wearing his Medal of Honor, he told his audience of young Marne men that his heart would always belong to the "dogface soldiers" of the 3rd Division. He did not normally wear the medal at his neck. But this evening was special. His was talking to infantrymen with the finest heritage in the US military.

"There was no better division in Europe than the 3rd Division of my day," said Daly. "I had the good fortune to serve with the First and Third Divisions—both excellent—but my heart will always be with the Third. They had some of the most difficult tasks—they took many casualties but in the end they always prevailed. We lost some of our best people. As you know they were often men who took the most chances and without them you could never win a battle. As a platoon leader and company commander they sustained me then just as their memory sustains me now.

"Now standing here with me tonight are all the great Third Division soldiers of the past—some of their faces flash through my memory—some still alive and many gone and those gone must be standing with the angels. . . . Remember that wonderful line . . . 'Courage is the thing. Everything goes if courage goes.' Without courage there is no protection for our other virtues. Every man loses his courage at times. All of us should pray every morning that God will give us the courage to do what is right."

He had never made a speech that meant so much.

Civilians had never understood the brotherhood of soldiers.[62]

Each man, Daly added, "deserves a cause greater than self."

His men in World War II had been that greater cause.

His audience stood and applauded for a long time.

"Remember us for as long as you can," Daly asked the young Marne men.[63]

MAURICE BRITT ALSO drew closer to his fellow warriors as the decades passed, regularly attending reunions and annual meetings of the Congressional Medal of Honor Society. His wounds still pained him but he never complained—not once in the fifty years since he'd had his arm blown off. A grandson, Chris Britt, recalled asking his grandfather: "'How come you're not a movie star like Audie Murphy?' . . . He [was] happy to be in second place and be quiet and calm and family-focused instead of being paraded around the country."[64]

Maurice Britt squeezed as much as he could from life, getting along as best as he could with one lung, one arm. The scars of war still covered his aging frame but not his psyche. Whenever he stood up, he felt the past—a piece of shrapnel was still lodged in his left foot. Other than each medal for valor, Maurice Britt had received four Purple Hearts, one more than Audie Murphy.

The piece of German metal in his foot was finally removed in October 1995. There were complications during the surgery and he needed further operations to combat infection to his old wound. But it all proved too much for his heart, no longer so stout, and he passed away in Little Rock, Arkansas, on November 26, 1995, aged seventy-six.[65] Britt was laid in state, his coffin left open, his World War II combat jacket hanging from the back of his favorite rocking chair, which had been placed close by. Each of his medals was on display.

The *New York Times* reported on his extraordinary war record and noted that he had been "the first Republican elected lieutenant governor in Arkansas since Reconstruction . . . and paved the way for a new generation of Arkansas politicians, including Democrats in a new mold, like Bill Clinton."[66] In another obituary, he was described not as the bravest of the so-called Greatest Generation but as the "First of the Bravest," the first American in history to win every medal for valor in a single war.[67]

Each Memorial Day, for as long as his legs could carry him, Michael Daly paid his respects to his fallen comrades in Fairfield, Connecticut.[68] Then he would get into his car and drive through the towns and villages along the coast of Long Island Sound, sometimes stopping to take a long walk on a beach, alone with his memories. He would then head home, returning after dark to his wife, Maggie. "He really mourns," she told one reporter. "Everybody else is having picnics, but he's alone, mourning."[69]

Although several decades had passed, Daly's feelings about West Point remained complicated.[70] Invited to visit the academy in 2002, along with other Medal of Honor recipients, he asked that cadets currently being punished, as he had, receive an amnesty during his visit. To his dismay, he was told that amnesties were given only when heads of state and royalty visited. "I went to West Point and was a failure at the academy," Daly told an audience of high school students at Fairfield High School in 2004. He had been "a mediocre student with severe disciplinary problems, on special confinement, continuously walking off punishment tours. At the end of my plebe year I left and was glad to leave. But there is something about the place that sticks to your ribs."

The high school students listened in rapt attention.

"We all lose our courage at times. It is something we pray for in the morning—that God will give us the strength and courage to do what is right."[71]

Four years later, in 2008, Michael Daly learned that he had pancreatic cancer. His last fight did not last long.[72] He faced the end with the same courage he had summoned in combat, pointing out that he should by rights have died in Nuremberg. As the end approached, his daughter Deirdre comforted him at his bedside. The pain medication sometimes made him hallucinate, taking him to "another place." One day, his daughter asked what he had seen in the beyond. He described a tunnel. At the end of it, there stood a young man.

"How did the young man look?"

"Forlorn."

Perhaps he was remembering the young private, his own age, whom he'd watched drift off into death in the Colmar Pocket in the last, bitter winter of the war.

The afterlife finally beckoned, a place according to his daughter "where he would take care of people."[73]

A priest gave Michael Daly last rites that July 2008 as he lay on his deathbed in his home. Before saluting the priest, Daly told him that the "world needs peacemakers. Anyone can shoot a gun."[74]

ACKNOWLEDGMENTS

Many thanks to Bob Maxwell, the oldest living recipient of the Medal of Honor before he passed in 2019. Bob hosted me in Oregon for two wonderful days. He was both inspiration and vital source, providing a vivid picture of life on the front lines with the 3rd Division in World War II. While in Oregon, Dick Tobiason was also most gracious. I am grateful to Anse Speairs and Louis Graziano for recounting their time in combat. I am indebted to the Society of the 3rd Division, particularly Henry Bodden and Toby Knight. Melissa Van Drew provided great information about Audie Murphy and pointed me to wonderful new materials held at the Audie Murphy Research Foundation. 15th Infantry Regiment historian Tim Stoy provided incredible help and support, including several hundred vital documents, after-action reports, unpublished accounts gathered from his many years of research, and photos from the National Archives. His wisdom and passion were invaluable. Tim Frank, historian at Arlington National Cemetery, took me to the graves of Audie Murphy and Keith Ware and also unearthed an invaluable interview he conducted back in the nineties with Michael Daly.

The following institutions provided critical archival materials: the National Archives, West Point, the Smithsonian, the Library of Congress, Geoffrey Stark at the University of Arkansas, the First Infantry Division Museum, the 3rd Infantry Division Museum, and the George Marshall Foundation. Melissa Smith sent wonderful images. Ryan Smith unearthed great material in Arkansas. Andrew Woods, research historian, Colonel Robert R. McCormick Research Center, First Division Museum at Cantigny Park, provided fine detail about Keith Ware and his time in Vietnam. Chris Britt was most generous in explaining his grandfather's family and postwar history. Deirdre Daly spoke to me at length about her father and sent a beautiful speech from which I have quoted extensively. Joyce Ware talked with great lucidity and detail about her husband, Keith Ware. Lottie Landra did great photo research. Amy Squiers transcribed many hours of interviews. My wife, Robin, did fantastic design work. John Snowdon helped greatly as I walked the battlefields in Europe. In Alsace, Patrick Baumann showed me where Audie Murphy earned the Medal of Honor. My agent, Jim Hornfischer, was awesome. Again, the team at Dutton has been fantastic to work with, in particular, my editor, Brent Howard.

SELECTED BIBLIOGRAPHY

Adleman, Robert H., and Colonel George Walton. *The Champagne Campaign*. New York: Little, Brown, 1969.

———. *The Devil's Brigade*. New York: Chilton Books, 1966.

Allen, William L. *Anzio: Edge of Disaster*. New York: Dutton, 1978.

Arnold-Foster, Mark. *The World at War*. New York: Stein & Day, 1973.

Atkinson, Rick. *The Day of Battle*. New York: Henry Holt, 2007.

———. *The Guns at Last Light*. New York: Henry Holt, 2013.

Bessel, Richard. *Germany 1945*. New York: HarperCollins, 2009.

Biddle, George. *Artist at War*. New York: Viking Press, 1944.

Bishop, Leo V., George A. Fisher, and Frank J. Glasgow. *The Fighting Forty-Fifth: The Combat Report of an Infantry Division*. Baton Rouge, LA: Army & Navy Publishing, 1946.

Blumenson, Martin. *Bloody River*. Boston: Houghton Mifflin, 1970.

———. *Patton*. New York: William Morrow, 1985.

———. *The Patton Papers*. Boston: Houghton Mifflin, 1974.

———. *U.S. Army in World War II: Mediterranean Theater of Operations, Salerno to Cassino*. Washington, DC: Center of Military History, United States Army, 1993.

Bonn, Keith E. *When the Odds Were Even: The Vosges Mountains Campaign, October 1944–January 1945*. Novato, CA: Presidio Press, 1994.

Bowditch, John, III, ed. *Anzio Beachhead* (vol. 14 in the American Forces in Action series). Washington, DC: Department of the Army Historical Division, 1947.

Bradley, Omar N. *A Soldier's Story*. Chicago: Rand McNally, 1951.

Bradley, Omar N., and Clay Blair. *A General's Life*. New York: Simon & Schuster, 1983.

Brighton, Terry. *Patton, Montgomery, Rommel*. New York: Three Rivers Press, 2008.

Bull, Stephen. *World War II Infantry Tactics: Company and Battalion*. Oxford, UK: Osprey, 2005.

Bullock, Alan. *Hitler*. New York: Konecky and Konecky, 1962.

Capa, Robert. *Slightly Out of Focus*. New York: Henry Holt, 1947.

Cave Brown, Anthony. *The Last Hero*. New York: Times Books, 1982.

Champagne, Daniel R. *Dogface Soldiers*. Bennington, VT: Merriam Press, 2011.

Chandler, Alfred. *The Papers of Dwight David Eisenhower, vol. 3*. Baltimore: Johns Hopkins University Press, 1970.

Churchill, Winston S. *The Second World War: Closing the Ring*. Boston: Houghton Mifflin, 1951.

Clark, Lloyd. *Anzio: Italy and the Battle for Rome—1944*. New York: Grove Press, 2006.

Clark, Mark W. *Calculated Risk*. New York: Harper & Bros., 1950.

Clodfelter, Michael. *Warfare and Armed Conflicts: A Statistical Reference to Casualty and Other Figures, 1500–2000*. Jefferson, NC: McFarland, 2002.

Collier, Peter. *Medal of Honor: Portraits of Valor Beyond the Call of Duty*. New York: Artisan, 2006.

Cox, Troy D. *An Infantryman's Memories of World War II*. Booneville, MS: Brown-Line Printing, 2003.

Darby, William O., and William H. Baumer. *Darby's Rangers: We Led the Way*. Novato, CA: Presidio Press, 1980.

DePastino, Todd. *Bill Mauldin: A Life Up Front*. New York: W. W. Norton, 2008.

D'Este, Carlo. *Bitter Victory: The Battle for Sicily, 1943*. New York: Dutton, 1988.

———. *Fatal Decision: Anzio and the Battle for Rome*. New York: HarperCollins, 1991.

———. *Patton: A Genius for War*. New York: HarperCollins, 1995.

Duffy, Christopher. *Red Storm on the Reich*. New York: Da Capo Press, 1993.

Eisenhower, Dwight D. *Crusade in Europe*. New York: Doubleday, 1948.

———. *Letters to Mamie*. New York: Doubleday 1978.

Eisenhower, John S. D. *The Bitter Woods*. New York: G. P. Putnam's Sons, 1969.

———. *They Fought at Anzio*. Columbia: University of Missouri Press, 2007.

Ellis, John. *The Sharp End: The Fighting Man in World War II*. London: Aurum Press, 1990.

Evans, Richard J. *The Third Reich at War*. New York: Penguin Press, 2009.

Ferguson, Harvey. *The Last Cavalryman: The Life of General Lucian K. Truscott, Jr*. Norman: University of Oklahoma Press, 2015.

Fest, Joachim. *Speer: The Final Verdict*. Translated by Ewald Osars and Alexandra Dring. New York: Harcourt, 2001.

The Fifth Army at the Winter Line. Washington, DC: Center of Military History, United States Army, 1990.

Franklin, Robert. *Medic!* Lincoln: University of Nebraska Press, 2006.

Fritz, Stephen G. *Endkampf*. Lexington: University Press of Kentucky, 2004.

Fussell, Paul. *Doing Battle*. New York: Little, Brown, 1996.

——. *Wartime.* New York: Oxford University Press, 1989.

Gervasi, Frank. *The Violent Decade.* New York: W. W. Norton, 1989.

Gilbert, Martin. *Churchill: A Life.* New York: Henry Holt, 1991.

——. *The Second World War* (rev. ed.). New York: Henry Holt, 1989.

——. *Winston Churchill's War Leadership.* New York: Vintage, 2004.

——. *Winston S. Churchill, vol. 7: Road to Victory, 1941–1945.* Boston: Houghton Mifflin, 1986.

Graham, Don. *No Name on the Bullet.* New York: Viking, 1989.

Grossman, Dave. *On Killing* (rev. ed.). New York: Little, Brown, 2009.

Hastings, Max. *Armageddon.* New York: Knopf, 2004.

——. *Winston's War.* New York: Vintage, 2011.

Hickey, Des, and Gus Smith. *Operation Avalanche: The Salerno Landings, 1943.* New York: McGraw-Hill, 1984.

Hitchcock, William I. *The Bitter Road to Freedom.* New York: Free Press, 2008.

Jones, James. *WWII: A Chronicle of Soldiering.* New York: Ballantine, 1975.

Keegan, John. *The Second World War.* New York: Penguin, 1989.

Kemp, Ted. *A Commemorative History: First Special Service Force.* Dallas: Taylor Publishing, 1995.

Kershaw, Alex. *The First Wave.* New York: Dutton Caliber, 2019.

——. *The Liberator.* New York: Crown, 2012.

Kershaw, Ian. *Hitler 1936–1945: Nemesis.* New York: W. W. Norton, 2000.

Kesselring, Albert. *The Memoirs of Field-Marshal Kesselring.* Novato, CA: Presidio Press, 1989.

Langworth, Richard, ed. *Churchill by Himself.* New York: PublicAffairs, 2008.

Lewis, Norman. *Naples '44.* New York: Carroll & Graf, 2005.

Lucas, James. *Experiences of War: The Third Reich.* London: Arms and Armour Press, 1990.

MacDonald, Charles, B. *The Last Offensive.* Washington, DC: Center of Military History, United States Army, 1973.

——. *The Mighty Endeavor.* New York: Da Capo Press, 1992.

Marshall, S. L. A. *Men Against Fire.* Norman: University of Oklahoma Press, 2000.

Mauldin, Bill. *Up Front.* New York: W. W. Norton, 1991.

McFarland, Robert C., ed. *The History of the 15th Regiment in World War II.* La Grande, OR: Society of the Third Infantry Division, 1990.

Middleton, Drew. "The Seventh Army." *Combat Forces Journal,* August 1952.

Molony, C. J. C. *The Mediterranean and Middle East,* vol. VI, part II: *Victory in the Mediterranean.* Uckfield, East Sussex: Naval & Military Press, 2004.

Moorehead, Alan. *Eclipse.* New York: Harper & Row, 1968.

Morison, Samuel Eliot. *History of United States Naval Operations in World War II, vol. 9: Sicily-Salerno-Anzio.* Boston: Little, Brown, 1954.

——. *The Invasion of France and Germany, 1944–1945.* Edison, NJ: Castle Books, 1957.

Morris, Eric. *Circles of Hell: The War in Italy 1943–1945.* New York: Crown, 1993.

——. *Salerno: A Military Fiasco.* New York: Stein & Day, 1983.

Mossack, Erhard. *Die Letzen Tage von Nürnberg.* Nuremberg: Noris-Verlag, 1952.

Murphy, Audie. *To Hell and Back*. London: Corgi, 1950.

Nichols, David, ed. *Ernie's War: The Best of Ernie Pyle's World War II Dispatches*. New York: Random House, 1986.

Nolan, Keith William. *The Battle for Saigon: Tet 1968*. New York: Pocket Books, 1996.

Ochs, Stephen J. *A Cause Greater Than Self*. College Station: Texas A&M University Press, 2012.

Oleck, Major Howard, ed. *Eye-Witness World War II Battles*. New York: Belmont Books, 1963.

Overy, Richard. *Why the Allies Won*. New York: W. W. Norton, 1995.

Patch, Alexander. "The Seventh Army: From the Vosges to the Alps." *Army and Navy Journal*, December 1945.

Patton, George S., Jr. *War As I Knew It*. Boston: Houghton Mifflin, 1947.

Prefer, Nathan N. *Eisenhower's Thorn on the Rhine*. Havertown, PA: Casemate Publishers, 2015.

Prohme, Rupert. *History of 30th Infantry Regiment, World War II*. Washington, DC: Infantry Journal Press, 1947.

Pyle, Ernie. *Brave Men*. New York: Henry Holt, 1944.

Rawson, Andrew. *In Pursuit of Hitler*. Barnsley, UK: Pen & Sword, 2008.

Reynolds, Quentin. *The Curtain Rises*. New York: Random House, 1944.

Roberts, Mary Louise. *What Soldiers Do*. Chicago: University of Chicago Press, 2013.

Salerno: American Operations from the Beachhead to the Volturno. Washington, DC: Military Intelligence Division, War Department, 1944.

Sevareid, Eric. *Not So Wild a Dream*. New York: Knopf, 1946.

Shapiro, L. S. B. *They Left the Back Door Open*. Toronto: Ryerson Press, 1944.

Sheehan, Fred. *Anzio: Epic of Bravery*. Norman: University of Oklahoma Press, 1964 (reprint 1994).

Shepard, Ben. *A War of Nerves*. London: Jonathan Cape, 2000.

Silvestri, Ennio. *The Long Road to Rome*. Latina, Italy: Etic Grafica, 1994.

Simpson, Harold B. *Audie Murphy, American Soldier*. Dallas: Alcor Publishing, 1982.

Smith, David A. *The Price of Valor: The Life of Audie Murphy, America's Most Decorated Hero of World War II*. Washington, DC: Regnery History, 2015.

Speer, Albert. *Inside the Third Reich*. New York: Macmillan, 1970.

Stanton, Shelby L. *World War II Order of Battle*. New York: Galahad Books, 1984.

Starr, Chester G., ed. *From Salerno to the Alps—A History of the Fifth Army, 1943–1945*. Washington, DC: Infantry Journal Press, 1948.

Taggart, Donald G., ed. *History of the Third Infantry Division in World War II*. Washington, DC: Infantry Journal Press, 1947.

Terkel, Studs. *The Good War*. London: Hamish Hamilton, 1985.

Tobin, James. *Ernie Pyle's War*. New York: Free Press, 1997.

Toland, John. *The Last 100 Days*. New York: Random House, 1966.

Tregaskis, Richard. *Invasion Diary*. New York: Random House, 1944.

Trevelyan, Raleigh. *The Fortress: A Diary of Anzio and After*. London: Collins, 1956.

Trevor Roper, Hugh. *The Last Days of Hitler.* New York: Macmillan, 1965.

Truscott, Lucian K. *Command Missions.* New York: Dutton, 1954.

Vaughan-Thomas, Wynford. *Anzio.* London: Longmans, Green, 1961.

Verney, Peter. *Anzio 1944: An Unexpected Fury.* London: B. T. Batsford, 1978.

Wallace, Robert. *The Italian Campaign.* New York: Time-Life Books, 1981.

Walters, Vernon A. *Silent Missions.* New York: Doubleday, 1978.

Warlimont, Walter. *Inside Hitler's Headquarters, 1939–45.* Novato, CA: Presidio Press, 1964.

Westphal, Siegfried. *The German Army in the West.* London: Cassel, 1951.

Whicker, Alan. *Whicker's War.* London: HarperCollins, 2006.

Whiting, Charles. *American Hero.* York, England: Kerslake, 2000.

———. *America's Forgotten Army.* New York: St. Martin's Press, 2001.

———. *Paths of Death & Glory: The Last Days of the Third Reich.* Havertown, PA: Casemate Publishers, 2003.

———. *Siegfried: The Nazis' Last Stand.* New York: Stein & Day, 1982.

Whitlock, Flint. *Rock of Anzio.* New York: Basic Books, 1998.

Whitman, Bill. *Scouts Out!* Los Angeles: Authors Unlimited, 1990.

Wilson, George. *If You Survive.* New York: Ivy Books, 1987.

Wyant, William K. *Sandy Patch: A Biography of Lt. Gen. Alexander M. Patch.* New York: Praeger, 1991.

NOTES

CHAPTER 1: BAPTISM OF FIRE

1. Maurice Britt, "Captain Maurice Britt, Most Decorated Infantryman, Begins His Story of War Experiences," Maurice Britt papers, University of Arkansas, box 6.
2. Lt. Colonel Jack C. Mason, "My Favorite Lion," *Army*, May 2008.
3. "The History of the 15th Infantry Regiment in WWII" (unpublished manuscript, courtesy of Tim Stoy), 1.
4. Prohme, *History of 30th Infantry Regiment, World War II*, 24.
5. Britt, "Captain Maurice Britt, Most Decorated Infantryman," 6.
6. Britt, "Captain Maurice Britt, Most Decorated Infantryman," 6.
7. "Former University Athlete Aboard Sunken Transport," undated press clipping, Maurice Britt collection, University of Arkansas, box 2.
8. Britt, "Captain Maurice Britt, Most Decorated Infantryman," 6.
9. "Journalism Major Awarded Congressional Medal," *The Arkansas Publisher*, April 1944.
10. "The History of the 15th Infantry Regiment in WWII," 4.
11. *The Commercial Appeal* (Memphis), December 8, 1944.
12. *Army*, May 2008.
13. "The History of the 15th Infantry Regiment in WWII," 4.
14. "The History of the 15th Infantry Regiment in WWII," 5.
15. On the banks of the Marne in 1918, the 3rd Division held as two German divisions assailed it. The Germans finally pulled back and Paris was saved. The 3rd Division also took part in other key battles on the Somme, at Château-Thierry and Saint-Mihiel, and in the Champagne-Marne, Meuse-Argonne, and Aisne-Marne offensives. The division had a long and storied history,

fighting against the British in 1812 and in the Spanish-American War, the Indian Wars, the Mexican-American War, and the Civil War. One of the division's three regiments, the 15th, spent twenty-six years in China, leaving in 1938.

16. Britt, "Captain Maurice Britt, Most Decorated Infantryman," 6.
17. "Journalism Major Awarded Congressional Medal."
18. "Were 'Soft Underbelly' and 'Fortress Europe' Churchill Phrases?," The Churchill Project, April 1, 2016, https://winstonchurchill.hillsdale.edu/soft-underbelly-fortress-europe/.
19. Britt, "Captain Maurice Britt, Most Decorated Infantryman," 7.
20. Britt, "Captain Maurice Britt, Most Decorated Infantryman," 7.
21. Ferguson, *The Last Cavalryman*, 150.
22. Taggart, *History of the Third Infantry Division in World War II*, 47–48.

CHAPTER 2: SICILY

1. Lucian Truscott to Sarah Truscott, July 7, 1943, Lucian K. Truscott papers, George C. Marshall Foundation.
2. Truscott, *Command Missions*, 220.
3. "Audie Murphy: Great American Hero," *Biography*, July 1, 1996.
4. Audie Murphy Research Foundation Newsletter, vol. 1, winter 1997, 7.
5. Murphy, *To Hell and Back*, 4–5.
6. Murphy, *To Hell and Back*, 4.
7. Prohme, *History of 30th Infantry Regiment, World War II*, 47.
8. Prohme, *History of 30th Infantry Regiment, World War II*, 92.
9. "The History of the 15th Infantry Regiment in WWII" (unpublished manuscript, courtesy of Tim Stoy), 22.
10. "The History of the 15th Infantry Regiment in WWII," 22.
11. "Audie Murphy: Great American Hero."
12. Murphy, *To Hell and Back*, 7.
13. "Audie Murphy: Great American Hero."
14. Murphy, *To Hell and Back*, 7.
15. Audie Murphy Research Foundation Newsletter, vol. 4, spring 1998, 2.
16. Regimental papers, 15th Infantry Regiment, Record Group 407, National Archives.
17. "The History of the 15th Infantry Regiment in WWII," 4.
18. Ferguson, *The Last Cavalryman*, 163.
19. *Army Times*, July 1964.
20. *Time*, September 20, 1968.
21. "The History of the 15th Infantry Regiment in WWII," 11.
22. "Keith Lincoln Ware," Hall of Valor Project, https://valor.militarytimes.com/hero/2162#241446.
23. Murphy, *To Hell and Back*, 10–11.
24. Five other enemy soldiers were shot dead that day by one of Murphy's comrades in the 15th Infantry Regiment—2nd Lieutenant Robert Craig, who

single-handedly took on a force of around a hundred men. Scottish-born Craig, who had lived in Toledo, Ohio, before the war, came under intense fire that pinned down his company. Three other junior officers tried to advance but were wounded, so Craig snaked his way forward through a field of waist-high wheat until he got to around forty yards from the enemy. Then the Germans spotted him and opened fire, their bullets scything through the wheat, flattening it inches from his feet. Craig jumped up and charged the machine gun, letting rip with his carbine, killing the crew. Then he signaled for his men to advance and was moving forward again, out in the open, down a dusty slope. Again a hail of enemy bullets. He shouted to the men following him. They were to pull back. He'd go ahead on his own. On the outskirts of the village of Favoratta, twenty-five yards from German defenders, Craig knelt down and took aim. Again, he was extraordinarily accurate, killing five and wounding three. Meanwhile, his platoon managed to find cover. Then Craig was shot dead. He would be posthumously awarded the Medal of Honor, the first man in the 15th Infantry Regiment to earn it while liberating Europe. Taggart, *History of the Third Infantry Division in World War II*, 57.

25. Like Audie Murphy, Truscott was disappointed by the interior of Sicily, home of Cyclops, a fabled island at the crossroads of history for more than two millennia. He had expected the countryside to be far more beautiful. "Believe me," he wrote his wife, "when I am once more home again I shall never have any desire to leave the feel and smell of good clean American air." Source: Truscott, *Command Missions*, 236.

26. Ferguson, *The Last Cavalryman*, 169.

27. Taggart, *History of the Third Infantry Division in World War II*, 58.

28. Maurice Britt, "Captain Maurice Britt, Most Decorated Infantryman, Begins His Story of War Experiences," Maurice Britt papers, University of Arkansas, MC box 6, folder 1, 7.

29. Britt, "Captain Maurice Britt, Most Decorated Infantryman," 6.

30. Morison, *History of United States Naval Operations in World War II, vol. 9: Sicily-Salerno-Anzio*, 183.

31. Champagne, *Dogface Soldiers*, 47.

32. Ferguson, *The Last Cavalryman*, 174.

33. Patton, *War As I Knew It*, 61–62.

34. Biddle, *Artist at War*, 66.

35. Capa, *Slightly Out of Focus*, 71.

36. Ferguson, *The Last Cavalryman*, 174.

37. Vert Enis, diary, July 23, 1943 (courtesy of Tim Stoy), 9.

38. Biddle, *Artist at War*, 68.

39. Morison, *History of United States Naval Operations in World War II, vol. 9: Sicily-Salerno-Anzio*, 187.

40. Atkinson, *The Day of Battle*, 143.

41. Murphy, *To Hell and Back*, 10–11.

42. Major General Eugene Salet, unpublished memoir (courtesy of Tim Stoy), 220.

43. Salet, unpublished memoir, 221.

44. Regimental papers, 15th Infantry Regiment.
45. Pyle, *Brave Men*, 92.
46. Michael Gallagher, email to author, December 11, 2020.
47. Champagne, *Dogface Soldiers*, 53.
48. Vert Enis, diary, August 9, 1943, 22.
49. "The History of the 15th Infantry Regiment in WWII," 49–50.
50. "The History of the 15th Infantry Regiment in WWII," 56.
51. Murphy, *To Hell and Back*, 15.
52. Blumenson, *The Patton Papers*, 319.
53. Truscott, *Command Missions*, 182–83.
54. Atkinson, *The Day of Battle*, 163.
55. Blumenson, *The Patton Papers*, 319.
56. Salet, unpublished memoir, 222.
57. Vert Enis, diary, August 14, 1943, 24.
58. Regimental papers, 15th Infantry Regiment.
59. Morison, *History of United States Naval Operations in World War II, vol. 9: Sicily-Salerno-Anzio*, 216.
60. MacDonald, *The Mighty Endeavor*, 186.
61. Biddle, *Artist at War*, 113.
62. Anse Speairs, interview with author.
63. Ferguson, *The Last Cavalryman*, 182.
64. MacDonald, *The Mighty Endeavor*, 14–15.
65. Vert Enis, diary, September 15, 1943, 30–31.
66. Vert Enis, diary, September 15, 1943, 30–31.
67. Britt later recalled Miller with great affection and respect: "My executive officer was Lieutenant Jack Miller of Vincennes, Ind. 'I don't believe I could do without him,' I told my wife in a letter. And I meant it. In battle, Lieutenant Miller was as cool as any man in the company, but after the fighting was over he would break out in a cold sweat and shake, talking a blue streak about his narrow escapes—real and imagined. Three times he was wounded—in Sicily, at Acerno, and later at Anzio. At Acerno he won the silver star for carrying two badly wounded men to safety from an exposed position. While he was doing it, a shell landed so close he was knocked flat by the concussion." Source: Britt, "Captain Maurice Britt, Most Decorated Infantryman," 13.
68. Britt, "Captain Maurice Britt, Most Decorated Infantryman," 3–5.

CHAPTER 3: MUD, MULES, AND MOUNTAINS

1. Harold Lundquist, "Random Thoughts of Days Gone By" (unpublished memoir, courtesy of Tim Stoy), 1.
2. Taggart, *History of the Third Infantry Division in World War II*, 79.
3. "Tribute to Captain Britt by Coach Who Recalls He Was Fine Player," undated press clipping, Maurice Britt papers, University of Arkansas, box 2.
4. Major General Eugene Salet, unpublished memoir (courtesy of Tim Stoy), 233.

5. Maurice Britt, "Captain Maurice Britt, Most Decorated Infantryman, Begins His Story of War Experiences," Maurice Britt papers, University of Arkansas, box 6.
6. Prohme, *History of 30th Infantry Regiment, World War II*, 87.
7. Prohme, *History of 30th Infantry Regiment, World War II*, 87.
8. Pyle, *Brave Men*, 68.
9. Salet, unpublished memoir, 236.
10. Murphy, *To Hell and Back*, 15.
11. Eisenhower, *Crusade in Europe*, 203.
12. "Journalism Major Awarded Congressional Medal," *The Arkansas Publisher*, April 1944, Maurice Britt papers, University of Arkansas, box 2.
13. Smith, *The Price of Valor*, 32–33.
14. Champagne, *Dogface Soldiers*, 63.
15. Smith, *The Price of Valor*, 32–33.
16. Tregaskis, *Invasion Diary*, 168–69.
17. Atkinson, *The Day of Battle*, 249.
18. Taggart, *History of the Third Infantry Division in World War II*, 385.
19. *Life*, October 2, 1944.
20. Blumenson, *U.S. Army in World War II: Salerno to Cassino*, 200.
21. Kesselring, *The Memoirs of Field-Marshal Kesselring*, 188.
22. Britt, "Captain Maurice Britt, Most Decorated Infantryman," 13.
23. Britt, "Captain Maurice Britt, Most Decorated Infantryman," 8–9.
24. Ferguson, *The Last Cavalryman*, 201.
25. Taggart, *History of the Third Infantry Division in World War II*, 385.
26. Britt, "Captain Maurice Britt, Most Decorated Infantryman," 12.
27. Prohme, *History of 30th Infantry Regiment, World War II*, 92.
28. "Lieutenant Maurice Britt of Fort Smith Now Is One of the Battle Toughened Veterans of the Italian Front," undated press clipping, Maurice Britt papers, University of Arkansas, box 2.
29. Britt, "Captain Maurice Britt, Most Decorated Infantryman," 10.
30. Murphy, *To Hell and Back*, 34.
31. Truscott, *Command Missions*, 284.
32. Taggart, *History of the Third Infantry Division in World War II*, 97.
33. *The Fifth Army at the Winter Line*, 1.
34. Britt, "Captain Maurice Britt, Most Decorated Infantryman," 11.

CHAPTER 4: BLOODY RIDGE

1. "Audie Murphy: Great American Hero," *Biography*, July 1, 1996.
2. "Our commanding officer, Lt. Colonel Edgar C. Doleman of Mount Holly, N.J., studied the problem for a full day," remembered Britt, "going over every foot of the mountain with field glasses. Then he called in all his company commanders, asking their opinions. His decision was that further frontal assaults would be too costly: it would be better to make a flanking movement across the mountains and try to seize the German positions from the rear. In the previous six weeks of fighting, the ranks of Company L had been reduced

from 198 to 140 by deaths, wounded, sickness, and battle fatigue. Now we had to give up a platoon to guard the regimental mule train that was bringing up supplies, so we entered the battle with only about 100 men." Source: Maurice Britt, "Captain Maurice Britt, Most Decorated Infantryman, Begins His Story of War Experiences," Maurice Britt papers, University of Arkansas, box 6.

3. Prohme, *History of 30th Infantry Regiment, World War II*, 96.
4. Shepard, *A War of Nerves*, 252.
5. William Weinberg, unpublished memoir (courtesy of Tim Stoy), 33.
6. Britt, "Captain Maurice Britt, Most Decorated Infantryman," 11.
7. Taggart, *History of the Third Infantry Division in World War II*, 100.
8. In a letter from Italy to W. M. Pratt, a pastor in his hometown of Lonoke, where he first attended church aged nine, Britt wrote: "The man who said 'there are no atheists in foxholes' hit the nail on the head. If every soldier would only remember his reactions when the bullets whistle over his head, and carry that impression with him through life, I feel confident that ninety-nine out of one hundred would live a true Christian life, thereafter. I have felt many times that I was actually near death. Without realizing what I was doing, I prayed, not once but many times. I remember on one particular occasion, large artillery shells caught me out in the open in full view without any cover. In my fright, I prayed. All at once, during the height of the intense shelling, a wonderful calm came over me and I was quite happy. I have since tried to analyze the cause, whether I became afraid to die or whether I knew in my own heart that I would not die, I do not know. There was a peace of mind and spirit." Source: "Home and Church Made This Hero," undated press clipping, Maurice Britt papers, University of Arkansas, box 2.
9. Britt, "Captain Maurice Britt, Most Decorated Infantryman," 12.
10. Britt, "Captain Maurice Britt, Most Decorated Infantryman," 12.
11. "The Watch on the Rhine," vol. 100, no. 2, October 2018, 4–5.
12. Prohme, *History of 30th Infantry Regiment, World War II*, 98.
13. Britt, "Captain Maurice Britt, Most Decorated Infantryman," 12.
14. Undated press clipping, Maurice Britt papers, University of Arkansas, box 2.
15. Britt, "Captain Maurice Britt, Most Decorated Infantryman," 11–14.
16. Undated press clipping, Maurice Britt papers, University of Arkansas, box 2.
17. *The Arkansas Traveler* (Fayetteville), December 1, 1944.
18. Taggart, *History of the Third Infantry Division in World War II*, 101.
19. Britt and his battalion would receive the Distinguished Unit Citation for their actions between November 7 and 12. "With fire sweeping its ranks from the rear and from an exposed flank, the battalion launched its attack up the forward slope of the mountain [Rotondo] and doggedly advanced to the crest in the face of stubborn enemy resistance," read the citation. "Although depleted heavily in effective strength and having neither food nor water for a period of two days, the intrepid infantrymen of the 3rd Battalion met the onslaught of the enemy over the six-day period and repelled each assault with heavy losses to the attackers." Source: Taggart, *History of the Third Infantry Division in World War II*, 101.
20. Britt, "Captain Maurice Britt, Most Decorated Infantryman," 11–14.

21. Kesselring, *The Memoirs of Field-Marshal Kesselring*, 188.
22. Lucian Truscott to Sarah Truscott, November 10, 1943, Lucian K. Truscott papers, George C. Marshall Foundation.
23. US Treasury, *Treasury Salute!* "Captain Maurice Britt," August 28, 1944.

Chapter 5: Naples

1. Tregaskis, *Invasion Diary*, 193.
2. Kesselring, *The Memoirs of Field-Marshal Kesselring*, 187.
3. Tregaskis, *Invasion Diary*, 195.
4. Blumenson, *U.S. Army in World War II: Salerno to Cassino*, 234.
5. Champagne, *Dogface Soldiers*, 73.
6. Maurice Britt, "Captain Maurice Britt, Most Decorated Infantryman, Begins His Story of War Experiences," Maurice Britt papers, University of Arkansas, box 6, folder 1, 14.
7. Prohme, *History of 30th Infantry Regiment, World War II*, 102.
8. Moorehead, *Eclipse*, 67.
9. Moorehead, *Eclipse*, 69.
10. Mark Clark, diary, January 2, 1944, Mark Clark papers, the Citadel.
11. Britt, "Captain Maurice Britt, Most Decorated Infantryman," 14.
12. Prohme, *History of 30th Infantry Regiment, World War II*, 102.
13. Britt, "Captain Maurice Britt, Most Decorated Infantryman," 15.
14. Ferguson, *The Last Cavalryman*, 212.
15. John P. Lucas, "From Algiers to Anzio" (unpublished manuscript), US Army Military History Institute, 353.

Chapter 6: The Agony of Anzio

1. "The History of the 15th Infantry Regiment in WWII" (unpublished manuscript, courtesy of Tim Stoy), 203.
2. Truscott, *Command Missions*, 309.
3. "The History of the 15th Infantry Regiment in WWII," 224.
4. "The History of the 15th Infantry Regiment in WWII," 226.
5. Prohme, *History of 30th Infantry Regiment, World War II*, 130.
6. Lt. Colonel Jack C. Mason, "My Favorite Lion," *Army*, May 2008.
7. Taggart, *History of the Third Infantry Division in World War II*, 111.
8. One veteran described Britt's exercises as "jump-up-and-down-spradle-your-legs." Source: Major General Eugene Salet, unpublished memoir (courtesy of Tim Stoy), 283.
9. Prohme, *History of 30th Infantry Regiment, World War II*, 111.
10. Maurice Britt, "Captain Maurice Britt, Most Decorated Infantryman, Begins His Story of War Experiences," Maurice Britt papers, University of Arkansas, box 6, folder 1, 17.
11. Prohme, *History of 30th Infantry Regiment, World War II*, 130–32.
12. Britt, "Captain Maurice Britt, Most Decorated Infantryman," 17.

13. "Same Old 'Footsie' Britt—He Played in Germans' Backfield," undated press clipping, Maurice Britt papers, University of Arkansas, box 2.
14. Britt, "Captain Maurice Britt, Most Decorated Infantryman," 18.
15. US Treasury, *Treasury Salute!* "Captain Maurice Britt," August 28, 1944.
16. Major General Lucian Truscott to Captain Maurice Britt, February 28, 1944, Maurice Britt papers, University of Arkansas, box 2.
17. "News of the Week for Those in Service," undated press clipping, Maurice Britt papers, University of Arkansas archives, box 2.
18. Major General Lucian Truscott to Captain Maurice Britt.
19. *Arkansas Democrat* (Little Rock), April 30, 1944.
20. Undated press clipping, Maurice Britt papers, University of Arkansas, box 2.
21. "Captain Britt Given Highest Army Medal," undated press clipping, Maurice Britt papers, University of Arkansas, box 2.
22. Sgt. Dan Polier, "Story of Footsy Britt, Congressional Winner," *Yank*, June 18, 1944, Maurice Britt papers, University of Arkansas, box 2.
23. Undated press clipping, Maurice Britt papers, University of Arkansas, box 2.
24. Graham, *No Name on the Bullet*, 51.
25. Audie Murphy Research Foundation Newsletter, vol. 4, spring 1998, 2.
26. "The History of the 15th Infantry Regiment in WWII," 209.
27. "The History of the 15th Infantry Regiment in WWII," 210.
28. "Blue and White Devils: The Story of the 3rd Infantry Division," Lone Sentry, https://www.lonesentry.com/gi_stories_booklets/3rdinfantry/index.html.
29. Graham, *No Name on the Bullet*, 54.
30. "The History of the 15th Infantry Regiment in WWII," 242.
31. "The History of the 15th Infantry Regiment in WWII," 226.
32. Kesselring, *The Memoirs of Field-Marshal Kesselring*, 195.
33. "Blue and White Devils."
34. Taggart, *History of the Third Infantry Division in World War II*, 121.
35. Whicker, *Whicker's War*, 123.
36. "Blue and White Devils."
37. Morison, *History of United States Naval Operations in World War II, vol. 9: Sicily-Salerno-Anzio*, 365.
38. "Blue and White Devils."
39. William Weinberg, unpublished memoir (courtesy of Tim Stoy), 30.
40. Graham, *No Name on the Bullet*, 57.
41. Audie Murphy Research Foundation Newsletter, vol. 4, 2.
42. Audie Murphy Research Foundation Newsletter, vol. 4, 3.
43. Murphy, *To Hell and Back*, 111.

CHAPTER 7: BREAKOUT

1. Atkinson, *The Day of Battle*, 514.
2. "The History of the 15th Infantry Regiment in WWII" (unpublished manuscript, courtesy of Tim Stoy), 223.
3. "The History of the 15th Infantry Regiment in WWII," 227.

4. Truscott, *Command Decisions*, 393.
5. Taggart, *History of the Third Infantry Division in World War II*, 149.
6. Truscott, *Command Missions*, 392.
7. Murphy, *To Hell and Back*, 156.
8. Truscott, *Command Missions*, 393.
9. Atkinson, *The Day of Battle*, 541.
10. "The History of the 15th Infantry Regiment in WWII," 247.
11. Taggart, *History of the Third Infantry Division in World War II*, 164.
12. Taggart, *History of the Third Infantry Division in World War II*, 171.
13. "The History of the 15th Infantry Regiment in WWII," 248.
14. One of the men to earn the Medal of Honor during the breakout was twenty-five-year-old Private Henry Schauer. It was around noon when Schauer, armed with a Browning Automatic Rifle, came under fire from snipers to his rear. Four bullets from four German snipers. But where the hell were they? How to spot them? Schauer was, according to a sergeant, the "best BAR-man" going. He climbed out of the ditch and with back straight walked slowly for thirty yards out in the open, and sure enough each German sniper opened up on him, one after another. Schauer spotted two snipers in a house to his rear. Another was in a wheat field beside the house and yet another on a road nearby. "Schauer was made of ice," remembered one soldier. "He stood upright, raised his BAR to his shoulder and went to work. The snipers 170 yards away alongside the house were low to the ground, blending in with the grass." Two bursts from the BAR killed both snipers. Schauer turned his body slightly. The sniper lying on the shaded road was only a dark shadow. Another burst from the BAR finished him. The last sniper, the one in the field, was almost impossible to spot. Schauer fired. Again, one burst was enough. The next day, the attack resumed. Private Schauer's heroics continued. A Mark VI tank opened up on Schauer and his men. Schauer was back on form, crawling through the dirt and grass before once again standing, this time around eighty yards from the target. Bullets ripped around him again and then four shells—fired at him directly—exploded close by. He was the master of the BAR and he stood up once more, and firing from his shoulder, he took out another German machine-gun crew. It was as if he was "taking aim at target practice on the firing range," recalled one eyewitness, a young lieutenant whose testimony, with that of others, would lead to Schauer receiving the Medal of Honor. Source: Taggart, *History of the Third Infantry Division in World War II*, 164.
15. Murphy, *To Hell and Back*, 133.
16. On May 24, another man from the 15th Infantry Regiment went beyond the call of duty. Private James Mills, from Fort Meade, Florida, was only in his second day of combat as he went ahead of his platoon from F Company near Cisterna, which was still held in force by the Germans. He had gone three hundred yards when a German machine gunner tried to kill him. The German was only five yards away but somehow had missed with his first volleys. Mills was quick enough on the draw to shoot the machine gunner dead with

a single shot. Another German nearby quickly surrendered. A lieutenant in Mills's patrol turned a corner in the road and found Mills aiming his rifle at the German prisoner. The lieutenant looked at the dead gunner. Mills had shot him between the eyes. "I had to do it, sir," Mills apologized. "He almost got me." Mills then moved on toward Cisterna, knowing every yard gained was important if the German defenses were to be breached. He soon spotted another German—hiding in a bush, pulling the pin on a grenade. He aimed at the German, who decided wisely to surrender rather than be killed. It quickly proved to be the right move as Mills then drilled another German who was about to throw a grenade. That made three Germans with three bullets. Enemy machine-gun fire intensified and several German riflemen also started to aim at Mills from around fifty feet. Mills rushed them, firing an M-1 rifle from the hip. Who was this crazed American? The Germans quickly put their hands above their heads, all six of them. Mills kept on charging down a draw and came under fire from yet another machine gunner. Crack. Another German down. A couple of Germans fired at him wildly. Snap. Another dead Nazi. Mills looked ahead at the German strongpoint. His men would be mowed down if they charged it. There was a drainage ditch alongside the road. They were to use it, Mills ordered, then scramble forward, keeping their heads down. They set off and Mills jumped up, out into the open, and fired and shouted at the enemy, drawing fire. Bullets ricocheted off rocks near his feet and tracers whipped past him. Mills fired back. Another clip soon emptied. Time to reload. He dived into the ditch, slotted another clip into his M-1, and then climbed back onto the road. Four times in all, Mills made himself a target until he ran out of clips. His platoon meanwhile reached the strongpoint without being spotted and seized it along with two dozen Germans. Not a single Marne man was wounded. Mills would survive the war and receive the Medal of Honor only to be killed, aged fifty. One day, he pulled up in his car to help an apparently stranded motorist who then murdered him. Source: Taggart, *History of the Third Infantry Division in World War II*, 169.

17. Atkinson, *The Day of Battle*, 543.
18. Murphy, *To Hell and Back*, 156.
19. Champagne, *Dogface Soldiers*, 113.
20. In the early hours of June 3, using the cover of night, a small German force counterattacked the 15th Infantry Regiment. So began, according to the 3rd Division's official history, "one of the most stirring tales of courage and self-sacrifice in the annals of United States military history." E Company's Private Herbert Christian, a dab hand with a tommy gun, belonged to a patrol that was assaulted on three sides by more than fifty Germans and three tanks. "The enemy had prepared an ambush and had sprung the trap," recalled a sergeant in the patrol. "The only way out was to the rear." The patrol leader was killed, and to buy others time to get away Christian and another man, Private Elden Johnson, a BAR gunner, chose to make themselves targets. A 20mm round blew most of Christian's lower leg away and he fell to the ground but then crawled toward the enemy, firing his tommy gun. Flares exploded above,

lighting up the area as if it were daytime. Christian's leg wound was nauseating. "Blood was gushing from the stump," remembered a soldier. "Shreds of flesh dangled from his leg. The pain must have been intense. This man Christian was like a wounded animal, instead of calling for aid he took his Thompson submachine gun and made his way forward on one knee and the bloody stump, firing his weapon as rapidly as possible." Christian was around ten yards from a German armed with a machine pistol. He emptied his gun into the man and reloaded, fired another burst, and was then raked by German fire. The BAR gunner Johnson was also killed but the others in the patrol managed to escape the ambush. Both Christian and Johnson would receive the Medal of Honor posthumously. Christian's medal would be presented to his five-year-old son in June 1945 on what would have been his thirty-third birthday. Source: Taggart, *History of the Third Infantry Division in World War II*, 182–89.

21. Kesselring, *The Memoirs of Field-Marshal Kesselring*, 205.
22. Truscott, *Command Decisions*, 397.
23. "The History of the 15th Infantry Regiment in WWII," 257.
24. Champagne, *Dogface Soldiers*, 116.
25. "Capt. Britt, Officer to Be in Wheel Chair for Ceremony," undated press clipping, Maurice Britt papers, University of Arkansas, box 2.
26. "Britt Receives Congressional Medal of Honor," undated press clipping, Maurice Britt papers, University of Arkansas, box 2.
27. "Britt Receives Congressional Medal in Ceremony at Razorback Stadium," undated clipping, Maurice Britt papers, University of Arkansas, box 2.
28. Untitled, undated press clipping, Maurice Britt papers, University of Arkansas, box 2.
29. Kershaw, *The First Wave*, 8.

CHAPTER 8: LA BELLE FRANCE

1. "Dwight D. Eisenhower, Order of the Day, June 6, 1944," American Rhetoric, https://www.americanrhetoric.com/speeches/dwighteisenhowerorderofdday.htm.
2. Michael Daly, interview with Tim Frank (courtesy of Tim Frank).
3. Michael Daly, interview with Tim Frank.
4. Deirdre Daly, interview with author.
5. *Yankee*, May 1983.
6. Ochs, *A Cause Greater Than Self*, 55–58.
7. Michael Daly, interview with Tim Frank.
8. Michael Daly, interview with Tim Frank.
9. Michael Daly, interview with Tim Frank.
10. MacDonald, *The Mighty Endeavor*, 333.
11. Ochs, *A Cause Greater Than Self*, 68.
12. Champagne, *Dogface Soldiers*, 117–18.
13. Taggart, *History of the Third Infantry Division in World War II*, 203.

14. Graham, *No Name on the Bullet*, 81.
15. Taggart, *History of the Third Infantry Division in World War II*, 203.
16. Morison, *The Invasion of France and Germany, 1944–1945*, 258.
17. Morison, *The Invasion of France and Germany, 1944–1945*, 257.
18. Simpson, *Audie Murphy, American Soldier*, 120.
19. Audie Murphy Research Foundation Newsletter, vol. 4, spring 1998, 3.
20. Audie Murphy Research Foundation Newsletter, vol. 4, 1.
21. Champagne, *Dogface Soldiers*, 128.
22. Champagne, *Dogface Soldiers*, 129.
23. Murphy's Distinguished Service Cross recommendation reads: "Sergeant Murphy silenced the enemy weapon, killed two of the crew and wounded a third. As he proceeded, two Germans advanced toward him. Quickly destroying both of them, he dashed alone toward the enemy strong point, disregarding bullets which glanced off rocks around him and hand grenades which exploded so close as 15 yards away. Closing in, he wounded two Germans with carbine fire, killed two more in a fierce, brief fire-fight, and forced the remaining five to surrender. His extraordinary heroism resulted in the capture of a fiercely contested enemy-held hill and the annihilation or capture of the entire enemy garrison." Simpson, *Audie Murphy, American Soldier*, 121.
24. David "Spec" McClure, "How Audie Murphy Won His Medals," Audie Murphy Research Foundation Newsletter, vol. 3, winter 1998.

CHAPTER 9: BLITZKRIEG IN PROVENCE

1. Graham, *No Name on the Bullet*, 67.
2. "The History of the 15th Infantry Regiment in WWII" (unpublished manuscript, courtesy of Tim Stoy), 276.
3. Taggart, *History of the Third Infantry Division in World War II*, 210–11.
4. "The History of the 15th Infantry Regiment in WWII," 296.
5. Communication was also a problem. The retreating Germans had destroyed all telephone lines and Truscott's Signal Corps was forced to frantically lay mile after mile of wire in record time. Technical Sergeant Robert Maxwell, a wireman in the 3rd Division, crawled between vines and along hedgerows that skirted bone white roads, caked in dust, unrolling wire. Not since the breakout from Anzio had he worked so hard, hanging wire from tree to tree above roads and through hedges and undergrowth. A devout Quaker who had been badly injured at Anzio, Maxwell could have avoided combat because of his religious beliefs, but had chosen to serve anyway. He prayed almost every hour of every day, sometimes constantly mumbling homilies. Laying wire was a harrowing occupation, especially if he was spotted by the enemy when out in the open, but Maxwell much preferred it to the grim hand-to-mouth graft of his youth at the height of the Depression. He had grown up in the Dust Bowl, groping his way along a rope from barn to farmhouse in the worst dust storms when he could see no more than a few feet in front of his face. One day, a young officer approached Maxwell. "Hey, sounds like a fire-

fight up there," said the officer. "We should go up and join them. See if we can help." . . . "Lieutenant, I don't think our job is get into firefights. I thought we were in communication?" . . . "No, come on. Let's go." . . . "I don't think we need to get involved in this." The officer ignored Maxwell and started toward the firing. Maxwell followed, worried the green officer would get them both killed. Enough was enough. "Lieutenant," said Maxwell. The officer turned around and saw Maxwell pointing his pistol at him. "I think we ought to go back to the command post." . . . "OK." . . . Maxwell was surprised that he was not then court-martialed. "I expected a royal reaming out for that one—at least to get drummed out of the service. But nothing happened. A day or two after that, the officer was transferred into an infantry unit." Source: Robert Maxwell, interview with author.

6. Whiting, *American Hero*, 100.
7. Audie Murphy Research Foundation Newsletter, vol. 4, spring 1998, 3.
8. "The History of the 15th Infantry Regiment in WWII," 304.
9. Audie Murphy Research Foundation Newsletter, vol. 4, 4.
10. Murphy, *To Hell and Back*, 188–89.
11. Champagne, *Dogface Soldiers*, 133.
12. Taggart, *History of the Third Infantry Division in World War II*, 223.
13. Interview with Major Keith Ware by Lt. Colonel Goddard, 7th Army Historical Section, on actions of 1st Battalion, 15th Infantry, Besancon, Fall 1944, 2. "European Theater of Operations Combat Interviews, 1944–1945," Records Group 407, National Archives.
14. "The History of the 15th Infantry Regiment in WWII," 321.
15. Major Keith Ware, interview with Lt. Colonel Goddard, 2.
16. On September 6, a forward command post came under fierce assault. A platoon from a communications company went to the rescue. It included twenty-three-year-old Technical Sergeant Robert Maxwell, a devout Quaker who had fought all the way from Casablanca. He and his fellow wiremen in the 3rd Division had laid well over twenty-five hundred miles of wire since arriving in France, so fast had been the advance. Maxwell got to within fifteen yards of the command post, where senior officers were trapped. Machine-gun bullets whipped past him. "He was the coolest customer I've ever seen," recalled a soldier nearby. "Tracer bullets were barely clearing his head, yet he didn't seem to notice it." Maxwell sought shelter with several other men behind a wall. He had received the Purple Heart, the Bronze Star, and two Silver Stars since arriving in Casablanca in November 1942, what felt like an eternity ago. As the Germans closed on his position, Maxwell spotted German grenades landing nearby, bouncing off some chicken wire. He was able to grab several that came too close and throw them back. Then another grenade landed. He couldn't reach it in time. "It dropped among us," he recalled, aged ninety-eight, in November 2018. "When I heard it land, I didn't know where it was, so I shoved my blanket down to my stomach and fell on the ground. My right foot caught the grenade. It blew my combat boot all to smithereens and took a big chunk out of the bottom of my right foot. And I had one piece right in

my temple, missed my eye. It was a pretty close call." A private nearby, a wire-man like Maxwell, lay still for a couple of seconds and then realized, although stunned, that he was alive. "Maxwell had deliberately drawn the full force of the explosion on himself," he remembered, "in order to protect us and make it possible for us to continue at our posts and fight." Maxwell survived, although much of his foot was blown off and he was severely wounded in the upper body. Several men nearby would certainly have been killed, had it not been for his selfless sacrifice. A commanding officer returned sometime later and carried Maxwell to safety. For his extraordinary courage, Maxwell would receive the Medal of Honor. He was the last living World War II recipient from the 3rd Division before he died in May 2019. Sources: Robert Maxwell, interview with author, and Taggart, *History of the Third Infantry Division in World War II*, 226.

17. "The History of the 15th Infantry Regiment in WWII," 329.
18. "The History of the 15th Infantry Regiment in WWII," 339–40.
19. "The History of the 15th Infantry Regiment in WWII," 339–40.
20. Taggart, *History of the Third Infantry Division in World War II*, 387.
21. Taggart, *History of the Third Infantry Division in World War II*, 237.
22. Audie Murphy Research Foundation Newsletter, vol. 4, 4.
23. Truscott, *Command Missions*, 470–71.
24. Lucian Truscott to Sarah Truscott, September 16, 1944, Lucian K. Truscott papers, George C. Marshall Foundation.
25. Truscott, *Command Missions*, 472–73.
26. Fussell, *Doing Battle*, 103.
27. Major Keith Ware, interview with Lt. Colonel Goddard, 2.
28. "After Action Report," 15th Infantry Regiment, Records Group 407, National Archives, March 1945.
29. Murphy, *To Hell and Back*, 202.
30. Simpson, *Audie Murphy, American Soldier*, 130.

Chapter 10: The Quarry

1. Audie Murphy Research Foundation Newsletter, vol. 6, winter 1998–99, 6–8.
2. "The History of the 15th Infantry Regiment in WWII" (unpublished manuscript, courtesy of Tim Stoy), 371.
3. "The History of the 15th Infantry Regiment in WWII," 371.
4. Audie Murphy Research Foundation Newsletter, vol. 6, 6–8.
5. "Paulick, Michael," TankDestroyer.net, https://www.tankdestroyer.net/honorees/p/777-paulick-michael-601st.
6. Graham, *No Name on the Bullet*, 75.
7. Murphy, *To Hell and Back*, 210.
8. Simpson, *Audie Murphy, American Soldier*, 437.
9. Audie Murphy Research Foundation Newsletter, vol. 6, 6–8.
10. "The History of the 15th Infantry Regiment in WWII," 374.
11. "The History of the 15th Infantry Regiment in WWII," 372.

12. Audie Murphy Research Foundation Newsletter, vol. 4, spring 1998, 4.
13. "The History of the 15th Infantry Regiment in WWII," 375.
14. *Farmersville* (TX) *Times*, August 9, 1945.
15. Audie Murphy Research Foundation Newsletter, vol. 4, 4.
16. Simpson, *Audie Murphy, American Soldier*, 136.
17. Graham, *No Name on the Bullet*, 78.
18. Fussell, *Doing Battle*, 123.
19. *Journal Gazette & Times-Courier* (Mattoon, IL), February 24, 2003.
20. "Audie Murphy: Great American Hero," *Biography*, July 1, 1996.
21. Audie Murphy Research Foundation Newsletter, vol. 4, 4.
22. Truscott, *Command Missions*, 475.
23. Lucian Truscott to Sarah Truscott, October 18, 1944, Lucian K. Truscott papers, George C. Marshall Foundation.
24. Audie Murphy Research Foundation Newsletter, vol. 8, 2000, 2.
25. Audie Murphy Research Foundation Newsletter, vol. 4, 1.
26. Champagne, *Dogface Soldiers*, 154.
27. "Audie Murphy: Great American Hero."
28. Audie Murphy Research Foundation Newsletter, vol. 6, 5.
29. Graham, *No Name on the Bullet*, 83.
30. *Photoplay*, June 1954.
31. Graham, *No Name on the Bullet*, 83.
32. "Recollections of Carolyn Price Ryan," February 12, 1973, AudieMurphy.com, http://www.audiemurphy.com/documents/doc038/CarolynPriceRyanRecollections_12Feb73.pdf.

CHAPTER 11: THE FROZEN CRUST

1. Alexander Patch to Julia Patch, November 6, 1944, Alexander Patch Jr. papers, United States Military Academy, West Point, Archives, box 1.
2. Atkinson, *The Guns at Last Light*, 362.
3. Atkinson, *The Guns at Last Light*, 362.
4. Alexander Patch to Julia Patch, November 14, 1944.
5. Ochs, *A Cause Greater Than Self*, 88.
6. *Yankee*, May 1983.
7. Ellis, *The Sharp End*, 332.
8. Murphy, *To Hell and Back*, 228.
9. Atkinson, *The Guns at Last Light*, 531.
10. "The History of the 15th Infantry Regiment in WWII" (unpublished manuscript, courtesy of Tim Stoy), 476.
11. Shepard, *A War of Nerves*, 245.
12. Shepard, *A War of Nerves*, 245.
13. *Saturday Evening Post*, September 15, 1945.
14. "The History of the 15th Infantry Regiment in WWII," 459.
15. William Weinberg, unpublished memoir (courtesy of Tim Stoy), 42.
16. "The History of the 15th Infantry Regiment in WWII," 461.

17. Champagne, *Dogface Soldiers*, 173.

18. "The Battle of Sigolsheim, December 1944, Then and Now," Stand Where They Fought, https://standwheretheyfought.jimdofree.com/alsace-2011-the-battle-of-sigolsheim-december-1944-then-and-now/.

19. Weinberg, unpublished memoir, 32.

20. Weinberg, unpublished memoir, 33–37.

21. McFarland, *The History of the 15th Regiment in World War II*, 245.

22. Weinberg, unpublished memoir, 36.

23. Vernon Rankin, "Complete Description of Service Rendered: Lt. Colonel Keith L. Ware's Medal of Honor Action," National Archives, 1945, 1–2.

24. "The History of the 15th Infantry Regiment in WWII," 465.

25. Taggart, *History of the Third Infantry Division in World War II*, 387.

26. Champagne, *Dogface Soldiers*, 173.

27. Weinberg, unpublished memoir, 41.

28. Dan Champaigne, "Bloody Fight for Hill 351: Skirmish in the Colmar Pocket," Warfare History Network, https://warfarehistorynetwork.com/2018/06/26/bloody-fight-for-hill-351/.

29. Taggart, *History of the Third Infantry Division in World War II*, 291.

30. Weinberg, unpublished memoir, 52.

31. Weinberg, unpublished memoir, 49.

32. Ware's Medal of Honor citation reads: "Commanding the 1st Battalion attacking a strongly held enemy position on a hill near Sigolsheim, France, on 26 December 1944, Lt. Col. Ware found that one of his assault companies had been stopped and forced to dig in by a concentration of enemy artillery, mortar, and machine-gun fire. The company had suffered casualties in attempting to take the hill. Realizing that his men must be inspired to new courage, Lt. Col. Ware went forward 150 yards beyond the most forward elements of his command, and for two hours reconnoitered the enemy positions, deliberately drawing fire upon himself which caused the enemy to disclose his dispositions. Returning to his company, he armed himself with an automatic rifle and boldly advanced upon the enemy, followed by two officers, nine enlisted men, and a tank. Approaching an enemy machine gun, Lt. Col. Ware shot two German riflemen and fired tracers into the emplacement, indicating its position to his tank, which promptly knocked the gun out of action. Lt. Col. Ware turned his attention to a second machine gun, killing two of its supporting riflemen and forcing the others to surrender. The tank destroyed the gun. Having expended the ammunition for the automatic rifle, Lt. Col. Ware took up an M1 rifle, killed a German rifleman, and fired upon a third machine gun 50 yards away. His tank silenced the gun. Upon his approach to a fourth machine gun, its supporting riflemen surrendered and his tank disposed of the gun. During this action Lt. Col. Ware's small assault group was fully engaged in attacking enemy positions that were not receiving his direct and personal attention. Five of his party of 11 were casualties and Lt. Col. Ware was wounded, but refused medical attention until this important hill position was cleared of the enemy and securely occupied by his command." Source: "Sto-

ries of Sacrifice: Keith Lincoln Ware," https://www.cmohs.org/recipients
/keith-l-ware.

33. "The History of the 15th Infantry Regiment in WWII," 466.
34. "The History of the 15th Infantry Regiment in WWII," 472.
35. Simpson, *Audie Murphy, American Soldier*, 140.
36. Taggart, *History of the Third Infantry Division in World War II*, 293.
37. Simpson, *Audie Murphy, American Soldier*, 140.
38. Weinberg, unpublished memoir, 15.
39. Ochs, *A Cause Greater Than Self*, 93.

CHAPTER 12: AT ALL COSTS

1. McFarland, *The History of the 15th Regiment in World War II*, 251–52.
 2. Regimental papers, 15th Infantry Regiment, Record Group 407, National Archives.
 3. Joyce Ware, interview with author.
 4. William Weinberg, unpublished memoir (courtesy of Tim Stoy), 56.
 5. Joyce Ware, interview with author.
 6. Private William Weinberg remembered: "The Company was in awe of Murphy. I found him rather reserved. He was not a braggart. His straight accounts needed no exaggeration. He seemed to favor incidents when he could shoot to kill. Few of us spoke about killing. He was a great marksman; few of us were. He could be caustic, but rarely would ride someone. He had a deeply ingrained, unflinching, immediate response to what needed to be done. You could always count on him. There was one major flaw that was said occasionally in admiration, or could be used as a fault, a dangerous blemish that could be an integral part of his sense of responsibility and a manifestation of his bravery: he seemed to be looking for a fight." Source: Weinberg, unpublished memoir, 73–74.
 7. Weinberg, unpublished memoir, 102.
 8. Don Kerr, "Soldiering with Audie Murphy," *The Plain Dealer Sunday Magazine* (Cleveland), November 11, 1984.
 9. Audie Murphy Research Foundation Newsletter, vol. 1, winter 1997, 3.
10. Weinberg, unpublished memoir, 74.
11. Lt. Melvin Lasky, "La Maison Rouge," After Action Report, National Archives, March 1945.
12. Prohme, *History of 30th Infantry Regiment, World War II*, 314.
13. Lasky, "La Maison Rouge."
14. Weinberg, unpublished memoir, 87.
15. Prohme, *History of 30th Infantry Regiment, World War II*, 316.
16. Weinberg, unpublished memoir, 30.
17. Citation, Record of Award of Decoration, Silver Star Medal, Second Lt. Michael J. Daly, January 25, 1945, National Archives.
18. Citation, Record of Award of Decoration, Silver Star Medal, Second Lt. Michael J. Daly.
19. Simpson, *Audie Murphy, American Soldier*, 153.

20. Audie Murphy Research Foundation Newsletter, vol. 4, spring 1998, 6.
21. Audie Murphy Research Foundation Newsletter, vol. 4, 7.
22. "The History of the 15th Infantry Regiment in WWII" (unpublished manuscript, courtesy of Tim Stoy), 488.
23. Taggart, *History of the Third Infantry Division in World War II*, 385.
24. Audie Murphy Research Foundation Newsletter, vol. 4, 7.
25. Weinberg, unpublished memoir, 99.
26. Simpson, *Audie Murphy, American Soldier*, 158.
27. Lt. Colonel Keith Ware, citation, 15th Infantry Commanding, April 13, 1945, Headquarters 2nd Battalion, 15th Infantry Regiment, APO#3, US Army, National Archives.
28. Champagne, *Dogface Soldiers*, 186.

CHAPTER 13: "MURPHY CROWDS BRITT"

1. "Meet Capt. Britt Who Left His Good Right Arm at Anzio," press clipping, Maurice Britt papers, University of Arkansas, box 2.
2. "Britt, in New York Interview, Tells How He Lost Right Arm," undated Associated Press clipping, Maurice Britt collection, University of Arkansas archives, scrapbook 4.
3. "Britt Gives Guardsmen the Lowdown on Fighting in Italy," press clipping, Maurice Britt papers, University of Arkansas, box 2.
4. Undated press clipping, Maurice Britt papers, University of Arkansas, box 2.
5. *The Arkansas Traveler* (Fayetteville), December 1, 1944.
6. Undated press clipping, Maurice Britt papers, University of Arkansas, box 2.
7. Maurice Britt, "Captain Maurice Britt, Most Decorated Infantryman, Begins His Story of War Experiences," Maurice Britt papers, University of Arkansas, box 6, folder 1, 13.
8. "'One Man Army' Completes Set of 3 Top Medals," December 6, 1944, press clipping, Maurice Britt papers, University of Arkansas, box 2.
9. "'One Man Army' Completes Set of 3 Top Medals."
10. "Meet Capt. Britt Who Left His Good Right Arm at Anzio."
11. Gerald Lyons, memo, December 11, 1944, Maurice Britt papers, University of Arkansas, box 2.
12. Lyons, memo.
13. Lyons, memo.
14. Maurice Britt to his mother, Mother's Day 1940, Maurice Britt papers, University of Arkansas, box 3.
15. *New York World-Telegram*, December 7, 1944.
16. *New York Daily News*, December 6, 1944.
17. "'One Man Army' Completes Set of 3 Top Medals."
18. Prefer, *Eisenhower's Thorn on the Rhine*, 234.
19. Ochs, *A Cause Greater Than Self*, 91.
20. Cox, *An Infantryman's Memories of World War II*, 156–57.
21. *Yankee*, May 1983.

22. "After Action Report," Regimental papers, 15th Infantry Regiment, Record Group 407, National Archives, March 1945.
23. *Yankee*, June 6, 2008.
24. "The History of the 15th Infantry Regiment in WWII" (unpublished manuscript, courtesy of Tim Stoy), 500.
25. Roberts, *What Soldiers Do*, 126.
26. Champagne, *Dogface Soldiers*, 207.
27. Whiting, *Paths of Death & Glory*, 88.
28. Whiting, *Paths of Death & Glory*, 88.
29. Graham, *No Name on the Bullet*, 96.
30. *Montgomery* (AL) *Journal Advertiser*, July 21, 1968.
31. Whiting, *America's Forgotten Army*, 169.
32. "The History of the 15th Infantry Regiment in WWII," 519.
33. Ellis, *The Sharp End*, 77.
34. "The History of the 15th Infantry Regiment in WWII," 520–21.
35. Simpson, *Audie Murphy, American Soldier*, 165.
36. Audie Murphy Research Foundation Newsletter, vol. 1, winter 1997, 5–6.
37. Regimental papers, 15th Infantry Regiment.
38. Cox, *An Infantryman's Memories of World War II*, 118–19.
39. *Front Line*, March 10, 1945.
40. *Front Line*, March 10, 1945.
41. "Gen. Marshall Defends Medals for U.S. Heroes," July 15, 1944, press clipping, Maurice Britt papers, University of Arkansas archive, box 2.
42. The Marne men's senior commanders in World War II—O'Daniel and Truscott—both believed in the value of awards. The division's awards section included a talented writer called Glendon Swarthout, who was badly injured while serving with the 30th Infantry Regiment; he penned many recommendations. Several of Swarthout's postwar books would be made into films, including 1975's *The Shootist*, John Wayne's last film, and 1959's *They Came to Cordura*, which starred Gary Cooper. Tim Stoy, interview with author.
43. Simpson, *Audie Murphy, American Soldier*, 164.
44. Ochs, *A Cause Greater Than Self*, 220–21.

Chapter 14: The Heart of Darkness

1. Taggart, *History of the Third Infantry Division in World War II*, 345.
2. "The History of the 15th Infantry Regiment in WWII" (unpublished manuscript, courtesy of Tim Stoy), 533.
3. Kesselring, *The Memoirs of Field-Marshal Kesselring*, 254.
4. Ellis, *The Sharp End*, 151.
5. Taggart, *History of the Third Infantry Division in World War II*, 346.
6. Taggart, *History of the Third Infantry Division in World War II*, 275.
7. Roger J. Spiller, "The Price of Valor," *Military History Quarterly*, spring 1993.
8. Kesselring, *The Memoirs of Field-Marshal Kesselring*, 272.
9. Graham, *No Name on the Bullet*, 95.

10. Murphy, *To Hell and Back*, 263.

11. Kesselring, *The Memoirs of Field-Marshal Kesselring*, 276.

12. "The History of the 15th Infantry Regiment in WWII," 563.

13. Whiting, *America's Forgotten Army*, 198–203.

14. Regimental papers, 15th Infantry Regiment, Record Group 407, National Archives.

15. *New Jersey Veteran Journal*, summer 2007.

16. *Yankee*, May 1983.

17. *New Jersey Veteran Journal*, summer 2007.

18. "The History of the 15th Infantry Regiment in WWII," 561

19. "The History of the 15th Infantry Regiment in WWII," 557.

20. Michael Daly, interview with Tim Frank (courtesy of Tim Frank).

21. Wyant, *Sandy Patch*, 191.

22. Wyant, *Sandy Patch*, 191.

23. Cox, *An Infantryman's Memories of World War II*, 145.

24. Taggart, *History of the Third Infantry Division in World War II*, 358.

25. Champagne, *Dogface Soldiers*, 228.

26. "The History of the 15th Infantry Regiment in WWII," 560.

27. Taggart, *History of The Third Infantry Division in World War II*, 381.

28. Taggart, *History of the Third Infantry Division in World War II*, 381.

29. Another Marne man received the Medal of Honor for actions that day: eighteen-year-old Private Joseph F. Merrell of I Company. On April 18, his company came under fierce attack on the outskirts of Nuremberg. Two German machine guns were particularly effective. Merrell ran for a hundred yards in the open, under fire, and got to within a few feet of four Germans who were armed with machine pistols. With his rifle, he killed all four as their bullets tore through his trousers. Then he was on the move again. His rifle was broken by a sniper's bullet. Now he only had grenades. He ran from cover to cover for another couple of hundred yards.

    The two machine guns were still in action and he was soon within ten yards of one. He threw two grenades, ready to fight with his hands. One grenade exploded and the Germans manning it were killed or wounded. He grabbed a Luger from one of them and shot the survivors. He then scrambled toward the next machine gun, some thirty yards away. But there were Germans hidden in a foxhole nearby. He killed four of them before being hit in the stomach. According to his Medal of Honor citation, he "went on staggering, bleeding, and disregarding bullets which tore through the folds of his clothing and glanced off his helmet. He threw his last grenade into the machinegun nest and stumbled on to wipe out the crew. He had completed this self-appointed task when a machine-pistol burst killed him instantly . . ." Source: Taggart, *History of the Third Infantry Division in World War II*, 384.

30. "The History of the 15th Infantry Regiment in WWII," 560.

31. *Yankee*, May 1983.

32. *Yankee*, May 1983.

33. Deirdre Daly, interview with author.

34. Deirdre Daly, interview with author.
35. Alexander Patch to Julia Patch, November 6, 1944, Alexander Patch Jr. papers, United States Military Academy, West Point, Archives, box 1.
36. Speer, *Inside the Third Reich*, 473.
37. Whiting, *America's Forgotten Army*, 203.
38. Taggart, *History of the Third Infantry Division in World War II*, 361.
39. Simpson, *Audie Murphy, American Soldier*, 171.
40. John Heintges, unpublished memoir, 189.
41. Daly was recovering, getting speech therapy, when that July in the hospital in Massachusetts he learned he would receive the Medal of Honor.
42. Regimental papers, 15th Infantry Regiment.
43. Taggart, *History of the Third Infantry Division in World War II*, 370.
44. Luciano Charles Graziano, interview with author.
45. Kershaw, *The Liberator*, 324.
46. Kershaw, *The Liberator*, 324.
47. Taggart, *History of the Third Infantry Division in World War II*, 373.

Chapter 15: No Peace Within

1. Michael Daly, interview with Tim Frank (courtesy Tim Frank).
2. Murphy, *To Hell and Back*, 273.
3. Murphy, *To Hell and Back*, 274.
4. "The History of the 15th Infantry Regiment in WWII" (unpublished manuscript, courtesy of Tim Stoy).
5. Lt. Colonel Keith Ware, citation, 15th Infantry Commanding, April 18, 1945, Headquarters 2nd Battalion, 15th Infantry Regiment, APO#3, US Army, National Archives.
6. Vaughan-Thomas, *Anzio*, 182.
7. Ferguson, *The Last Cavalryman*, 366.
8. Bill Mauldin, *The Brass Ring*, 272.
9. Ferguson, *The Last Cavalryman*, 335.
10. List of junior officers in the 15th Infantry Regiment in 1944 (courtesy of Tim Stoy).
11. Audie Murphy Research Foundation Newsletter, vol. 2, spring 1997, 11.
12. Henry R. Bodson, "Anecdotes About Audie Murphy," AudieMurphy.com, http://www.audiemurphy.com/documents/doc049/HenryBodsonRecolle tions.pdf.
13. Vic Dallaire, "Murphy Ties Britt's Record," *Stars and Stripes*, May 27, 1945.
14. *Front Line*, May 26, 1945.
15. "Champion of Champions," undated press clipping, Maurice Britt papers, University of Arkansas, box 2.
16. According to one account: "The Legion of Merit was the icing on the cake for it officially made him the most decorated US soldier of WWII. It was noted that the man he had beaten to that prize was Captain Maurice Britt. Inexplicably, Britt did not receive the Legion of Merit although he certainly deserved

it. Britt suffered another injustice—he was not awarded a second Silver Star, although he had earned it. With the Legion of Merit, Audie became the soldier most decorated for valor in the entire American armies of World War II. His nearest competitor was Captain Maurice Britt, also of the 3rd Infantry Division. For some reason, Britt apparently did not get the Legion of Merit, which he undoubtedly deserved." Source: Audie Murphy Research Foundation Newsletter, volume 4, spring 1998, 8.

17. Audie Murphy Research Foundation Newsletter, vol. 4, 8.
18. Lyrics to "Dog Face Soldier," International Military Forums, https://www.military-quotes.com/forum/lyrics-dog-face-soldier-t397.html.
19. Audie Murphy Research Foundation Newsletter, vol. 4, 8.
20. He appeared on the cover of *Life* on July 16, 1945.
21. Graham, *No Name on the Bullet*, 102.
22. Simpson, *Audie Murphy, American Soldier*, 219.
23. Simpson, *Audie Murphy, American Soldier*, 220.
24. Graham, *No Name on the Bullet*, 106.
25. Graham, *No Name on the Bullet*, 8.
26. Simpson, *Audie Murphy, American Soldier*, 221.
27. Graham, *No Name on the Bullet*, 105.
28. Graham, *No Name on the Bullet*, 105.
29. *Fort Worth Star-Telegram*, July 8, 1945.

CHAPTER 16: COMING HOME

1. "Flashback: Valor 28 WWII Veterans in Medal of Honor Ceremony August 23, 1945," Medal of Honor News, https://medalofhonornews.com/2014/04/flashback-valor-28-wwii-veterans-in.html.
2. The full list of those decorated on August 23 is as follows:

Pfc. Silvestre S. Herrera, Phoenix, AZ
T/Sgt. Bernard P. Bell, New York City, NY
S/Sgt. Paul L. Bolden, Madison, AL
First Lieut. Cecil H. Bolton, Huntsville, AL
S/Sgt. Herschel F. Briles, Ankeny, IA
Capt. Bobbie E. Brown, Columbus, GA
Pfc. Herbert H. Burr, Kansas City, MO
Second Lieut. Edward C. Dahlgren, Caribou, ME
T/Sgt. Peter J. Dalessondro, Watervliet, NY
Capt. Michael J. Daly, Southport, CT
S/Sgt. Macario Garcia, Sugarland, TX
T/Sgt. Robert E. Gerstung, Chicago, IL
S/Sgt. James R. Hendrix, Lepanto, AK
S/Sgt. Robert E. Laws, Altoona, PA
Sgt. Charles A. MacGillivary, Charlottetown, PEI, Canada
Pvt. Lloyd C. McCarter, Tacoma, WA

Lieut. Col. George L. Mabry, Hagood, SC
Second Lieut. Donald E. Rudolph, Minneapolis, MN
T/Sgt. Forrest E. Everhart, Bainbridge, OH
Capt. Jack L. Treadwell, Snyder, OK
Pfc. George B. Turner, Los Angeles, CA
First Lieut. Eli Whiteley, Georgetown, TX
First Sgt. Leonard Funk Jr., Wilkinsburg, PA
T/Sgt. Francis J. Clark, Salem, NY
S/Sgt. Clyde L. Choate, Anna, IL
S/Sgt. Raymond H. Cooley, South Pittsburgh, TN
Sgt. Ralph G. Neppel, Glidden, IA
T/4th Class Arthur O. Beyer, Ogena, MN

3. *The Bridgeport* (CT) *Post*, August 25, 1945.
4. Deirdre Daly, interview with author.
5. Collier, *Medal of Honor*, 58.
6. *The Bridgeport* (CT) *Post*, August 25, 1945.
7. *The Bridgeport* (CT) *Telegram*, August 25, 1945.
8. *Yankee*, May 1983.
9. *Yankee*, May 1983.
10. Audie Murphy Research Foundation Newsletter, vol. 8, 2000, 13.
11. Joyce Ware, interview with author.
12. Audie Murphy Research Foundation Newsletter, vol. 8, 13.
13. Simpson, *Audie Murphy, American Soldier*, 410.
14. *Photoplay*, June 1954.
15. Graham, *No Name on the Bullet*, 190.
16. Graham, *No Name on the Bullet*, 191.
17. "Audie Murphy: Great American Hero," *Biography*, July 1, 1996.
18. "Audie Murphy: Great American Hero."
19. *World War II*, August 2019.
20. Joyce Ware, interview with author.
21. "Audie Murphy: Great American Hero."
22. Deirdre Daly, interview with author.
23. Deirdre Daly, interview with author.
24. Associated Press, August 2, 2008.
25. *New York Times*, March 26, 1964.
26. *Army Times*, July 1964.
27. Joyce Ware, interview with author.
28. "Major General Keith L. Ware, 1st Infantry Division commanding general, was killed in action September 13th, 1968. The North Vietnamese shot down MG Ware's command helicopter, 'Danger 77.' MG Ware was directing the division in the Battle of Loc Ninh IV against the *7th NVA Division* when his helicopter crashed at 1300 hours. Killed in with MG Ware were LTC Henry M. Oliver, G-4 (Supply); CPT Gerald W. Plunkett, aircraft commander; 1LT Steven L. Beck, aide-de-camp; CWO2 William Manzanares, Jr., pilot; CSM

Joseph A. Venable, division command sergeant major; SP5 Jose D. Guitierrez-Valaques, crew chief; and SP4 Raymond E. Lanter, door gunner. The 52-year-old Ware was the only draftee ever to rise from private to general. Inducted in 1941, Ware was commissioned in 1942 at Officer's Candidate School, Fort Benning, GA." Source: Andrew Woods, research historian, Colonel Robert R. McCormick Research Center First Division Museum at Cantigny Park, email to author, November 2, 2020.

29. According to Britt's daughter Andrea: "My dad was vice president of Mitchell Mfg Co that was owned by my grandfather, Albert Mitchell . . . my mother's father. They manufactured a variety of things including bedsprings, well buckets and air cooled seat cushions (a very popular item since most cars didn't have a/c back then)." Source: Andrea Schafer, email to author, June 3, 2021.

30. President Nixon asked Britt in 1971 to become district director of the Arkansas Small Business Administration. He gladly accepted and spent the next fourteen years in that role, retiring in 1985, receiving high praise and thanks from President Reagan. In Little Rock, Arkansas, he had meanwhile befriended a young Democratic politician called Bill Clinton, whose centrist politics were similar to his. Britt would provide key advice and encouragement to Clinton when he later decided to run for president. Chris Britt, interview with author.

31. Graham, *No Name on the Bullet*, 119.

32. *Esquire,* December 1983.

33. *Esquire,* December 1983.

34. Graham, *No Name on the Bullet*, 313.

35. Graham, *No Name on the Bullet*, 313.

36. Joyce Ware, interview with author.

37. Nolan, *The Battle for Saigon*, 147–48.

38. Vietnam Veterans Memorial, "Keith Lincoln Ware," http://thewall-usa.com/guest.asp?recid=54558.

39. Ramrods, "General Keith L. Ware, First Inv. Div. Cmmdr," Second Infantry Regiment, https://secinfreg.websitetoolbox.com/post./general-keith-l-ware-first-inf-div-cmmdr-2285847.

40. Joyce Ware, interview with author.

41. Arlington National Cemetery Website, "Keith Lincoln Ware," http://www.arlingtoncemetery.net/klware.htm.

42. Wall of Faces, "Keith Lincoln Ware," Vietnam Veterans Memorial Fund, https://www.vvmf.org/Wall-of-Faces/54520/KEITH-L-WARE/page/5.

43. Ted Engelmann, interview with author.

44. Gail Parsons, "Remembering the Day Danger 6 Went Down," *Army,* September 11, 2018, https://www.army.mil/article/210991/remembering_the_day_danger_6_went_down.

45. Ted Engelmann, interview with author.

46. David T. Zabecki, "Fighting General Killed in Action," *Vietnam,* August 2020.

47. He also had three Purple Hearts. Ware's Distinguished Service Cross award reads: "Major General Ware distinguished himself by exceptionally valorous actions on 12 and 13 September 1968 as the Commanding General of the 1st Infantry Division during an operation in the vicinity of Loc Ninh. Elements of the division became heavily engaged with a reinforced North Vietnamese regiment. Although he knew the enemy was utilizing anti-aircraft weapons in the area, General Ware repeatedly directed his helicopter commander to fly at a minimum altitude so he could more effectively direct and coordinate his infantry units' fierce fight. On numerous occasions his ship received fire from the communists' anti-aircraft emplacements, but General Ware continued his low level flights, which gave him maximum control of his troops and the best observation of the North Vietnamese deployment. He was killed when the enemy fusillade directed at his craft hit the ship, causing it to crash and burn. General Ware's personal courage and leadership inspired his beleaguered men to ultimately gain a total victory over the aggressors. Major General Ware's extraordinary heroism and devotion to duty, at the cost of his life, were in keeping with the highest traditions of the military service and reflect great credit upon himself, his unit, and the United States Army." Source: Wall of Faces, "Keith Lincoln Ware."

48. Phillip T. Washburn, "Ware, Murphy: Patriotic, Courageous, They Became Legends Few Could Equal in Combat," *Fort Hood Sentinel*, January 15, 1998, https://www.audiemurphy.com/newspaper/news068/fts_15Jan98.pdf.

49. Audie Murphy Research Foundation Newsletter, vol. 4, 13.

50. *West Magazine*, July 18, 1971.

51. "Audie Murphy: Great American Hero."

52. Graham, *No Name on the Bullet*, 337–38.

53. Lyrics to "Dog Face Soldier."

54. *Life*, June 11, 1971.

55. *National Geographic*, June 1957.

56. Associated Press, August 2, 2008.

57. Michael Daly, interview with Tim Frank (courtesy Tim Frank).

58. Deirdre Daly, interview with author.

59. *Yankee*, May 1983.

60. *Yankee*, May 1983.

61. *Yankee*, May 1983.

62. Daly also said, talking about becoming a professional war hero: "You've got to be careful. You can become a professional hero. There's an awful sadness with that. You spend your life going from ceremony to ceremony. You have to move on. Life is a long distance race. If too much of your life is centered on things you did early—there's a sadness. You can only stand up and hear what you did a few times. It's something you did at one time." Source: *Yankee*, May 1983.

63. Michael Daly, speech, Würzburg, Germany, August 28, 1982 (text provided by Deirdre Daly).

64. Chris Britt, interview with author.

65. Chris Britt, interview with author.
66. *New York Times*, November 29, 1995.
67. Lt. Colonel Jack C. Mason, "My Favorite Lion," *Army*, May 2008.
68. Deirdre Daly, interview with author.
69. *Yankee*, May 1983.
70. Deirdre Daly, interview with author.
71. *New York Times*, July 29, 2008.
72. Deirdre Daly, interview with author.
73. Deirdre Daly, interview with author.
74. "Daly, Michael Joseph," Together We Served, https://army.togetherweserved
    .com/army/servlet/tws.webapp.WebApp?cmd=ShadowBoxProfile&type=Per
    son&ID=213168.

INDEX

ABOUT THE AUTHOR

ALEX KERSHAW is a journalist and a *New York Times* best-selling author of books on World War II. Born in York, England, he is a graduate of Oxford University and has lived in the United States since 1994.